Microsoft Visio 2010 Business Process Diagramming and Validation

Create custom Validation Rules for structured diagrams and increase the accuracy of your business information with Visio 2010 Premium Edition

David J. Parker

BIRMINGHAM - MUMBAI

Microsoft Visio 2010 Business Process Diagramming and Validation

First published: July 2010

Production Reference: 1020710

Published by Packt Publishing Ltd.
32 Lincoln Road
Olton
Birmingham, B27 6PA, UK.

ISBN 978-1-849680-14-1

www.packtpub.com

Cover Image by Sandeep Babu (sandyjb@gmail.com)

Credits

Author
David J. Parker

Reviewers
Dr. Stephanie L. Horn
John Marshall

Acquisition Editor
Kerry George

Development Editor
Stephanie Moss

Technical Editor
Vinodhan Nair

Indexer
Rekha Nair

Editorial Team Leader
Gagandeep Singh

Project Team Leader
Lata Basantani

Project Coordinator
Poorvi Nair

Graphics
Nilesh Mohite

Production Coordinators
Kruthika Bangera
Adline Swetha Jesuthas

Cover Work
Kruthika Bangera

Foreword

I met the author through the Visio MVP community — a group of elite Visio experts who actively share their technical expertise with others. David Parker is a long-time Visio MVP, and we first discussed the new Diagram Validation functionality shipped with Microsoft Visio Premium 2010 almost two years before its release. As a Visio MVP, David provides input for new functionality and early feedback on features as they are developed. Diagram Validation was one of the features I worked on for Visio 2010, and David was keen to learn about its functionality.

The Visio team had heard from our customers that they spend a lot of time manually checking diagrams to find even simple problems like shapes without labels and unconnected shapes. Companies were also struggling to ensure that diagrams met certain compliancy requirements or business standards. With Diagram Validation, Visio automatically verifies properties of a diagram and displays diagramming issues. It is then easy to review the issues and fix the problems in the diagram. This automatic detection of diagramming errors is a big time saver and can greatly increase diagram quality.

Microsoft Visio Premium 2010 provides built-in validation support for Basic Flowchart, Cross-Functional Flowchart, Six Sigma, Microsoft SharePoint Workflow, and **Business Process Modeling Notation (BPMN)** diagrams. What intrigued David most, though, was the ability for anyone to create custom validation logic — you can specify your own custom diagram requirements, for any type of diagram, and Visio will verify these requirements for you. Moreover, once you have created custom validation logic, you can use it in all your diagrams, share it with others, distribute it within your company, or even sell it as part of a Visio solution. As most diagrams have some logical structure to them, there are many opportunities to create your own custom validation logic and extend the built-in functionality of Diagram Validation.

Although Visio 2010 has just recently been released, David is already an expert in the area of Diagram Validation. He has created new validation logic for several different diagram types, created a tool to work with validation logic in Visio, and written articles about Diagram Validation. Outside of the Visio team itself, David is probably most versed in this area of Visio 2010. It was not surprising then that David chose this area for his new book. This is David Parker's second book—he is also the author of *Visualizing Information with Microsoft Office Visio 2007.*

As a technical reviewer for this book, I had a chance to read the book from cover to cover. As I read, there were a couple of key things that impressed me about its contents. First, this is more than a book about Diagram Validation; it also introduces Visio users to an assortment of new Visio 2010 features. Second, it presents a nice balance between the Visio Object Model and the Visio ShapeSheet. These two powerful tools combine to provide a unique development experience within Visio. Finally, the book provides coded examples, and even a chapter devoted to a worked example. These clear, well thought out examples are great for those who want to experiment in Visio as they read the book.

David begins this book with an overview of process management in Visio 2010. Diagram Validation is one of many features developed for business process users. In fact, business process management is a cornerstone of Microsoft Visio Premium 2010. The Visio team spent a lot of time reflecting on how we could best enhance the experience for our business process users—we added new diagram types like BPMN and SharePoint workflow, redesigned our **Cross-Functionality Flowchart (CFF)** support to make it easier to use, and created new support for concepts like sub-processes and Diagram Validation. Readers of this book will be introduced to a breadth of new Visio 2010 functionality, thanks to David's considerable knowledge of Visio 2010.

David next devotes a chapter each to the Visio Object Model and the Visio ShapeSheet. Microsoft Visio is unique as a diagramming application, because of the joint power of the Visio Object Model and Visio shapes. Beginners to Visio are often surprised by the amount of data and behavioral logic that can be specified on a shape, through the ShapeSheet. For example, the way a shape interacts with other shapes and the drawing page and the way users can interact with the shape are often implemented by formulas entered in the ShapeSheet. David is well aware of the balance between creating smart shapes and writing solution code.

A similar balance exists between the Visio ShapeSheet and validation logic — the validation logic can often be made simpler if the data or logic specified on shapes is slightly more complex. Unless you write code to specify your diagram requirements, this realization is fundamental to writing validation logic for your requirements. Appropriately, the worked example for data flow model diagrams at the end of the book shows how the shape properties specified in the ShapeSheet can be leveraged when writing validation logic.

Having written a significant amount of the validation logic shipped with Visio 2010, I am familiar with the learning curve associated with writing validation logic. It was daunting, at first to ponder expressing the validation logic to check the visual correctness of a diagram based on the diagramming rules specified in the BPMN standard. Perhaps surprisingly, this task turned out to be rather straightforward — Microsoft Visio Premium 2010 shipped this BPMN validation logic and it is also written out in this book's appendix.

To write even very complex validation logic, it is simply a matter of clearly understanding the fundamentals of Diagram Validation. This book presents these fundamentals and, through examples, shows you how to create custom validation logic. David enjoyed the challenge of writing complex diagram requirements as validation logic, and the satisfaction of having these requirements forevermore verified automatically and I hope you have a similar experience with Diagram Validation. It is very rewarding to have the ability to express diagram requirements to meet your needs, and to know these requirements will be automatically verified by Microsoft Visio Premium 2010.

Dr. Stephanie L. Horn

VISIO MVP Coordinator and Program Manager on the Visio development team

About the Author

David J. Parker explored linking Unix CAD and SQL databases in the early '90s for facilities and cable management, as he was frustrated as an architect in the late '80s, trying to match 3D building models with spreadsheets.

In '96 he discovered the ease of linking data to Visio diagrams of personnel and office layouts. He immediately became one of the first Visio business partners in Europe, and was soon invited to present his applications at worldwide Visio conferences. He started his own Visio-based consultancy and development business, **bVisual ltd** (`http://www.bvisual.net`), applying analysis, synthesis, and design to various graphical information solutions.

He has presented Visio solution provider courses for Microsoft EMEA, adding personal anecdotes and previous mistakes hoping that all can learn from them.

He wrote his first book, *Visualizing Information with Microsoft Office Visio 2007* (`http://www.visualizinginformation.com`), to spread the word about data-linked diagrams in business, and is currently writing his second book, which is about creating custom rules for validating structured diagrams in Visio 2010.

David wrote WBS Modeler for Microsoft, which integrates Visio and Project, and many other Visio solutions for various vertical markets.

David has been regularly awarded Most Valued Professional status for his Visio community work over the years, and maintains a Visio blog at `http://bvisual.spaces.live.com`.

Based near to Microsoft UK in Reading, he still sees the need for Visio evangelism throughout the business and development community.

I would like to thank the Microsoft Visio for continuing to develop such a great application, and in particular, Stephanie Horn for agreeing to edit this book. Similarly, I would like to thank my fellow Visio MVP, John Marshall, for his help and encouragement.
Most of all, I would like to thank my wife, Beena, for allowing me to write another book!

About the Reviewers

Dr. Stephanie L. Horn is a Program Manager on the Visio team at Microsoft and coordinated the Diagram Validation feature introduced in Microsoft Visio 2010. She is also responsible for the programmability aspects of Visio and is the coordinator for the Visio MVPs — a small group of recognized Visio community leaders that includes the author, David Parker. She holds a Ph.D. in Computer Science from the University of Toronto.

John Marshall apprenticed as a Civil Engineer and early on learned the power of computers. Many of the tedious tasks that were routine in Civil Engineering could be automated and done in less time with better accuracy.

After university, he switched to OS development on mainframes and continued to work in various aspects of the computer industry on wide variety of platforms. One area of interest has always been graphics and he wrote several applications to create business graphics in the pre-PC days.

In 1993, shortly before Visio was released, he was introduced to the product by a sample copy of Visio that was included on a Microsoft Windows 3 upgrade disk. It provided a far easier solution to business diagrams and the user was not restricted to the shapes that came with the application. When he checked out Visio on the Visio forum on CompuServe, he ended up answering more questions than he asked. This started an almost twenty year involvement as an online volunteer helping the Visio community. When Visio was acquired by Microsoft he received the first Visio MVP award and has received one annually ever since.

With Visio, he has a strong interest in automation and shape creation. He maintains a website, `Visio.MVPs.Org` that lists the collection of Visio stencils he has found online.

He has worked on the following books:

- *Visio 2007 Bible*, Wiley
- *Visualizing Information with Microsoft Office Visio 2007*, McGraw Hill
- *Special Edition Using Microsoft Office Visio 2007*, QUE

Table of Contents

Preface

Once the creators of Aldus PageMaker had delivered Desktop publishing to the masses, they decided that they could make a smarter diagramming application. Eighteen months later, they emerged with the Visio product. Now they needed to get a foothold in the market, so they targeted the leading process flow diagramming package of the day, ABC FlowCharter, as the one to outdo. They soon achieved their aim to become the number one flowcharting application and so they went after other usage scenarios, such as network diagramming, organization charts, and building plans. In 1999, Microsoft bought Visio Corporation and Visio gradually became Microsoft Office Visio, meaning that all add-ons had to be written in a certain manner, and the common Microsoft Office core libraries like the Fluent UI were ever more increasingly employed.

Flowcharting still accounts for 30% of the typical uses that Visio is put to, but the core product did not substantially enhance its flowcharting abilities. There were some add-ons that provided rules, perhaps most notably for Data Flow Diagrams (which came and went); UML and Database Modelling, and many third parties have built whole flowcharting applications based on Visio. What all of these enhancements have in common is the imposition of a structure to the diagrams, which necessarily means the adoption of one rule set or another. There are a lot of competing and complementary rule sets in use, but what is important is that the chosen rule set fits the purpose it is being used for, and that it can be understood by other related professionals.

It is true that a picture is worth a thousand words, but the particular thousand words understood by each individual are more likely to be the same if the picture was created with commonly available rules. The structured diagramming features and Validation API in Visio 2010 enable business diagramming rules to be developed, reviewed, and deployed. The first diagramming types to have these rules applied to are process flowcharts, reminiscent of the vertical markets attacked by the first versions of Visio itself, but these rules can and will be extended beyond this discipline.

What this book covers

Chapter 1, Overview of Process Management in Microsoft Visio 2010, introduces the new features that have been added to Microsoft Visio to support structured diagrams and validation. You will see where Visio fits in the Process Management stack, and explore the relevant out of the box content.

Chapter 2, Understanding the Microsoft Visio Object Model, explains the Microsoft Visio 14.0 Type Library and the key objects, collections, and methods in the programmer's interface of Visio, where relevant for structured diagrams.

Chapter 3, Understanding the ShapeSheet™, explains the Microsoft Visio ShapeSheet™ and the key sections, rows, and cells, along with the functions available for writing ShapeSheet™ formulae, where relevant for structured diagrams.

Chapter 4, Understanding the Validation API, explains the Microsoft Visio Validation API and the key objects, collections, events, and methods in the programmer's interface for Visio diagram validation.

Chapter 5, Developing a Validation API Interface, is devoted to building a useful tool, called Rules Tools, to enable the tasks to be performed easily as Microsoft Visio 2010 does not provide a user interface to the Validation API for rules developers to use.

Chapter 6, Reviewing Validation Rules and Issues, will extend the tool, started in *Chapter 5,* to provide an import/export routine of rules to an XML file or to an HTML report, and a feature to add issues as annotations in Visio diagrams.

Chapter 7, Creating Validation Rules, will use the tool created in the previous chapter to create rules for structured diagramming. This chapter will look at common ShapeSheet™ functions that will be useful for rules, and the new Validation functions. It will also go through different scenarios for creating rules, especially with regard to Filter and Test Expressions.

Chapter 8, Publishing Validation Rules and Diagrams, will go through different methods for publishing Visio validation rules for others to use.

Chapter 9, A Worked Example for Data Flow Model Diagrams, presents a complete cycle for writing validation rules for the Data Flow Model Diagram methodology. Validation rules are created using the Rules Tools add-in developed in previous chapters, although alternative VBA code is provided.

What you need for this book

The following software products are used in this Microsoft Visio 2010 Business Process Diagramming and Validation book:

- Microsoft Visio 2010 (Premium Edition for some of the content)
- Microsoft Visio 2010 SDK
- Optionally, Microsoft Visual Studio 2010 (with knowledge of C#)

Who this book is for

This book is primarily for Microsoft Office Visio users or developers who want to know how to use and extend the new Validation Rules in Microsoft Office Visio 2010 Premium Edition. There are some rule sets available out of the box, but the capability can be added to many sorts of diagramming, whether they are process flows, network cabling drawings, or risk dependency diagrams, for example. This is not a Visio SmartShape developer manual or a Visio automation guide, although these subjects are explored when relevant for writing validation rules, but it does shed light on the possibilities with this new powerful feature of Microsoft Office Visio 2010. This book will be an essential guide to understanding and creating structured diagramming rules, and will add developer tools that are not in the out of the box product.

Conventions

In this book, you will find a number of styles of text that distinguish between different kinds of information. Here are some examples of these styles, and an explanation of their meaning.

Code words in text are shown as follows: " The following class diagram displays the methods of the VEDocuments class."

A block of code is set as follows:

```
private void VisioEvents_Connect()
{
    Globals.ThisAddIn.Application.DocumentOpened +=
        new Visio.EApplication_DocumentOpenedEventHandler(
        VisioApplication_DocumentOpened);
    Globals.ThisAddIn.Application.DocumentCreated +=
        new Visio.EApplication_DocumentCreatedEventHandler(
        VisioApplication_DocumentCreated);
    Globals.ThisAddIn.Application.BeforeDocumentClose +=
        new Visio.EApplication_BeforeDocumentCloseEventHandler(
```

```
              VisioApplication_BeforeDocumentClose);
      //Listen for selection changes
      Globals.ThisAddIn.Application.SelectionChanged +=
          new Visio.EApplication_SelectionChangedEventHandler(
          Window_SelectionChanged);
    }
```

When we wish to draw your attention to a particular part of a code block, the
relevant lines or items are set in bold:

```
For Each shp In shps
    If shp.CellExistsU("User.UMLShapeType",
      Visio.visExistsAnywhere) Then
        Select Case shp.Cells("User.UMLShapeType").ResultIU
            Case 97
                shapeID = shp.ID
            Case 98, 99, 100
                shapeID = shp.ID
                flowchartShapes.Add shapeID
                hshTable.Add shapeID, shapeStatus.[New]
        End Select
    End If
Next
```

New terms and **important words** are shown in bold. Words that you see on
the screen, in menus or dialog boxes for example, appear in the text like this:
"Let us create a test rule by selecting the **Add** button on the **Rules Tools**
ribbon group.".

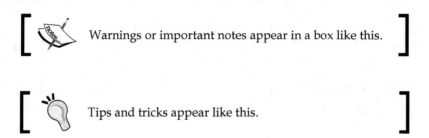

Warnings or important notes appear in a box like this.

Tips and tricks appear like this.

Reader feedback

Feedback from our readers is always welcome. Let us know what you think about this book—what you liked or may have disliked. Reader feedback is important for us to develop titles that you really get the most out of.

To send us general feedback, simply send an e-mail to feedback@packtpub.com, and mention the book title via the subject of your message.

If there is a book that you need and would like to see us publish, please send us a note in the **SUGGEST A TITLE** form on www.packtpub.com or e-mail suggest@packtpub.com.

If there is a topic that you have expertise in and you are interested in either writing or contributing to a book on, see our author guide on www.packtpub.com/authors.

Customer support

Now that you are the proud owner of a Packt book, we have a number of things to help you to get the most from your purchase.

Downloading the example code for this book

You can download the example code files for all Packt books you have purchased from your account at http://www.PacktPub.com. If you purchased this book elsewhere, you can visit http://www.PacktPub.com/support and register to have the files emailed directly to you.

Errata

Although we have taken every care to ensure the accuracy of our content, mistakes do happen. If you find a mistake in one of our books—maybe a mistake in the text or the code—we would be grateful if you would report this to us. By doing so, you can save other readers from frustration and help us improve subsequent versions of this book. If you find any errata, please report them by visiting http://www.packtpub.com/support, selecting your book, clicking on the **let us know** link, and entering the details of your errata. Once your errata are verified, your submission will be accepted and the errata will be uploaded on our website, or added to any list of existing errata, under the Errata section of that title. Any existing errata can be viewed by selecting your title from http://www.packtpub.com/support.

Piracy

Piracy of copyright material on the Internet is an ongoing problem across all media. At Packt, we take the protection of our copyright and licenses very seriously. If you come across any illegal copies of our works, in any form, on the Internet, please provide us with the location address or website name immediately so that we can pursue a remedy.

Please contact us at `copyright@packtpub.com` with a link to the suspected pirated material.

We appreciate your help in protecting our authors, and our ability to bring you valuable content.

Questions

You can contact us at `questions@packtpub.com` if you are having a problem with any aspect of the book, and we will do our best to address it.

1
Overview of Process Management in Microsoft Visio 2010

Process flow diagrams have long been a cornerstone of Visio's popularity and appeal, and, although there have been some usability improvements over the years, there have been few enhancements to turn the diagrams into models that can be managed efficiently. Microsoft Visio 2010 sees the introduction of two features that make process management achievable and customizable.

In this chapter, you will be introduced to the new features that have been added to Microsoft Visio to support structured diagrams and validation. You will see where Visio fits in the **Process Management** stack, and explore the relevant out of the box content.

What is new in Visio 2010 for Process Management?

Firstly, Microsoft Visio 2010 introduces the new **Validation API** for structured diagrams, and provides several examples of this in use, for example with the new **BPMN Diagram** and **Microsoft SharePoint Workflow** templates, and the improvements to the **Basic Flowchart** and **Cross-Functional Flowchart** templates, all of which are found in the **Flowchart** category.

Templates in Visio consist of a predefined Visio document that has one or more pages, and may have a series of docked stencils (usually positioned on the left-hand side of workspace area). The template document may have an associated list of add-ons that are active whilst it is in use, and, with Visio 2010 Premium Edition, an associated list of structured diagram validation rule sets as well.

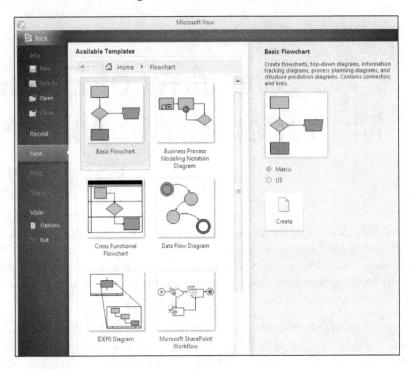

Secondly, the concept of a **Subprocess** has been introduced. This enables processes to hyperlink to other pages describing the subprocesses in the same document, or even across documents. This latter point is necessary if subprocesses are stored in a document library, such as Microsoft SharePoint.

The following screenshot illustrates how an existing subprocess can be associated with a shape in a larger process:

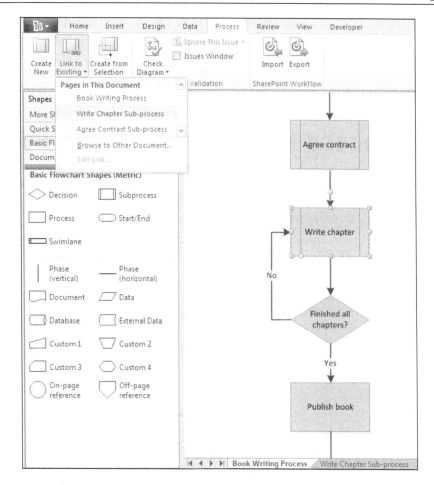

In addition, a subprocess page can be created from an existing shape, or a selection of shapes, in which case they will be moved to the newly-created page.

There are also a number of new ease-of-use features in Microsoft Visio 2010 to assist in the creation and revision of process flow diagrams. These include:

- Easy auto-connection of shapes
- Aligning and spacing of shapes
- Insertion and deletion of connected shapes
- Improved cross-functional flowcharts
- Subprocesses
- An infinite page option, so you need not go over the edge of the paper ever again

However, this book is not about teaching the user how to use these features, since there will be many other authors willing to show you how to perform tasks that only need to be explained once. This book is about understanding the **Validation API** in particular, so that you can create or amend, the rules to match the business logic that your business requires.

Visio Process Management capabilities

Microsoft Visio now sits at the top of the **Microsoft Process Management Product Stack**, providing a **Business Process Analysis (BPA)** or **Business Process Modeling (BPM)** tool for business analysts, process owners/participants, and line of business software architects/developers.

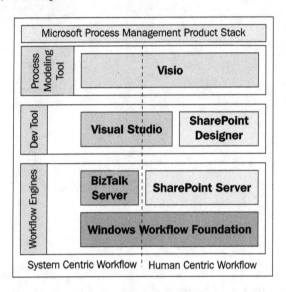

Of course, your particular business may not have all, or parts, of the stack, but you will see in later chapters how Visio 2010 can be used in isolation for business process management to a certain depth.

If we look at the **Visio BPM Maturity Model** that Microsoft presented to their partners, then we can see that Visio 2010 has filled some of the gaps that were still present after Visio 2007. However, we can also see that there are plenty of opportunities for partners to provide solutions on top of the Visio platform.

Level		Visio 2007	Visio 2010	Opportunities
	Visio BPM Maturity Model			

8	Monitor business activity by integrating BPMS and LOB applications	• Pivot Diagram
		• DataGraphics
		• Data Link
			• Visio Services
			• Excel Services
			• Mash-up API
			• SPD integration
			• Workflow visualization
				• Integration with other biz apps
				  · SQL AS/RS · SAP
				  · Dynamics · FileNet
				  · BizTalk · Documentum
				• Industry standard language
				  · Xml · XLANG
				  · BPEL · XPDL
				  · UML · WWF

7	Execute process models to process engine with round trip capability			
6	Manage standardized business process within process repository		• SharePoint Repository	• Process Repository • Multi-user editing • Model merge support • Versioning / Lockout
5	Integrate business rules and validate the business models based on the rules		• Validation	• Business Rule Modeling • Business Rule Visualization • Import Rules
4	Simulate process models with analytical algorithms within Visio	• Pivot Diagram • DataGraphics • Data Link		• Static analysis • Dynamic simulation • Animation • Financial analysis • Risk analysis
3	Create Custom Shape and ShapeData set to standardize process notation	• Custom Shape • New stencil • ShapeData set		• Critical path analysis • Value-chain analysis • Resource use optimization • Matrix support

2	Add process information into ShapeData and export it to Excel for process analysis	• ShapeData
		• Reporting to Excel/XML
			• Auto Layout
			• Sub process
			• BPMN
			• Six Sigma
			• Cross Functional Flowchart
				• Pre-defined industry templates
				  · Supply Chain Management
				  · Discrete manufacturing control
				  · Mortgage approval
				  · Claims Processing
				  · Six Sigma/ISO/Quality
				  · Compliance
				  · IT Processes

1	Capture paper-based process into Visio to streamline business processes	• Templates and Stencils • Auto Connector		

Throughout this book we will be going into detail about Level 5 (**Validation**) in Visio 2010, because it is important to understand the core capabilities provided in Visio 2010. We will then be able to take the opportunity to provide custom **Business Rule Modeling** and **Visualization**.

The foundations of structured diagrams

A **structured diagram** is a set of logical relationships between items, where these relationships provide visual organization or describe special interaction behaviors between them.

The Microsoft Visio team analyzed the requirements for adding structure to diagrams, and came up with a number of features that needed to be added to the Visio product to achieve this:

- **Container Management**: The ability to add labeled boxes around shapes to visually organize them

- **Callout Management**: The ability to associate callouts with shapes to display notes

- **List Management**: To provide order to shapes within a container
- **Validation API**: The ability to test the business logic of a diagram
- **Connectivity API**: The ability to create, remove, or traverse connections easily

The following diagram demonstrates the use of **Containers** and **Callouts** in the construction of a basic flowchart, which has been validated using the **Validation API**, that in turn uses the **Connectivity API**.

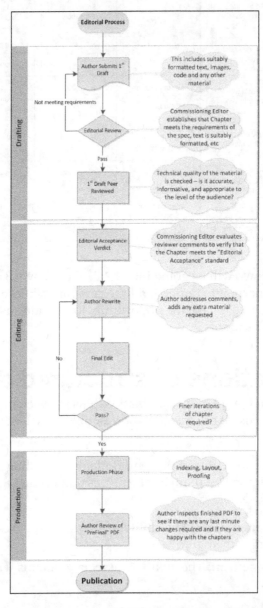

Enhanced process flow templates

There are two process flow diagram templates in Visio 2010 Premium edition that have been enhanced since the previous versions of Visio to include validation rules.

The Flowchart templates

There is now very little difference between the **Basic Flowchart** template and the **Cross-Functional Flowchart** template in the **Flowchart** category. In fact, they are identical apart from the latter opening with a couple of **Swimlane** shapes already placed on the page. Any **Basic Flowchart** diagram can become a **Cross-Functional Flowchart** diagram with the dragging-and-dropping of a **Swimlane** shape onto the page, at which point the new **Cross-Functional Flowchart** tab will appear.

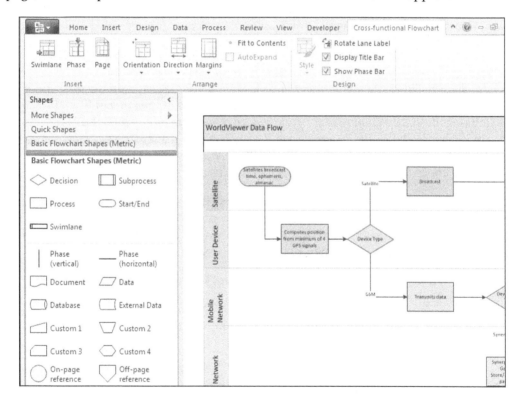

In addition, parts of the new **Six Sigma** template in the **Business** category, which is Visio 2010 Premium edition only, use the same flowchart rules.

New process flow templates

There are two new process flow diagram templates in addition to the **Six Sigma Diagram** template, in the **Flowchart** category of Visio 2010 Premium edition that include their own validation rules. The first, **BPMN Diagram**, provides native Visio support for an important and widely-used process flow notation, and the second, **Microsoft SharePoint Workflow** enables visual development of SharePoint workflows that integrates closely with Visual Studio 2010 and SharePoint 2010.

BPMN Diagram template

The **Object Management Group/Business Process Management Initiative** (http://bpmn.org/) promotes the **BPMN** standards. The BMPN version in Microsoft Visio 2010 is 1.2. There is no better short description of BPMN than the charter from the **OMG**'s website, which states:

> *A standard Business Process Modeling Notation (BPMN) will provide businesses with the capability of understanding their internal business procedures in a graphical notation and will give organizations the ability to communicate these procedures in a standard manner. Furthermore, the graphical notation will facilitate the understanding of the performance collaborations and business transactions between the organizations. This will ensure that businesses will understand themselves and participants in their business and will enable organizations to adjust to new internal and B2B business circumstances quickly.*

Having been involved in the creation of two other BPMN solutions based on earlier versions of Visio, I believe that the native support of BPMN is a very important development for Microsoft, because it is obviously a very popular methodology for the description of an interchange of business processes.

The BMPN template in Visio 2010 contains five docked stencils, each of them containing a logical set of shapes.

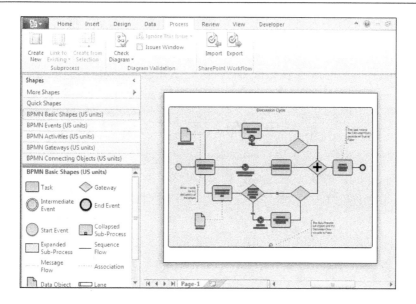

Each of the shapes has **BPMN attributes** in the form of a set of **Shape Data**, which can be edited using the **Shape Data** window or dialog. Some shapes can also be edited using the right-mouse menu.

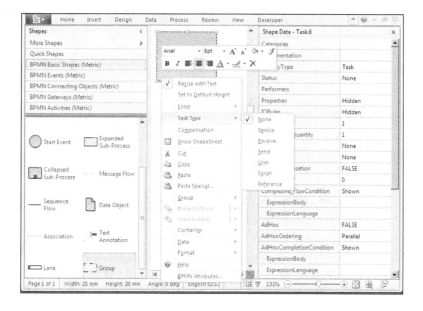

These **Shape Data** rows correspond to BPMN attributes, as specified by the OMG specification. In the above diagram, a **Task** shape is selected revealing that there are many permutations that can be set. A few of these permutations are made easily accessible by laying them out in the **BPMN Activities** stencil as different shapes.

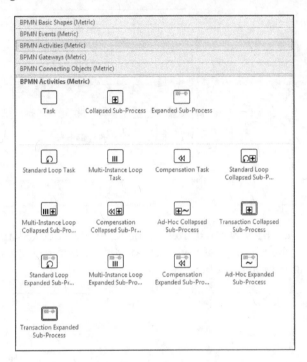

In reality, any of these Task/Activity shapes can be changed into any of the other shapes in the **BPMN Activities** stencil by amending the **Shape Data.** Thus, the original name of the **Master** shape is really immaterial, since it is the **Shape Data** that determines how it should be understood.

SharePoint Workflow Designer template

Microsoft Visio 2010 also includes a template and shapes for designing workflows that can be imported into **Microsoft SharePoint Designer**. You can also take workflow files that were created in Microsoft SharePoint Designer and open them in Visio, which generates a diagram of the workflow that you can view and modify. You can pass the workflow back and forth between the two with no loss of data or functionality, by using a **Visio Workflow Interchange** (*.vwi) file.

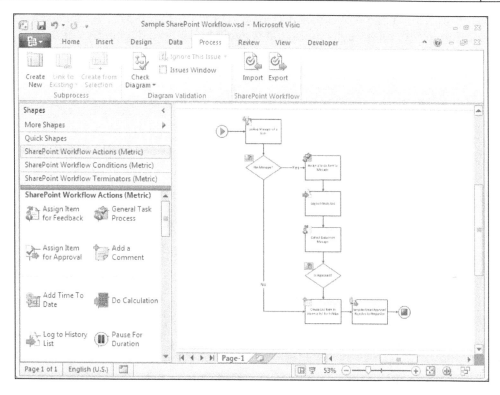

Validation of process diagrams

Validation ensures that the diagram is compliant with the required business logic by checking that it is properly constructed. Therefore, you need to be able to verify that the rule set being used is the one that your business requires. Visio will not provide instant feedback at the moment when you transgress a rule. However, it will check your diagram against a rule set only when you select **Check Diagram**. It will then provide you with feedback on why any given rule has been broken.

Some of the **Validation API** can be accessed via the **Process** tab on the **Diagram Validation** group, but there is more that is available only to developers, thus enabling you to automate some tasks if necessary.

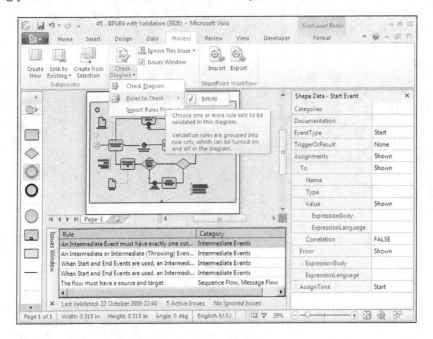

The first group on the **Process** tab, **Subprocess**, is for the creation of subprocesses, and the third group is for the **Import** and **Export** of a **SharePoint Workflow**, but it is the second group, **Diagram Validation**, that is of most interest here.

In this second group, the first button, **Check Diagram**, validates the whole document against the selected rule set(s). You can have more than one rule set in a document, which can be enabled or disabled as required. The drop-down menu on the **Check Diagram** button enables you to select which **Rules to Check**, and also to **Import Rules From** another open Visio document. It is a pity that you cannot export to/import from XML, but we will create our own tool to do that in a later chapter.

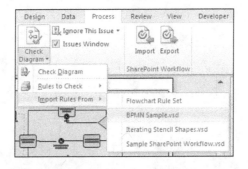

At this point, we should be aware that Visio documents can either be saved as binary (normally with a *.vsd extension) or XML format (normally with a *.vdx extension). So, if we save a Visio document that contains a rule set in XML format, then it can be opened in an XML viewer or editor, such as Microsoft's **XML Notepad**. Here we can see that the new Validation extensions for Microsoft Visio 2010 (internally, version 14) are clearly visible in XML:

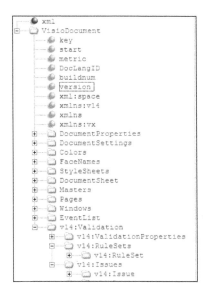

If we expand a **v14:RuleSet** branch, and one of the **v14:Rule** sub-branches, then we can see how a rule is defined.

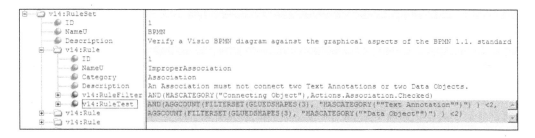

Later, we will be going into these definitions in much greater detail, but for now, notice that the **v14:RuleFilter** and **v14:RuleTest** elements contain formulae that precisely define what constitutes the particular rule.

The **Diagram Validation** group also has the option to show/hide the **Issues Window**, which has a right-mouse menu that is identical (apart from the additional **Arrange by** menu option) to the drop-down menu on the **Ignore This Issue** button.

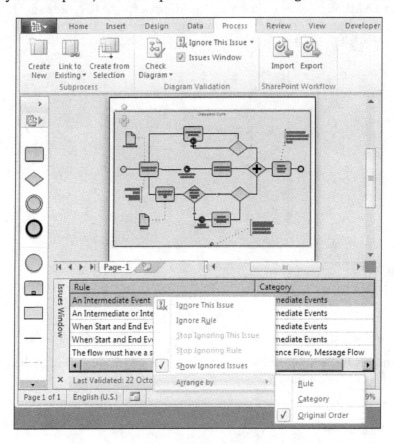

Now that we can see that a **Rule** has an **ID**, and belongs to a **RuleSet** that also has an **ID**, we can begin to understand how an issue can be associated with a shape. So, if we expand an **v14:Issue** element in the Visio document XML, we can see that **v14:Issue** has **v14:IssueTarget** and **v14:RuleInfo** elements.

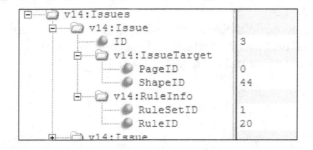

If we were to look for the **Shape** in the document XML, we can find it by its **ID** under the **Shapes** collection of the **Page**, also identified by its **ID**.

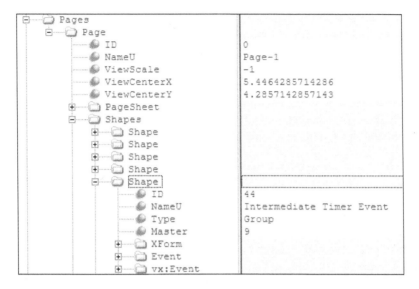

In fact, the **PageID** and **ShapeID** element of an **IssueTarget** are optional because an issue may just be associated with a page, or even with the whole document.

We will use the new Validation API to explore these **RuleSets**, **Rules**, and **Issues** in later chapters, and we will expose them to scrutiny so that your business can be satisfied that you have modeled the business logic correctly.

Visio Process Repository

There is also a new **Visio Process Repository**, which is a site template that is included with Microsoft SharePoint 2010. It provides a place to share and collaborate on process diagrams. The repository has built-in file access control and version control — users can view the process diagram simultaneously and edit the diagram without corrupting the original.

This repository can therefore ensure that a user is editing the most recent version of a process diagram, and enables a user to find out about updates that have been made to processes of interest to them.

In addition, administrators can monitor whether diagrams comply with a business's internal standards or not, or discover, for example, which processes apply to a specified department.

Visio services

Microsoft Visio has had, for several versions, a useful **Save As** Web feature that creates a mini-website, complete with widgets for pan and zoom, **Shape Data**, and shape reports. This has worked best using the **Vector Markup Language** (**VML**) in Microsoft Internet Explorer, or in **Scalable Vector Graphics** (**SVG**) using a web browser plugin in IE, although it has native support in some other browsers. This is quite powerful, but it does require that the native Visio file is republished if any changes are made to the document. Visio 2010 has introduced the increasingly adopted **XAML** format, which actually means that the Visio file will be rendered for viewing in **Silverlight**. This is a very useful addition.

In addition, Microsoft has an ActiveX **Visio Viewer** control that can display native Visio files that are in both binary and XML format. This control is installed as default with Microsoft Outlook 2007+, but is also available as a separate free download from Microsoft. In fact, the Visio Viewer control has a programmable API that enables Shape Data to be extracted and exposed too. While this viewer has the advantage that the native file does not have to be republished, its reach is limited by the choice of browsers available, and the willingness to make the native Visio file accessible — this is not always the best strategy.

Microsoft Visio 2010 provides Visio Services for Microsoft SharePoint. Therefore, with rendering on the server, any client that accesses the Microsoft SharePoint site will have the ability to view Visio diagrams without having to install anything locally.

The user can interact with the diagrams by clicking on shapes to view the **Shape Data**, navigating any embedded hyperlinks, as well as pan/zoom and print capabilities. These are capabilities of the **Save As** Web and **Visio Viewer** options too.

Microsoft Visio 2007 introduced the ability to add a data recordset to a diagram and refresh the data so that the diagram could be kept up-to-date, but the **Save As Web html pages** and the **Visio Viewer ActiveX** control are not able to automatically respond to any data changes. Therefore, the diagram can quickly become outdated, thus requiring you to refresh the diagram in Visio, and then to republish it.

Now with Visio Services, that same data recordset can be refreshed by the server, thus providing everyone who views the diagram using the new Visio web part with the latest information. This is extremely nice, but be aware that there are some limitations, such as no shapes will be added, moved, or deleted in this operation, as only linked Shape Data and Data Graphics are updated and all layers will be visible. Still, you no longer have to republish just to refresh the data set!

Visio has a complex layering system. Most CAD systems, for example, insist that all diagram elements belong to a single layer. This layer can either be made visible or not, or all elements on a layer have a specified color. Drawing elements in Visio can belong to none, one, or many layers! Visio Services, however, simply ignores layers.

What are the Visio 2010 editions?

Microsoft decided to split Visio 2010 into three editions, so you need to be aware of the relevant features that are in each of them. In the following matrix, a black dot denotes which features are present:

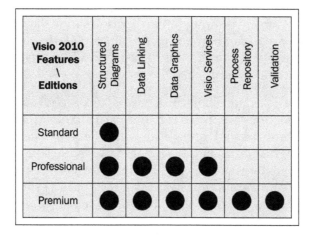

Visio 2010 Features \ Editions	Structured Diagrams	Data Linking	Data Graphics	Visio Services	Process Repository	Validation
Standard	●					
Professional	●	●	●	●		
Premium	●	●	●	●	●	●

Although you will need Microsoft Visio 2010 Premium edition to use the Validation capabilities, the other editions will be able to review any of the diagrams created.

Planning your own solutions

By now, you should be eager to explore the out of the box structured diagram functionality, and perhaps be considering how to create validation rules for your own business. In doing so, I would advise that you always look to build upon what Visio provides—do not try to replicate it! I believe that trying to create your own Shape Data objects, or your own line routing algorithms, for example, is ultimately a waste of time as they will lead you down some dead-ends, some of which still exist within the boxed Visio product. For example, the following three legacy diagram templates in Visio have their own limitations. They are:

- The **Software and Database | UML Model Diagram** solution within Visio is essentially a closed third-party add-on that was purchased, and has seen very little development since then. However, all sets of rules need to be updated from time to time, and so the UML version in Visio will always lag behind those of the leading developers of the UML standard. In addition, there are some elements of the UML solution in Visio that leaves the users constantly frustrated — such as the inability to get at the model composition programmatically.

- The **Software and Database | Database Model Diagram** solution has a few annoyances, such as the inability to print any table or field notes, and the disappearance of any forward engineering capabilities.

- The **Software and Database | Data Flow Model Diagram** solution is one that has been reassessed. We still have the template and stencil for this, but the add-on has not made it through the Microsoft rationalization of Visio add-ons. Therefore, you can now construct DFD models badly without realizing it. We will attempt to remedy this omission in a later chapter by constructing a rule set that can be used with DFD models.

One of the frequently asked questions by a newbie to Visio when confronted by the multiple diagram categories and types is how a particular template is supposed to be used? Often, they are directed to the Visio online help for examples of how to create certain types of diagrams, but this is not always sufficient because they are really asking for automatic assistance as they create the diagram. What they usually want is in fact a guided diagramming system; they require a system that provides them with some feedback on the way that they are composing a diagram. It is easy to drag-and-drop shapes in Visio, to connect them together, to make a diagram pretty with embellishments, or to add text in a variety of ways. However, this loosely-created drawing cannot consistently convey any semantic meaning unless it follows generally accepted rules. It is the imposition of rules that turns a pretty picture into a meaningful mesh of semantic symbology. This is where Microsoft Visio 2010 has made a great advance because it has provided us with the ability to create validation rules for different types of behaviors. In fact, these new features are worthy of a brand new tab, the **Process** tab, which although automatically applied to several drawing templates, is also available for use on any type of diagram.

Summary

In this chapter, we looked at an overview of the new capabilities and process diagram types in Visio 2010, especially with regard to structured and validated diagrams.

Microsoft Visio 2010 provides considerable ease-of-use features to the end user, a rich programming model for the developer, and greater capabilities for document management and sharing than ever before.

In the next chapter, we will need to delve deeper into the internal structure of a Visio document and the use of its various APIs so that you can best understand how to formulate your own rules to represent the business logic that you require.

Summary

2
Understanding the Microsoft Visio Object Model

Whatever programming language you code in, you need to understand the objects, properties, methods, relationships, and events of the application that you are working with. Without this knowledge, the development process is slow and any code you use is going to be inefficient. Visio is no different, in that it provides the **Visio Type Library** with all of its elements, but Visio also has a programmable ShapeSheet behind every shape. Therefore, the Visio Type Library can only be used efficiently if you understand the ShapeSheet, and in turn, the ShapeSheet formulae can only be used fully if you understand the Visio Type Library.

Also, if you are going to create validation rules to check the relationships and properties of structured diagrams, then you will need to understand how to traverse the Visio object model.

Therefore, this chapter is going to explain the **Microsoft Visio 14.0 Type Library** (VisLib.dll), and the key objects, collections, and methods in the programmer's interface of Visio, and the next chapter will reveal the ShapeSheet.

The Visio Type libraries

The publicly displayed version number of an application like Visio can be quite different from the internal version number that is revealed to programmers. For example, Microsoft Visio 2010 is the public version number for the internal version number 14. Therefore, programmers need to know that the Visio Type Library version is 14, although their users will know it as Visio 2010.

There were no 13 versions prior to 14 because Visio was at version 6 (externally Visio 2000) when Microsoft bought the company in 1999. At that time, Microsoft Office was internally at version 9, so Microsoft Visio 2002 was internally hiked up to version 10 to be at the same version number as Microsoft Office 2002. At this point, Microsoft Visio 2003 was internally version number 11, and Microsoft Visio 2007 was internally 12. Version 13 went the same way as the thirteenth floors in high-rise buildings in the States—pandering to the superstitions of the masses.

Microsoft Visio 2010 may also install the following type libraries, depending upon the edition installed.

Name	File	Visio Editions
Microsoft Visio 14.0 Drawing Control Library	`VisOcx.dll`	All editions
Microsoft Visio 14.0 Save As Web Type Library	`SaveAsWeb.dll`	All editions
Microsoft Visio Database Modeling Engine Type Library	`ModelEng.dll`	Professional and Premium editions only
Microsoft Visio UML Add-In for Microsoft Visual C++ 6.0	`UmlVC60.dll`	Professional and Premium editions only
Microsoft Visio UML Solution for Visual Basic Type Library	`UmlVB.dll`	Professional and Premium editions only

In addition, since version 2007, Microsoft Outlook installs the Microsoft Visio Viewer (`Vviewer.dll`), which has a useful programming interface itself. It allows pages, shapes, and data to be explored, even without Visio being installed. It is also available as a separate, free download from Microsoft, should you wish to use it on Windows desktops that do not have Microsoft Outlook installed.

But all I need is the object model

Some programmers think that Visio is present just to provide a graphical canvas with symbols and lines that they need to manipulate or interrogate. Perhaps they have been used to draw items in Windows Forms applications or even XAML-based development with WPF or Silverlight. To think like this is to misunderstand Visio because Visio has a rich diagramming engine, coupled with the ability to encapsulate data and custom behaviors in every element, not to mention the inheritance between certain types of objects. This has resulted in a fairly complex structure in parts of the object model, so that all of the desired functionality can be described fully.

Programmers who look at the Visio object model for the first time may be full of pre-conceptions and look in vain for the x and y coordinate of a shape on a page. They are surprised and a little frustrated that the x coordinate of a shape on a page is:

```
shape.CellsSRC(VisSectionIndices.visSectionObject,
  visRowIndices.visRowXFormOut,
  visCellIndices.visXFormPinX).ResultIU
```

The SRC part of the CellsSRC method is an acronym for **Section Row Column**, which will be explained later.

There is an alternative shorter form namely:

```
Shape.Cells("PinX").ResultIU
```

However, the shorter form is intrinsically more inefficient since the name has to be interpreted into the SRC indices by Visio anyway. Therefore, it is recommended that you work with the indices rather than the names, if at all possible.

The Visio object model is quite large, so I shall be selective by only discussing the parts that I think will assist in understanding and developing validation rules. There are other type libraries installed with Visio, but these are not relevant to the scope of this book. In addition, the Visio edition installed has an impact on the Visio type library itself. For example, the **Validation** objects and collections are only available if you have the **Premium** edition installed, and the **Data Linking** features are not available if you have only the **Standard** edition installed.

The other difference between the different Visio editions is the add-ons, templates, and stencils installed with it. But as these could be moved around and copied between users (illegally), their presence (or lack of presence) cannot be relied on to ascertain the edition installed. One way to ascertain the version is to check a specific registry setting (which is the only way if you are writing an installation script), or using the CurrentEdition property of the Application object.

```
HKEY_CURRENT_USER\Software\Microsoft\Office\14.0\Visio\
Application\LicenseCache
```

The expected values are STD, PRO, or PRM.

Types of Visio document

Before we get into the object model, we need to remind ourselves of the formats and types of Visio documents. Traditionally, Visio used its own binary format (which usually has an extension * . vsd for drawings), and then the XML format was introduced (* . vdx for drawings). The latter is approximately ten times larger in size than the former, although it often compresses to be smaller than the binary equivalent. The XML format is very verbose because it needs to describe the complexity of the graphics and the inheritance of elements within the document. In addition, it is not in the same zipped-up XML files in sub-folders format as most of the Microsoft Office applications.

The **Visio Web Drawing** is new in Visio 2010, which, when published to SharePoint 2010, allows certain elements that are linked to data recordsets to be automatically refreshed when the underlying data is updated, without using Visio. This Visio Services feature however, does not enable new shapes to be created, moved, or deleted, or for connections to be varied during the refresh. But it can be edited by the Visio client application to make these sorts of changes. This new file format has a * . vdw extension, and it contains **XAML** for rendering in Silverlight (or PNG format if required), in addition to the Visio document. These Visio files can be rendered by a new standard web part in Microsoft SharePoint 2010, which can be set to refresh either on a timer event, or manually.

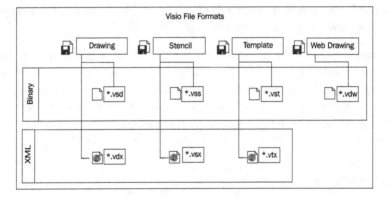

A Visio drawing document can save its workspace along with it, which usually means that there is a collection of docked stencils, which contain the shapes (properly referred to as **Masters** when they are in a stencil).

A Visio stencil is just a Visio document with the pages hidden, and is normally saved with a * . vss extension in the binary format, or * . vsx for the XML format.

A Visio template is just a Visio drawing document saved with a different extension, * . vst for binary and * . vtx for XML, so that Visio knows that the default action is to open a copy of it, rather than the original document.

I mentioned that a stencil is just a Visio document with the drawing pages hidden. Well a drawing is just a Visio document which normally has its stencil hidden. However, you can reveal this in the UI with **More Shapes/Show Document Stencil**.

 Any shape in a page in the document that is an instance of a **Master**, must be an instance of a **Master** in the document stencil. It is not an instance of a **Master** in the stencil from which it was originally dragged and dropped from.

Which programming language should you use with Visio?

Microsoft Visio comes with **Visual Basic for Applications** (**VBA**) built into it, which is a very useful interface for exploring the object model, and testing out ideas. In addition, Visio has a macro recorder that can provide a quick and dirty way of exploring how some of the actions are performed. However, the resultant code from the macro recorder can be very verbose in parts, and completely miss out some bits because Visio is running code inside one of the many **Add-ons** or **COM add-ins** that may be installed.

If you want to use VBA then you will need to run Visio in **Developer Mode** by checking the option available from the **Visio Options** dialog (use **File | Options** to display this), in the **Advanced** group.

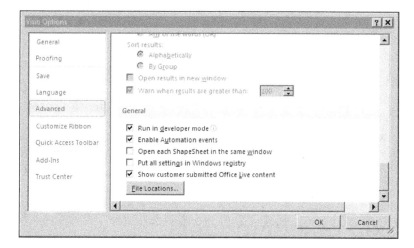

Developer Mode will also add some features to other parts of the Visio interface, such as additional options on the right-mouse menu when a page and shape is selected.

The Drawing Explorer window

The **Drawing Explorer** window can be opened in the Visio UI in the **Show/Hide** group on the **Developer** tab. It is an extremely useful method for visually navigating some of the collections and objects in the Visio application.

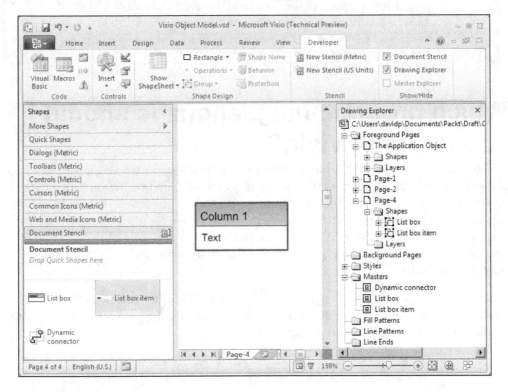

It starts with the active document object, and displays the **Masters, Pages** and **Shapes** collections, amongst others.

 There are two different page collections, **Foreground Pages** and **Background Pages**. You will normally find all of the interesting shapes in the **Foreground Pages** collection, since the **Background Pages** are usually used for backgrounds and titles.

The Visio object model

We will now examine some of the key properties of the main objects in the Visio Type Library. Please note that I have highlighted the collections in the diagrams of these objects.

I have also formatted the output in the following code examples as a table for legibility, because the text will mostly wrap within the **Immediate Window**.

The Application object

The Application object is the root of most collections and objects in Visio, including the Active objects, two of which are useful for traversing structured diagrams — ActiveDocument and ActivePage.

The following sub-function in VBA prints out the salient information to the **Immediate Window**:

```
Public Sub DebugPrintApplication()
Debug.Print "DebugPrintApplication"
    With Visio.Application
        Debug.Print , "ActiveDocument.Name", .ActiveDocument.Name
        Debug.Print , "ActivePage.Name", .ActivePage.Name
        Debug.Print , "Addons.Count", .Addons.Count
        Debug.Print , "COMAddIns.Count", .COMAddIns.Count
        Debug.Print , "CurrentEdition", .CurrentEdition
        Debug.Print , "DataFeaturesEnabled", .DataFeaturesEnabled
        Debug.Print , "Documents.Count", .Documents.Count
        Debug.Print , "TypelibMinorVersion", .TypelibMinorVersion
        Debug.Print , "Version", .Version
    End With
End Sub
```

An example output is:

DebugPrintApplication	
ActiveDocument.Name	Visio Object Model.vsd
ActivePage.Name	The Application Object
Addons.Count	96
COMAddIns.Count	2
CurrentEdition	2
DataFeaturesEnabled	True
Documents.Count	7
TypelibMinorVersion	14
Version	14.0

The ActiveDocument and ActivePage objects

These objects can be referenced from the global object in VBA, but they are only available via the `Application` object in other languages.

The Addons collection

Microsoft writes all of its additional code as C++ add-ons to Visio as **Visio Solution Library files** (`*.vsl`), which are standard DLLs with specific header information in them. Others may write them as executable files (`*.exe`), which are generally slower because they are not running within the Visio process thread.

You can list the `Add-ons` that are loaded in your Visio installation like this:

```
Public Sub EnumerateAddons()
Dim adn As Visio.Addon
    Debug.Print "EnumerateAddons : Count = " &
        Application.Addons.Count
    Debug.Print , "Index", "Enabled", "NameU", "Name"
    For Each adn In Application.Addons
        With adn
            Debug.Print , .Index, .Enabled, .NameU, .Name
        End With
    Next
End Sub
```

This will output a very long list to your **Immediate Window**, the first few items are as follows:

EnumerateAddons : Count = 96			
Index	Enabled	NameU	Name
1	-1	Aec	Aec
2	-1	AutoSpaceConvert	AutoSpaceConvert
3	-1	AutoSpaceDrop	AutoSpaceDrop
4	-1	AutoSpaceResize	AutoSpaceResize
5	-1	Move Shapes...	Move Shapes...
6	-1	Shape Area and Perimeter...	Shape Area and Perimeter...
7	-1	Array Shapes...	Array Shapes...
8	-1	Measure Tool	Measure Tool
9	-1	BRAINSTORM	Brainstorming
10	-1	DB Engineer	DB Engineer
11	-1	DBWiz	Database Wizard

Note that the **NameU** (**Universal Name**) can be different than the **Name** property, although either can be used if you want to reference a particular add-on to run it. For example, if you select a shape in Visio, then type the following into the **Immediate Window**:

```
Application.Addons("Shape Area and Perimeter...").Run("")
```

This will cause the add-on to run, if you have a shape selected.

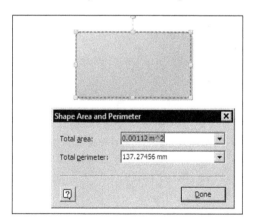

The COMAddIns collection

The COMAddIns collection is actually part of the Microsoft Office 14.0 Object Library, so you will need to set it correctly if you want **IntelliSense** to work in Visual Studio, or the VB Editor.

The following code will enumerate the loaded COMAddins in your Visio application:

```
Public Sub EnumerateCOMAddIns()
Dim adns As Office.COMAddIns
Dim adn As Office.COMAddIn
    Set adns = Application.COMAddIns
    Debug.Print "EnumerateCOMAddIns"
    Debug.Print , "Description"
    For Each adn In adns
        With adn
            Debug.Print , .Description
        End With
    Next
End Sub
```

The output in the **Immediate Window** will be something like this:

```
EnumerateCOMAddIns : Count = 2
        Description
        ValidationExplorer
        VisioAddIn1
```

The CurrentEdition property

Since the **Validation** object is only in Visio Premium edition, a further check could be included to ensure that CurrentEdition value is not Standard or Professional. It can be done using the following command:

```
If Application.CurrentEdition=visEdition.visEditionPremium Then
....
```

The DataFeaturesEnabled property

Data Linking and **Data Graphic** features are not available in Visio Standard, and they could be disabled in code, so you could check that this value is True if you want to interact with these particular features.

The Documents collection

The Documents collection contains all of the stencils and drawings that are currently open in the Visio application.

Consider this screenshot of a drawing that has been created from the **Software and Databases | Wireframe Diagram** template:

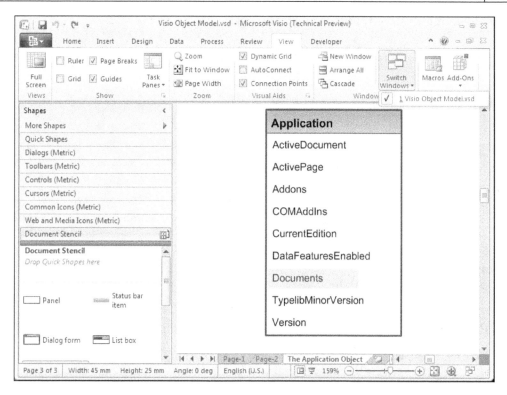

How many documents are open? Well, there is one showing, **Visio Object Model. vsd,** in the **Switch Windows** menu on the **View** tab. There appear to be seven docked stencils open too.

If you were to run the following code:

```
Public Sub EnumerateDocuments()
Dim doc As Visio.Document
    Debug.Print "EnumerateDocuments : Count = " &
      Application.Documents.Count
    Debug.Print , "Index", "Type", "ReadOnly", "Name", "Title"
    For Each doc In Application.Documents
        With doc
            Debug.Print , .Index, .Type, .ReadOnly, .Name, .Title
        End With
    Next
End Sub
```

Then you might get output that looks like this:

```
EnumerateDocuments : Count = 7
    Index      Type    ReadOnly   Name              Title
    1          1       0          Visio Object      The Visio Object
                                  Model.vsd         Model
    2          2       -1         WFDLGS_M.VSS      Forms and Dialogs
    3          2       -1         WFTLBR_M.VSS      Toolbars and Menus
    4          2       -1         WFCTRL_M.VSS      Controls
    5          2       -1         WFCRS_M.VSS       Cursors
    6          2       -1         WFCICN_M.VSS      Common Icons
    7          2       -1         WFWICN_M.VSS      Web and Media Icons
```

As you can see, there are seven documents in all, one of which is `Type = 1` (**Drawing**) and the rest are `Type = 2` (**Stencil**). The **Document Stencil** is part of the Drawing, **Visio Object Model.vsd.**

The TypelibMinorVersion and Version properties

It may also be helpful to check the version of Visio, since **Validation** was not available prior to Visio 2010:

```
Application.Version = "14.0"
```

Or

```
Application.TypelibMinorVersion = 14
```

The Document object

The `Application.Documents` collection, seen highlighted in the following diagram contains many `Document` objects. The `Document` object contains the collections of `DataRecordsets`, `Masters`, `Pages`, and other properties, that you may need if you are validating a document.

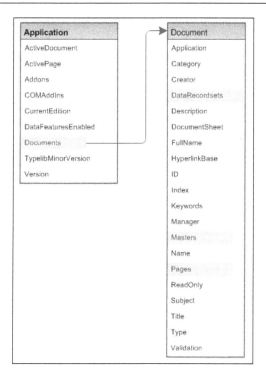

The Advanced Properties object

The **Advanced Properties**, which are the document properties in the UI, could be referenced by the **Validation** expressions, as follows:

- Category
- Creator displayed as **Author** in the **Properties** dialog
- Description displayed as **Comments** in the **Properties** dialog
- HyperlinkBase
- Keywords displayed as **Tags** in the **Properties** dialog
- Manager
- Subject
- Title

You can view these values in the backstage panel, and in the **Advanced Properties** option on the **Properties** button.

```
Public Sub DebugPrintDocumentAdvancedProperties()
    Debug.Print "DebugPrintDocumentAdvancedProperties : " &
      ActiveDocument.Name
    With ActiveDocument
        Debug.Print , "Title", .Title
        Debug.Print , "Subject", .Subject
        Debug.Print , "Author", .Creator
        Debug.Print , "Manager", .Manager
        Debug.Print , "Company", .Company
        Debug.Print , "Language", .Language
        Debug.Print , "Categories", .category
        Debug.Print , "Tags", .Keywords
        Debug.Print , "Comments", .Description
        Debug.Print , "HyperlinkBase", .HyperlinkBase
    End With
End Sub
```

The output would be as follows.

DebugPrintDocumentAdvancedProperties : Partial Visio Object Model and VBA Code.vsd	
Title	The Visio Object Model
Subject	Business Process Diagramming in Visio 2010
Author	David J Parker
Manager	Stephanie Moss
Company	bVisual ltd
Language	1033
Categories	Samples
Tags	Visio,Object Model,Type Library
Comments	This document contains sample VBA code
HyperlinkBase	http://www.bvisual.net

The DataRecordsets collection

If you are using the **Data Linking** features, then you may want to reference one or more of the DataRecordsets objects in the document.

```
Public Sub EnumerateRecordsets()
Dim doc As Visio.Document
Dim dst As Visio.DataRecordset
    Set doc = Application.ActiveDocument
    Debug.Print "EnumerateRecordsets : Count = " &
      doc.DataRecordsets.Count
    Debug.Print , "ID", "DataConnection", "Name"
```

```
    For Each dst In doc.DataRecordsets
        With dst
            Debug.Print , .ID, .DataConnection, .Name
        End With
    Next
End Sub
```

The output from the above will be similar to this:

EnumerateRecordsets : Count = 1		
ID	DataConnection	Name
2	2	XLEXTDAT9 DemoData NetworkStatus

Note that the **Pivot Diagram** feature in Visio creates multiple `DataRecordsets` which are not visible in the normal UI.

The DocumentSheet object

The `DocumentSheet` object is the **ShapeSheet** of `Documents`.

If you wanted to ensure that a document is uniquely identifiable, since its name can be changed, then you can use the `UniqueID` property to generate a **GUID** for the `DocumentSheet`, for example where `doc` is a Document object.

```
doc.DocumentSheet.UniqueID(VisUniqueIDArgs.visGetOrMakeGUID)
```

The ID and Index properties

An `ID` is assigned to a document when it is added to the `Documents` collection, and it will be kept so long as the document stays open, whereas the `Index` may change if other documents are closed.

The FullName and Name properties

The `Name` property is the file name without the path, whilst the `FullName` is the whole path, including the Name.

The Masters collection

The `Document` object contains the `Masters` collection.

```
Public Sub EnumerateMasters()
Dim doc As Visio.Document
Dim mst As Visio.Master
    Set doc = Application.ActiveDocument
    Debug.Print "EnumerateMasters : Count = " & doc.Masters.Count
    Debug.Print , "ID", "Type", "OneD", "Hidden", "Name"
    For Each mst In doc.Masters
        With mst
            Debug.Print , .ID, .Type, .OneD, .Hidden, .Name
        End With
    Next
End Sub
```

This code will produce output similar to the following:

EnumerateMasters : Count = 3				
ID	Type	OneD	Hidden	Name
6	1	0	0	List box
7	1	0	0	List box item
9	1	-1	0	Dynamic connector

The `Type=1` is the constant `visMasterTypes.visTypeMaster`. There are other types for fills, themes, and data graphics but they will usually be hidden to ensure that the user does not accidently drag-and-drop them off the document stencil in the UI.

The Pages collection

The `Pages` collection of the `Document` object contains all pages in the document, regardless of type, thus you may need to filter by type when you are traversing them.

The following code provides a simple enumeration of the pages:

```
Public Sub EnumeratePages()
Dim doc As Visio.Document
Dim pag As Visio.Page
    Set doc = Application.ActiveDocument
    Debug.Print "EnumeratePages : Count = " & doc.Pages.Count
    Debug.Print , "Index", "ID", "Type", "Name"
    For Each pag In doc.Pages
        With pag
            Debug.Print , .Index, .ID, .Type, .Name
```

```
        End With
    Next
End Sub
```

The output will be similar to this:

EnumeratePages : Count = 4			
Index	ID	Type	Name
1	5	1	The Application Object
2	0	1	Page-1
3	4	1	Page-2
4	6	1	Page-4

Notice that the ID property does not need to be contiguous!

The ReadOnly property

This is a Boolean (True/False) property.

The Type property

You can test for the type of document in code to ensure that it is the type that you want.

```
If doc.Type=VisDocumentTypes.visTypeDrawing Then
    . . .
```

The other types are visTypeStencil and visTypeTemplate.

The Validation object

The **Validation** object provides access to the **Validation API** and will be discussed at length in *Chapter 4*.

The Master object

When a **Master** shape is dragged-and-dropped from a stencil onto a page, (or by using any of the PageDrop methods) then Visio checks the local document stencil to see if the master already exists.

If a master name exists already and it has not been edited locally, or, even if it has and the MatchByName property is true, then the shape becomes an instance of the local master. If it does not exist, then the master is copied from the docked stencil to the local stencil, so that the shape can become an instance of it.

The `MatchByName` property can be set by editing a master's properties in the user interface, and changing the **Match Master By Name on Drop** checkbox in the **Master Properties** dialog.

If you open a **Master** on your local document stencil via **Edit Master | Edit Master Shape**, then you can open the **Master Explorer** window. You can then see that it is usually composed of a single **Shape** which often has a **Shapes** collection within it.

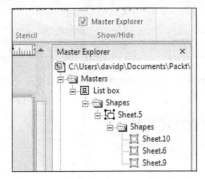

You can do a certain amount of editing to the shape in a local master, and have these changes propagated to all instances within the document. However, many users make the assumption that you can simply replace the master in a document to update the instances. This is not so, although some third-parties have attempted to make tools that can perform this task.

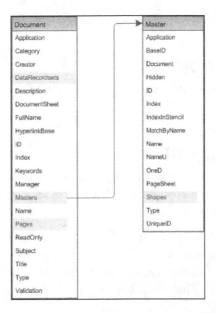

The BaseID property

It is possible that many Masters have been derived from the same root Master, in which case they would all have the same **BaseID**.

The Hidden property

If this value is true, then the Master is hidden in the UI, but it still can have shape instances. This is merely the display position of the Master in the stencil.

The ID, Index, and IndexInStencil properties

An ID is assigned to a master when it is added to the Masters collection, and it will be kept so long as the document exists. The Index is the read-only ordinal position in the stencil, but the IndexInStencil controls the display position in the stencil, and can be modified.

The Name and NameU properties

The Name property is the displayed name, which could be different to the universal NameU property.

The PageSheet object

The PageSheet object is the **ShapeSheet** of the Master (or a Page).

If you wanted to ensure that a page is uniquely identifiable, since its name can be changed, then you can use the UniqueID property to generate a GUID for the PageSheet, for example, where pag is a Page object.

```
pag.PageSheet.UniqueID(VisUniqueIDArgs.visGetOrMakeGUID)
```

The Type property

There are many different types of Master, since they are used to define **Data Graphics**, **Fills**, **Lines**, and **Themes** so it can be useful to check first.

```
If master.Type = Visio,visMasterTypes.visTypeMaster Then
...
```

The Page object

The Page object contains the Connects, Layers, and most importantly, the Shapes collections.

The Connects collection

The page has a Connects collection that contains all of the shape connections in it. A developer can now use the simpler ConnectedShapes and GluedShapes methods, described later in this chapter, but it is worth understanding this collection.

In a process diagram, most flowchart shapes are connected to each other via a **Dynamic Connector** shape. So, each **Dynamic Connector** (which is **OneD**) shape is usually connected to a flowchart shape at each end of it. The cell at the start of the line is called **BeginX**, and the cell at the end is called **EndX**.

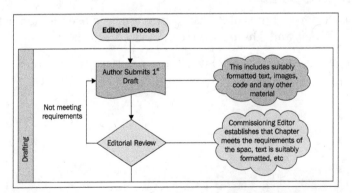

You can iterate the `Connects` collection with the following code:

```
Public Sub EnumeratePageConnects()
Dim pag As Visio.Page
Dim con As Visio.Connect
    Set pag = Application.ActivePage
    Debug.Print "EnumeratePageConnects : Count = " &
      pag.Connects.Count
    Debug.Print , "Index", "FromSheet.Name", "FromCell.Name",
      "FromSheet.Text ", _
        "ToSheet.Name", "ToCell.Name", "ToSheet.Text"
    For Each con In pag.Connects
        With con
            Debug.Print , .Index, .FromSheet.Name, .FromCell.Name,
              .FromSheet.Text, _
                .ToSheet.Name, .ToCell.Name, .ToSheet.Text
        End With
    Next
End Sub
```

This is the first few rows of the example output:

```
EnumeratePageConnects : Count = 32
```

Index	FromSheet. Name	FromCell. Name	FromSheet. Text	ToSheet. Name	ToCell. Name	ToSheet. Text
1	Dynamic connector	BeginX		Start/End	PinY	Editorial Process
2	Dynamic connector	EndX		Document	PinY	Author Submits 1st Draft
3	Dynamic connector.5	BeginX		Document	PinY	Author Submits 1st Draft
4	Dynamic connector.5	EndX		Decision	PinY	Editorial Review
5	Dynamic connector.7	BeginX	Pass	Decision	PinX	Editorial Review
6	Dynamic connector.7	EndX	Pass	Process	PinX	1st Draft Peer Reviewed

I have displayed the text on each shape to make it easier to understand, but it is more likely that you will need to read the **Shape Data** on each shape in more complex diagrams.

The ID and Index properties

An ID is assigned to a page when it is added to the Pages collection, and it will be kept, whereas the Index will change if the page order is modified.

The Layers collection

A page can contain many layers, which can have their Visible and Print setting toggled, amongst other options. However the display in Silverlight (as contained in the Visio drawing for web format) does not respect any of these settings. This is probably because a Visio shape can belong to none or many layers, making the correlation to XAML very difficult.

Users often confuse layers with the display order in the Z-order or index. The Z-index is controlled by the index of the shape within the page. The Move Forwards, Move To Front, Move Backwards, and Move to Back commands merely change the index of the affected shapes. However, Visio 2010 has introduced a new way to control the display level, which will be discussed in the next chapter.

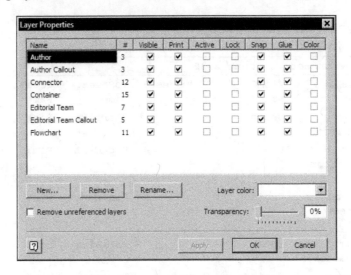

The sum of the number of shapes on each layer can be less or greater than the total number of shapes on a page because a shape can belong to none or multiple layers, and shapes with subshapes can have different layer membership.

The **Drawing Explorer** window provides an easy way of viewing the list of shapes assigned to each layer.

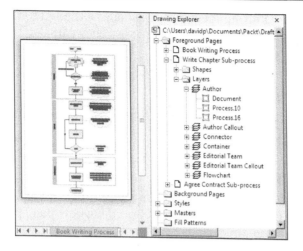

You can iterate the layers on a page in code:

```
Public Sub EnumeratePageLayers()
Dim pag As Visio.Page
Dim lyr As Visio.Layer
    Set pag = Application.ActivePage
    Debug.Print "EnumeratePageLayers : Count = " & pag.Layers.Count
Debug.Print , "Index", "Row", "Visible", "Print", "Name"
    For Each lyr In pag.Layers
        With lyr
            Debug.Print , .Index, .Row,
                .CellsC(VisCellIndices.visLayerVisible),
                .CellsC(VisCellIndices.visLayerPrint), .Name
        End With
    Next
End Sub
```

This could provide output like this:

EnumeratePageLayers : Count = 7				
Index	Row	Visible	Print	Name
1	0	1	1	Flowchart
2	1	1	1	Connector
3	2	1	1	Author
4	3	1	1	Editorial Team
5	4	1	1	Author Callout
6	5	1	1	Editorial Team Callout
7	6	1	1	Container

Layers are useful for controlling visibility of shapes assigned to them, and they provide a way of retrieving a selection of shapes. They can also be part of a validation expression.

The PageSheet object

The `PageSheet` object is the ShapeSheet of the `Master` (or a `Page`. See *The Master object* section covered previously).

The Reviewer property

When a user tracks markup using the **Review** tab in Visio on a page, then a new page is added to the document `Pages` collection. This new page provides a canvas for adding comments and any shapes over the top of the original page, but without adding anything to the original page.

If a page is a markup page, then the `ReviewerID` property is available in code. The `ReviewerID` is an index into specific cells in the `DocumentSheet`, as you will discover in the next chapter.

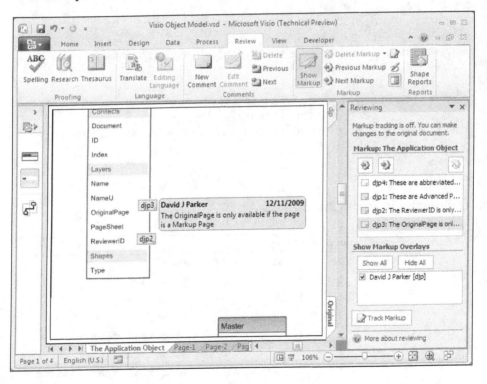

The following code can be run on a normal (non-markup) page:

```
Public Sub EnumeratePageMarkups()
Dim pag As Visio.Page
Dim pagTest As Visio.Page
    Set pag = Application.ActivePage
    Debug.Print "UserName : " & pag.Application.Settings.UserName
    Debug.Print "UserInitials : " &
      pag.Application.Settings.UserInitials
    Debug.Print "EnumeratePageMarkups for " & pag.Name

    Debug.Print , "Index", "ID", "ReviewerID", "Name"
    For Each pagTest In pag.Document.Pages
        With pagTest
            If .Type = VisPageTypes.visTypeMarkup Then
                If .OriginalPage Is pag Then
                    Debug.Print , .Index, .ID, .ReviewerID, .Name
                End If
            End If
        End With
    Next
End Sub
```

This will produce the following output:

UserName : David J Parker			
UserInitials : djp			
EnumeratePageMarkups for The Application Object			
Index	ID	ReviewerID	Name
5	7	1	The Application Object [djp]

Notice that the markup page name is the same as the `OriginalPage.Name`, but with the reviewers initials appended in square brackets.

It is possible to iterate through the comments too, but this requires some understanding of the ShapeSheet, which comes in the next chapter.

 Comments are not displayed in the new Microsoft SharePoint Web Part, which displays the Visio document for the web format (*.vdw).

The Shapes collection

Each `Page`, `Master`, or `Shape` can have a `Shapes` collection. The Shapes collections contains all of the shapes, whether they are instances of a `Master`, or simple drawn lines, rectangles, text, and so on.

In this example, I have simply shown how to iterate through the shapes on a page.

```
Public Sub EnumeratePageShapes()
Dim pag As Visio.Page
Dim shp As Visio.Shape
    Set pag = Application.ActivePage
    Debug.Print "EnumeratePageShapes : Count = " & pag.Shapes.Count
    Debug.Print , "Index", "ID", "Type", "OneD", "Is Instance",
"Name", "Text"
    For Each shp In pag.Shapes
        With shp
            Debug.Print , .Index, .ID, .Type, .OneD, Not .Master Is
Nothing, .Name, .Text
        End With
    Next
End Sub
```

Here are a few lines from the output as follows:

EnumeratePageShapes : Count = 35						
Index	ID	Type	OneD	Is Instance	Name	Text
1	34	2	0	True	Container 3	Drafting
2	39	2	0	True	Container 3.39	Editing
3	44	2	0	True	Container 3.44	Production
4	20	5	0	False	Sheet.20	
5	1	3	0	True	Start/End	Editorial Process
6	2	3	0	True	Document	Author Submits 1st Draft
7	3	3	-1	True	Dynamic connector	
8	4	3	0	True	Decision	Editorial Review

It may be necessary to test that specific shapes exist on a page during the validation process. For example, it may be a requirement that there is a Start and End flowchart shape.

The Type property

There are several types of `Page` in Visio, namely **Foreground**, **Background** and **Markup**. Any page in Visio can have an associated Background page, and any number of associated Markup pages used by reviewers. Therefore, it is usual to check the page type in code before continuing with any operations on it.

```
If pag.Type = visPageTypes.visTypeForeground Then
...
```

The Shape object

The `Shape` object is the most important object in the Visio application, and it needs to be seen as a whole with its member `Sections`, `Rows`, and `Cells` to understand its complexity.

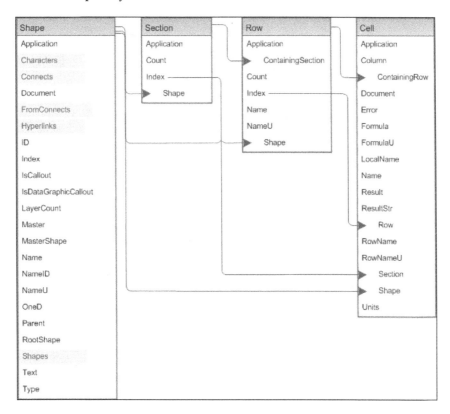

Here is a function that prints out basic information about a selected shape into the **Immediate Window** in **VBA**:

```
Public Sub DebugPrintShape()
If Application.ActiveWindow.Selection.Count = 0 Then
    Exit Sub
End If
Dim shp As Visio.Shape
    Set shp = Application.ActiveWindow.Selection.PrimaryItem
    Debug.Print "DebugPrintShape : " & shp.Name
    With shp
        Debug.Print , "Characters.CharCount", .Characters.CharCount
        Debug.Print , "Connects.Count", .Connects.Count
        Debug.Print , "FromConnects.Count", .FromConnects.Count
        Debug.Print , "Hyperlinks.Count", .Hyperlinks.Count
        Debug.Print , "ID", .ID
        Debug.Print , "Index", .Index
        Debug.Print , "IsCallout", .IsCallout
        Debug.Print , "IsDataGraphicCallout", .IsDataGraphicCallout
        Debug.Print , "LayerCount", .LayerCount
        Debug.Print , "Has Master", Not .Master Is Nothing
        Debug.Print , "Has MasterShape", Not .MasterShape Is Nothing
        Debug.Print , "Name", .Name
        Debug.Print , "NameID", .NameID
        Debug.Print , "NameU", .NameU
        Debug.Print , "OneD", .OneD
        Debug.Print , "Parent.Name", .Parent.Name
        Debug.Print , "Has RootShape", Not .RootShape Is Nothing
        Debug.Print , "Text", .Text
        Debug.Print , "Type", .Type
    End With
End Sub
```

This produces the following output in my sample workflow as follows, when the Document shape with the text Author Submits 1st Draft is selected before the code is run:

DebugPrintShape : Document	
Characters.CharCount	24
Connects.Count	0
FromConnects.Count	3
Hyperlinks.Count	0
ID	2

```
DebugPrintShape : Document
        Index                    6
        IsCallout                False
        IsDataGraphicCallout     False
        LayerCount               2
        Has Master               True
        Has MasterShape          True
        Name                     Document
        NameID                   Sheet.2
        NameU                    Document
        OneD                     0
        Parent.Name              Write Chapter Sub-process
        Has RootShape            True
        Text                     Author Submits 1st Draft
        Type                     3
```

The Characters and Text properties

Every shape in Visio has a text block, regardless of whether there are any characters in it. This text block can be multiple lines, contain different fonts and formats, and can even contain references to other cell values. Indeed, if a text block does contain references to other cells, then the shape.Text property in code will display special characters instead of the actual value. However, shape.Characters.Text will return the referenced cell's values. Therefore, it is usually better to use the shape.Characters.Text property.

The Connects and FromConnects collections

The Connects collection contains the connections that the source shape is connected to, whereas the FromConnects collection contains the connections that are connected to the source shape.

Sounds easy, but it isn't. Traversing a structured diagram using these collections gets terribly messy, so use the newly added ConnectedShapes and GluedShapes methods, as described in the *Connectivity API* section covered later in this chapter.

The Hyperlinks collection

Hyperlinks can be created in the UI, in code, or even automatically by using **Data Linking**. Hyperlinks can contain http:, https:, and even mailto: URLs. Therefore, you may need to be aware of, and even report on them.

The ID, Index, NameID, Name, and NameU properties

The Index is controlled by the Z-index or Z-order in the user interface (by using **Send To Back**, **Bring to Front**, and so on), whereas the ID is a sequential number that is assigned when the shape is created. The NameID is concatenation of Sheet and ID.

The Name and NameU are automatically created, usually as a concatenation of the Master.Name and ID, and are originally identical. These properties can be modified (even independently of each other), but they must be unique for the Shapes collection of the parent. The NameU is the Shapes' locale- independent name, but Name can be locale- specific.

The IsCallout and IsDataGraphicCallout properties

The IsCallout property is a new property for Visio 2010, implemented so that you can spot more easily if a shape is one of the new callout shapes. The IsDataGraphicCallout property was introduced in Visio 2007 so that you can identify if the parent shape is a **Data Graphic** shape.

The LayerCount property

A shape can be a member of none, one, or multiple layers, which can lead to great complexity. You may wish to have a rule that a shape must only belong to a single layer.

The Master, MasterShape, and RootShape objects

A shape in Visio can either be an instance of a Master, that is one that has been dragged-and-dropped from a stencil, or it is one that is just drawn, like a line, rectangle, ellipse, or text. You can test this by checking if the shape.Master or shape.MasterShape object exists (Is Nothing) or not.

If the shape is part of a Master instance, then the RootShape is the top-level shape of the instance.

The OneD property

The OneD property is true if the shape is set to behave like a line.

The Parent object

The Parent property is never Nothing, but it can be either a Page, Master, or Shape.

Note that the `Parent` object may also be one of the following `Containing` properties:

- A shape in `Page.Shapes` collection always has values for the `ContainingPage` and `ContainingPageID` properties
- A shape in `Master.Shapes` collection always has values for the `ContainingMaster` and `ContainingMasterID` properties
- A shape in `Shape.Shapes` collection always has values for the `ContainingShape` and `ContainingShapeID` properties

The Type property

A shape can be a group of other shapes, in which case the `shape.Type` property will be equal to `VisShapeTypes.visTypeGroup` and the `shape.Shapes` collection will probably contain other shapes.

There are other shape types too, such as **Guide** and **Ink**, but most will be `VisShapeTypes.visTypeShape` or `VisShapeTypes.visTypeGroup`.

The Section object

Visio ShapeSheets have two types of Sections—fixed and variable. You can always rely upon a fixed `Section` being present, thus you do not need to test for its existence before referencing it.

However, some sections are optional (and in the case of **Geometry**, there may be multiple occurrences). Therefore, you may need to test for their existence before referencing them. The most common variable sections that you will need to be aware of are for **Shape Data**, **User-defined Cells**, and less often, **Hyperlinks**. You will learn more about these in the next chapter.

Use the enum `VisSectionIndices` in the **Visio Type Library** to get the right integer value for the `Section.Index` property. For example, you could test for the presence of a **Shape Data** section in a shape as follows (where `shp` is a **Shape** object):

```
If shp.SectionExists(VisSectionIndices.visSectionProp, VisExistsFlags.
visExistsAnywhere) Then...
```

You can get the number of `Rows` in a `Section` using the `RowCount` method as follows:

```
For i = 0 to shp.RowCount(VisSectionIndices.visSectionProp) -1...
```

The Row object

Sections contain **Rows**, just like a worksheet in Excel, and each Row contains cells. All of the interesting information is at the Cell object level.

Take this example where I have selected a Document shape.

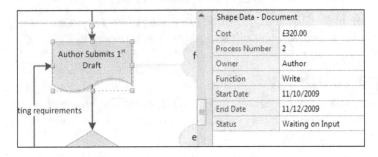

Shape Data - Document	
Cost	£320.00
Process Number	2
Owner	Author
Function	Write
Start Date	11/10/2009
End Date	11/12/2009
Status	Waiting on Input

I can enumerate through the cells of the **Shape Data** section using the following code:

```
Public Sub EnumerateShapePropRows()
If Application.ActiveWindow.Selection.Count = 0 Then
    Exit Sub
End If
Dim shp As Visio.Shape
Dim iRow As Integer
Dim cel As Visio.Cell
    Set shp = Application.ActiveWindow.Selection.PrimaryItem
    Debug.Print "EnumerateShapePropRows : " & shp.Name
    If Not shp.SectionExists(VisSectionIndices.visSectionProp, _
      VisExistsFlags.visExistsAnywhere) Then
        Debug.Print , "Does not contain any Shape Data rows"
        Exit Sub
    End If
    With shp
        Debug.Print , "Shape Data row count : ", _
          .RowCount(VisSectionIndices.visSectionProp)
        Debug.Print , "Row", "RowName", "Label"
      For iRow = 0 To .RowCount(VisSectionIndices.visSectionProp) - 1
            Set cel = .CellsSRC(VisSectionIndices.visSectionProp, _
              iRow, 0)
            Debug.Print , cel.Row, cel.RowName, _
              .CellsSRC(VisSectionIndices.visSectionProp, iRow, _
              VisCellIndices.visCustPropsLabel).ResultStr("")
        Next iRow
    End With
End Sub
```

This will produce the following output:

EnumerateShapePropRows : Document		
Shape Data row count :	7	
Row	RowName	Label
0	Cost	Cost
1	ProcessNumber	Process Number
2	Owner	Owner
3	Function	Function
4	StartDate	Start Date
5	EndDate	End Date
6	Status	Status

Notice that I had to use the `CellsSRC()` method to iterate through the `Row`, and that I need to understand what values to use for the third parameter.

Moreover, I know that the `RowName` is safe to use on the **Shape Data** section, but some **Sections** do not have names for their **Rows**.

I have also displayed the difference between the `RowName` and the `Label` of a **Shape Data** row. Note that the `RowName` cannot contain any special characters or spaces, whereas `Label` can.

The Cell object

We must look a little more closely at the `Cell` object.

The Column property

There are a different number of columns in different **Sections** of ShapeSheet. Therefore, you should use the `Section` specific values of the `VisCellIndices` enum to refer to a specific cell column. For example, the **User-defined Cells** section column indices begin with `visCellIndices.visUser`. However, all of the **Shape Data** section column indices begin with `visCellIndices.visCustProps` because **Shape Data** used to be called **Custom Properties**.

The Error property

If a `Cell` formula is unable to evaluate, then the `Error` value is one of the `VisCellError` enum values. This value is generated along with the result.

The Formula and FormulaU properties

Every `Cell` in Visio can contain a formula. This formula can contain references to other cells, and because Visio works with multiple languages the `Formula` string is the localized version of the `FormulaU` string, which is in English.

The Name and LocalName properties

For some languages, the `LocalName` property may be different to the English `Name` property.

The Result properties

There are quite a few different cell properties that begin `.Result` because the data type is agnostic. Generally, you can retrieve text values using the `.ResultStr("")` property, and numeric values using the `.ResultIU` property. **IU** stands for **Internal Units** in this case, but you could also use the `.Result("m")` property to return a numeric property formatted in the units of your choice.

Also, be aware that there is a powerful `Application.ConvertResult` method that you can use to convert values between units.

The Units property

This is an integer value from the `VisUnitCodes` enum.

Iterating through cells

Now that we understand a bit more about the `Cell` object, we can iterate through some cells in the **Shape Data** rows of a selected shape:

```
Public Sub EnumerateShapePropCells()
If Application.ActiveWindow.Selection.Count = 0 Then
    Exit Sub
End If
Dim shp As Visio.Shape
Dim iRow As Integer
Dim iCol As Integer
Dim cel As Visio.Cell
    Set shp = Application.ActiveWindow.Selection.PrimaryItem
    Debug.Print "EnumerateShapePropRows : " & shp.Name
    If Not shp.SectionExists(VisSectionIndices.visSectionProp,
      VisExistsFlags.visExistsAnywhere) Then
        Debug.Print , "Does not contain any Shape Data rows"
        Exit Sub
    End If
    With shp
        Debug.Print , "Shape Data row count : ",
          .RowCount(VisSectionIndices.visSectionProp)
        Debug.Print , "Row", "RowName"
        Debug.Print , , "Column", "Cell.Name", "Cell.Formula",
          "Cell.ResultIU", "Cell.ResultStr("""")"
        For iRow = 0 To .RowCount(VisSectionIndices.visSectionProp)-1
            For iCol = 0 To
          .RowsCellCount(VisSectionIndices.visSectionProp, iRow) - 1
                Set cel = .CellsSRC(VisSectionIndices.visSectionProp,
                  iRow, iCol)
                Debug.Print , , iCol, cel.Name, cel.Formula,
                  cel.ResultIU, cel.ResultStr("")
            Next iCol
        Next iRow
    End With
End Sub
```

On my selected Document shape, the top of the output looks like this:

Row	RowName				
	Column	Cell.Name	Cell.Formula	Cell.ResultIU	Cell.ResultStr("")
	0	Prop.Cost	CY(320,"GBP")	320	£320.00
	1	Prop.Cost.Prompt	""	0	
	2	Prop.Cost.Label	"Cost"	0	Cost
	3	Prop.Cost.Format	"@"	0	@
	4	Prop.Cost.SortKey	""	0	
	5	Prop.Cost.Type	7	7	7
	6	Prop.Cost.Invisible	FALSE	0	FALSE
	7	Prop.Cost.Verify	FALSE	0	FALSE
	8	Prop.G7	0	FALSE	
	9	Prop.H7	0	FALSE	
	10	Prop.I7	0	FALSE	
	11	Prop.J7	0	FALSE	
	12	Prop.K7	0	FALSE	
	13	Prop.L7	0	FALSE	
	14	Prop.Cost.LangID	1033	1033	1033
	15	Prop.Cost.Calendar	0	0	0

The table is preceded by:

```
EnumerateShapePropRows : Document
  Shape Data row count :     7
```

Cells 8 through 13 stick out because they do not appear in the UI at all. In fact, these are reserved for internal use or future use by Microsoft, so use them at your peril!

Connectivity API

All of the above sections were to get you used to the object model a bit, so that you can understand how to traverse a structured diagram and retrieve the information that you want. The **Connectivity API** also provides easy methods for creating and deleting connections, but we are simply interested in traversing connections in order to check or export the process steps to another application.

Here is the top part of my **Write Chapter Sub-process** page which demonstrates some of the key features of the Connectivity API. They are done in the following sequence:

1. The flow shapes are connected together creating a logical sequence of steps.

2. Some steps have an associated callout with extra Notes.

3. Some steps are within a Container shape to define the Phase.

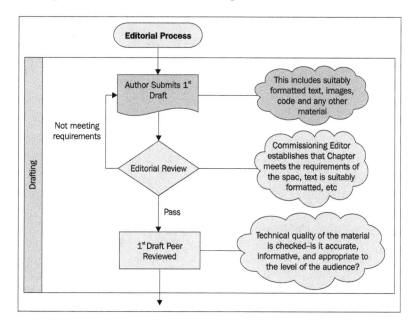

Now we will traverse the diagram in code, and list out the steps in their phases with any associated notes, but first we need to understand a few of the new methods in the Connectivity API.

The Shape.ConnectedShapes method

The `Shape.ConnectedShapes` method returns an array of **identifiers** (**IDs**) of shapes that are one degree of separation away from the given shape (that is, separated by a 1-D connector).

The method has two arguments, `Flags` and `CategoryFilter`.

- `Flags`: This filters the list of returned shape IDs by the directionality of the connectors, using the `VisConnectedShapesFlags` enum for All, Incoming, or Outgoing nodes.

- `CategoryFilter`: This filters the list of returned shape IDs by limiting it to IDs of shapes that match the specified category. A shape's categories can be found in the `User.msvShapeCategories` cell of its ShapeSheet.

So, we can use the new `ConnectedShapes` method to list all of the significant connections in my **Write Chapter Sub-process** page. I have used the existence of the `Prop.Cost` cell as a test for shape significance.

```
Public Sub ListNextConnections()
Dim shp As Visio.Shape
Dim connectorShape As Visio.Shape
Dim sourceShape As Visio.Shape
Dim targetShape As Visio.Shape
Dim aryTargetIDs() As Long
Dim arySourceIDs() As Long
Dim targetID As Long
Dim sourceID As Long
Dim i As Integer
Const CheckProp As String = "Prop.Cost"
For Each shp In Visio.ActivePage.Shapes
    If Not shp.OneD Then
        If shp.CellExists(CheckProp, Visio.visExistsAnywhere) Then
            Debug.Print "Shape", shp.Name, shp.Text
            arySourceIDs =
             shp.ConnectedShapes(visConnectedShapesOutgoingNodes, "")
            For i = 0 To UBound(arySourceIDs)
                Set sourceShape =
                   Visio.ActivePage.Shapes.ItemFromID(arySourceIDs(i))
                If sourceShape.CellExists(CheckProp,
                    Visio.visExistsAnywhere) Then
                    Debug.Print , "<", sourceShape.Name,
                        sourceShape.Text
                End If
            Next
            aryTargetIDs =
             shp.ConnectedShapes(visConnectedShapesIncomingNodes, "")
            For i = 0 To UBound(aryTargetIDs)
                Set targetShape =
                   Visio.ActivePage.Shapes.ItemFromID(aryTargetIDs(i))
                If targetShape.CellExists(CheckProp,
```

```
                    Visio.visExistsAnywhere) Then
                        Debug.Print , ">", targetShape.Name,
                            targetShape.Text
                    End If
                Next
            End If
        End If
    Next

    End Sub
```

The top of the output from this function will appear as follows:

Shape	Start/End	Editorial Process	
	<	Document	Author Submits 1st Draft
Shape	Document	Author Submits 1st Draft	
	<	Decision	Editorial Review
	>	Start/End	Editorial Process
	>	Decision	Editorial Review
Shape	Decision	Editorial Review	
	<	Document	Author Submits 1st Draft
	<	Process	1st Draft Peer Reviewed
	>	Document	Author Submits 1st Draft

The Shape.GluedShapes method

The Shape.GluedShapes method returns an array of identifiers for the shapes that are glued to a shape. For instance, if the given shape is a 2-D shape that has multiple connectors attached to it, this method would return the IDs of those connectors. If the given shape is a connector, this method would return the IDs of the shapes to which its ends are glued.

The method has three arguments, Flags, CategoryFilter, and OtherConnectedShape:

- Flags: This filters the list of returned shape IDs by the directionality of the connectors, using the VisGluedShapesFlags enum for All1D All2D, Incoming1D, Incoming2D, Outgoing1D, or Outgoing2D nodes.

- CategoryFilter: This filters the list of returned shape IDs by limiting it to IDs of shapes that match the specified category. A shape's categories can be found in the User.msvShapeCategories cell of its **ShapeSheet**.

- OtherConnectedShape: Optional additional shape to which returned shapes must also be glued.

The method is used as follows :

```
arIDs = Shape.GluedShapes(Flags, CategoryFilter,
  pOtherConnectedShape)
```

The Shape.MemberOfContainers property

We can return an array of IDs of the **Containers** that a shape is within.

You can use the ID to return the Container shape, get its ContainerProperties object, and, in this case, return the text from the shape.

Here is a private function that I will use in the main function in the following code:

```
Private Function getContainerText(ByVal shp As Visio.Shape) As String
'Return text of any containers,
'or an empty string if there are none
Dim aryTargetIDs() As Long
Dim targetShape As Visio.Shape
Dim returnText As String
Dim i As Integer
    returnText = ""
    aryTargetIDs = shp.MemberOfContainers
    On Error GoTo exitHere
    For i = 0 To UBound(aryTargetIDs)
        Set targetShape =
          shp.ContainingPage.Shapes.ItemFromID(aryTargetIDs(i))
        If Len(returnText) = 0 Then
            returnText = targetShape.ContainerProperties.Shape.Text
        Else
            returnText = returnText & vbCrLf &
                targetShape.ContainerProperties.Shape.Text
        End If
    Next

exitHere:
    getContainerText = returnText
End Function
```

The Shape.CalloutsAssociated property

This property will return an array of shape IDs of any associated callouts.

You can use the ID to return the callout shape, and, in this case, return the text from within that shape.

Here is a private function that I will use in the `main` function:

```
Private Function getCalloutText(ByVal shp As Visio.Shape) As String
'Return text of any connected callouts,
'or an empty string if there are none
Dim aryTargetIDs() As Long
Dim targetShape As Visio.Shape
Dim returnText As String
Dim i As Integer
    returnText = ""
    aryTargetIDs = shp.CalloutsAssociated
    On Error GoTo exitHere
    For i = 0 To UBound(aryTargetIDs)
        Set targetShape = _
          shp.ContainingPage.Shapes.ItemFromID(aryTargetIDs(i))
        If Len(returnText) = 0 Then
            returnText = targetShape.Characters.Text
        Else
            returnText = returnText & vbCrLf & _
              targetShape.Characters.Text
        End If
    Next

exitHere:
    getCalloutText = returnText
End Function
```

Listing the steps in a process flow

In order to create a sequential listing of the steps in the page, we need to create a function that will call itself to iterate through the connections out from the source shape.

```
Private Function getNextConnected(ByVal shp As Visio.Shape, ByVal
dicFlowShapes As Dictionary, ByVal colSteps As Collection) As
Collection
'Return a collection of the next connected steps
Dim aryTargetIDs() As Long
Dim targetShape As Visio.Shape
Dim returnCollection As Collection
Dim i As Integer
    dicFlowShapes.Add shp.NameID, shp

    aryTargetIDs = _
      shp.ConnectedShapes(visConnectedShapesOutgoingNodes, "")
    For i = 0 To UBound(aryTargetIDs)
```

```
        Set targetShape =
          Visio.ActivePage.Shapes.ItemFromID(aryTargetIDs(i))
        If Not targetShape.Master Is Nothing And
          dicFlowShapes.Exists(targetShape.NameID) = False Then
            colSteps.Add targetShape
            getNextConnected targetShape, dicFlowShapes, colSteps
        End If
    Next
    Set getNextConnected = colSteps
End Function
```

Finally, we can create the public function that will list the steps. For simplicity, I'm only following the direct route and not displaying the text on the connector lines.

I have introduced the `Visio.Selection` object because it contains a collection of shapes returned by the `Page.CreateSelection()` method, which is extremely useful for getting a filtered collection of shapes by **Layer**, **Master**, **Type**, and so on.

> I am also using the `Dictionary` object in the following code, so you will need to ensure that the **Microsoft Scripting Runtime** library (`C:\Windows\system32\scrun.dll`) is ticked in the **References** dialog opened from the **Tools** menu in the Visual Basic user interface.

```
Public Sub ListProcessSteps()
Dim sel As Visio.Selection
Dim pag As Visio.Page
Dim shp As Visio.Shape
Dim shpStart As Visio.Shape
Dim shpEnd As Visio.Shape
Dim iStep As Integer
Dim dicFlowShapes As Dictionary
    Set dicFlowShapes = New Dictionary
    Set pag = Visio.ActivePage
    'Find the Start and End shapes on the Page
    'Assume that they are the instances of the Master "Start/End"
    'Assume that the Start has no incoming connections
    'and the End shape has no outgoing connections
    Set sel = pag.CreateSelection(visSelTypeByMaster, 0,
      pag.Document.Masters("Start/End"))
    If Not sel.Count = 2 Then
        MsgBox "There must be one Start shape and one End shape
          only", vbExclamation, "ListProcessSteps"
        Exit Sub
    End If
```

```
    For Each shp In sel
        If shpStart Is Nothing Then
            Set shpStart = shp
            Set shpEnd = shp
        Else
            If UBound(shp.ConnectedShapes(
                visConnectedShapesOutgoingNodes, "")) > -1 _
                And UBound(shp.ConnectedShapes(
                    visConnectedShapesIncomingNodes, "")) = -1 Then
                Set shpStart = shp
            ElseIf UBound(shp.ConnectedShapes(
                visConnectedShapesIncomingNodes, "")) > -1 _
                And UBound(shp.ConnectedShapes(
                    visConnectedShapesOutgoingNodes, "")) = -1 Then
                Set shpEnd = shp
        End If
    Next
    iStep = 1
Dim nextSteps As Collection
Dim nextShp As Visio.Shape
Dim iNext As Integer
    Set nextSteps = New Collection
    Set nextSteps = getNextConnected(shpStart, dicFlowShapes,
      nextSteps)
    Debug.Print "Step", "Master.Name", "Phase", "Text", "Notes"
    Debug.Print iStep, shpStart.Master.Name,
      getContainerText(shpStart), shpStart.Text,
      getCalloutText(shpStart)
    For iNext = 1 To nextSteps.Count
        iStep = iNext + 1
        Set nextShp = nextSteps.Item(iNext)
        Debug.Print iStep, nextShp.Master.Name,
          getContainerText(nextShp), nextShp.Characters.Text,
          getCalloutText(nextShp)
    Next
    If Not nextShp Is shpEnd Then
        MsgBox "Theprocess did not finish on the End shape",
          vbExclamation, "ListProcessSteps"
    End If
End Sub
```

With a fanfare of trumpets, we get a simple listing of each step in order:

Step	Master.Name	Phase	Text	Notes
1	Start/End	Editorial Process		
2	Document	Drafting	Author Submits 1st Draft	This includes suitably formatted text, images, code and any other material
3	Decision	Drafting	Editorial Review	Commissioning Editor establishes that Chapter meets the requirements of the spec, text is suitably formatted, etc
4	Process	Drafting	1st Draft Peer Reviewed	Technical quality of the material is checked - is it accurate, informative, and appropriate to the level of the audience?
5	Process	Editing	Editorial Acceptance Verdict	Commissioning Editor evaluates reviewer comments to verify that the Chapter meets the "Editorial Acceptance" standard
6	Process	Editing	Author Rewrite	Author addresses comments, adds any extra material requested
7	Process	Editing	Final Edit	
8	Decision	Editing	Pass?	Finer iterations of chapter required?
9	Process	Production	Production Phase	Indexing, Layout, Proofing
10	Process	Production	Author Review of "PreFinal" PDF	Author inspects finished PDF to see if there are any last minute changes required and if they are happy with the chapters
11	Start/End	Publication		

Summary

In this chapter, we delved into the Visio object model, and looked at the hierarchy of the objects and collections.

We looked at the analytical parts of the Connectivity API, which enabled us to navigate connections and to retrieve surrounding containers and associated callouts.

We also used this knowledge to build a function that does some rudimentary checks of a diagram structure, and to list the steps in a process flow.

In the next chapter, we will look into the ShapeSheet and how to use the functions within it.

3
Understanding the ShapeSheet™

Microsoft Visio is a unique data diagramming system, and most of that uniqueness is due to the power of the **ShapeSheet,** which is a window on the Visio object model. It is the ShapeSheet that enables you to encapsulate complex behavior into apparently simple shapes by adding formulae to the cells using functions. The ShapeSheet was modeled on a spreadsheet, and formulae are entered in a similar manner to cells in an Excel worksheet.

Validation rules are written as quasi-ShapeSheet formulae so you will need to understand how they are written. Validation rules can check the contents of ShapeSheet cells, in addition to verifying the structure of a diagram. Therefore, in this chapter you will learn about the structure of the ShapeSheet and how to write formulae.

Where is the ShapeSheet?

There is a ShapeSheet behind every single Document, Page, and Shape, and the easiest way to access the ShapeSheet window is to run Visio in Developer mode. This mode adds the **Developer** tab to the Fluent UI, which has a **Show ShapeSheet** button. The drop-down list on the button allows you to choose which ShapeSheet window to open.

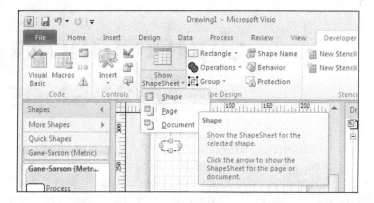

Alternatively, you can use the right-mouse menu of a shape or page, or on the relevant level within the **Drawing Explorer** window as shown in the following screenshot:

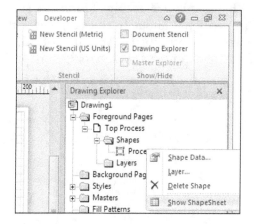

The ShapeSheet window, opened by the **Show ShapeSheet** menu option, displays the requested sections, rows, and cells of the item selected when the window was opened. It does not automatically change to display the contents of any subsequently selected shape in the Visio drawing page—you must open the ShapeSheet window again to do that. The **ShapeSheet Tools** tab, which is displayed when the ShapeSheet window is active, has a **Sections** button on the **View** group to allow you to vary the requested sections on display.

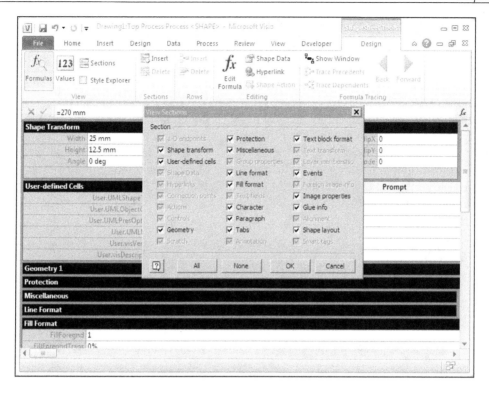

You can also open the **View Sections** dialog from the right-mouse menu within the ShapeSheet window.

You cannot alter the display order of sections in the ShapeSheet window, but you can expand/collapse them by clicking the section header.

The syntax for referencing the shape, page, and document objects in ShapeSheet formula is listed in the following table.

Object	ShapeSheet formula	Comment
Shape	`Sheet.n!`	Where n is the ID of the shape
		Can be omitted when referring to cells in the same shape.
Page.PageSheet	`ThePage!`	Used in the ShapeSheet formula of shapes within the page.
	`Pages[page name]!`	Used in the ShapeSheet formula of shapes in other pages.
Document.DocumentSheet	`TheDoc!`	Used in the ShapeSheet formula in pages or shapes of the document.

What are sections, rows, and cells?

There are a finite number of sections in a ShapeSheet, and some sections are mandatory for the type of element they are, whilst others are optional. For example, the **Shape Transform** section, which specifies the shape's size (that is, angle and position) exists for all types of shapes. However, the **1-D Endpoints** section, which specifies the co-ordinates of either end of the line, is only relevant, and thus displayed for **OneD** shapes. Neither of these sections is optional, because they are required for the specific type of shape. Sections like **User-defined Cells** and **Shape Data** are optional and they may be added to the ShapeSheet if they do not exist already. If you press the **Insert** button on the **ShapeSheet Tools** tab, under the **Sections** group, then you can see a list of the sections that you may insert into the selected ShapeSheet.

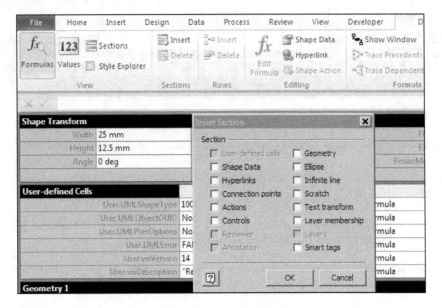

In the above example, **User-defined Cells** option is grayed out because this optional section already exists.

It is possible for a shape to have multiple **Geometry**, **Ellipse**, or **Infinite line** sections. In fact, a shape can have a total of 139 of them.

Reading a cell's properties

If you select a cell in the ShapeSheet, then you will see the formula in the formula edit bar immediately below the ribbon.

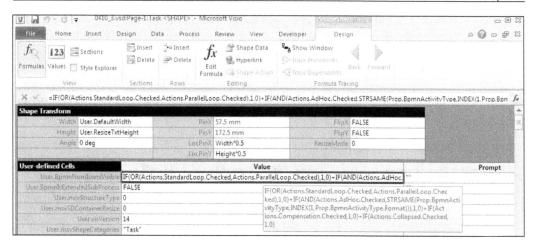

You can view the ShapeSheet **Formulas** (and I thought the plural was formulae!) or **Values** by clicking the relevant button in the **View** group on the **ShapeSheet Tools** ribbon.

Notice that Visio provides **IntelliSense** when editing formulae. This is new in Visio 2010, and is a great help to all ShapeSheet developers.

Also notice that the contents of some of the cells are shown in blue text, whilst others are black. This is because the blue text denotes that the values are stored locally with this shape instance, whilst the black text refers to values that are stored in the Master shape. Usually, the more black text you see, the more memory efficient the shape is, since less is needed to be stored with the shape instance. Of course, there are times when you cannot avoid storing values locally, such as the **PinX** and **PinY** values in the above screenshot, since these define where the shape instance is in the page. The following VBA code returns 0 (False):

```
ActivePage.Shapes("Task").Cells("PinX").IsInherited
```

But the following code returns -1 (True) :

```
ActivePage.Shapes("Task").Cells("Width").IsInherited
```

The **Edit Formula** button opens a dialog to enable you to edit multiple lines, since the edit formula bar only displays a single line, and some formulae can be quite large.

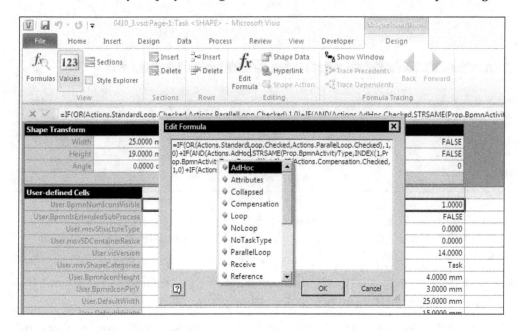

You can display the **Formula Tracing** window using the **Show Window** button in the **Formula Tracing** group on the **ShapeSheet Tools** present in **Design** tab. You can decide whether to **Trace Dependents**, which displays other cells that have a formula that refers to the selected cell or **Trace Precedents**, which displays other cells that the formula in this cell refers to.

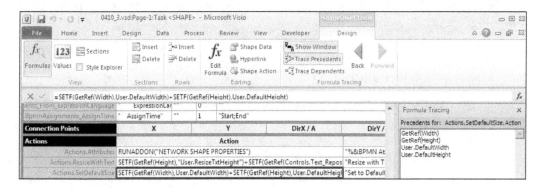

Of course, this can be done in code too. For example, the following VBA code will print out the selected cell in a ShapeSheet into the **Immediate Window**:

```
Public Sub DebugPrintCellProperties ()
'Abort if ShapeSheet not selected in the Visio UI
    If Not Visio.ActiveWindow.Type = Visio.VisWinTypes.visSheet Then
        Exit Sub
    End If
Dim cel As Visio.Cell
    Set cel = Visio.ActiveWindow.SelectedCell
'Print out some of the cell properties
    Debug.Print "Section", cel.Section
    Debug.Print "Row", cel.Row
    Debug.Print "Column", cel.Column
    Debug.Print "Name", cel.Name
    Debug.Print "FormulaU", cel.FormulaU
    Debug.Print "ResultIU", cel.ResultIU
    Debug.Print "ResultStr("""")", cel.ResultStr("")
    Debug.Print "Dependents", UBound(cel.Dependents)
'cel.Precedents may cause an error
On Error Resume Next
    Debug.Print "Precedents", UBound(cel.Precedents)

End Sub
```

In the previous screenshot, where the `Actions.SetDefaultSize.Action` cell is selected in the **Task** shape from the **BPMN Basic Shapes** stencil, the `DebugPrintCellProperties` macro outputs the following:

Section	240
Row	2
Column	3
Name	Actions.SetDefaultSize.Action
FormulaU	SETF(GetRef(Width),User.DefaultWidth)+SET F(GetRef(Height),User.DefaultHeight)
ResultIU	0
ResultStr("")	0.0000
Dependents	0
Precedents	4

 I have tried to be selective about the properties displayed to illustrate some points.

Firstly, any cell can be referred to by either its name, or section/row/column indices, commonly referred to as **SRC**.

Secondly, the **FormulaU** should produce a **ResultIU** of 0, if the formula is correctly formed and there is no numerical output from it.

Thirdly, the **Precedents** and **Dependents** are actually an array of referenced cells.

Can I print out the ShapeSheet settings?

You can download and install the Microsoft Visio SDK from the **Visio Developer Center** (visit `http://msdn.microsoft.com/en-us/office/aa905478.aspx`). This will install an extra group, **Visio SDK**, on the **Developer** ribbon and one extra button **Print ShapeSheet**.

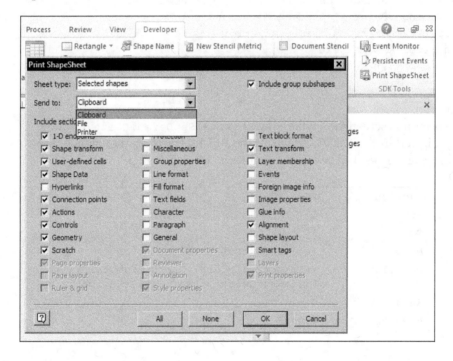

I have chosen the **Clipboard** option and pasted the report into an Excel worksheet, as in the following screenshot:

	A	B	C
1	SHAPESHEET : TASK SHEET.1		
2			
3	Start Section : USER-DEFINED CELLS		
4	Cell	Value	Formula
5	User.BpmnNumIconsVisible		1 IF(OR(Actions.StandardLoop.Checked,Actio
6	User.BpmnNumIconsVisible.Prompt	No Formula	No Formula
7	User.BpmnIsExtendedSubProcess	FALSE	FALSE
8	User.BpmnIsExtendedSubProcess.Prompt	No Formula	No Formula
9	User.msvStructureType	0	0
10	User.msvStructureType.Prompt	No Formula	No Formula
11	User.msvSDContainerResize	0	0
12	User.msvSDContainerResize.Prompt	No Formula	No Formula
13	User.visVersion	14	14
14	User.visVersion.Prompt	No Formula	No Formula
15	User.msvShapeCategories	Task	Task
16	User.msvShapeCategories.Prompt	No Formula	No Formula

The output displays the cell name, value, and formula in each section, in an extremely verbose manner. This makes for many rows in the worksheet, and a varying number of columns in each section.

What is a function?

A function defines a discrete action, and most functions take a number of arguments as input. Some functions produce an output as a value in the cell that contains the formula, whilst others redirect the output to another cell, and some do not produce a useful output at all.

The **Developer ShapeSheet Reference** in the Visio SDK contains a description of each of the 197 functions available in Visio 2010, and there are some more that are reserved for use by Visio itself.

Formulae can be entered into any cell, but some cells will be updated by the Visio engine or by specific add-ons, thus overwriting any formula that may be within the cell. Formulae are entered starting with the = (equals) sign, just as in Excel cells, so that Visio can understand that a formula is being entered rather than just a text. Some cells have been primed to expect text (strings) and will automatically prefix what you type with =" (equals double-quote) and close with "(double-quote) if you do not start typing with an equal sign.

For example, the function NOW(), returns the current date time value, which you can modify by applying a format, say, =FORMAT(NOW(),"dd//MM/YYYY"). In fact, the NOW() function will evaluate every minute unless you specify that it only updates at a specific event. You could, for example, cause the formula to be evaluated only when the shape is moved, by adding the DEPENDSON() function:

```
=DEPENDSON(PinX,PinY)+NOW()
```

The normal user will not see the result of any values unless there is something changing in the UI. This could be a value in the **Shape Data** that could cause linked **Data Graphics** to change. Or there could be something more subtle, such as the display of some geometry within the shape, like the **Compensation** symbol in the **BPMN Task** shape.

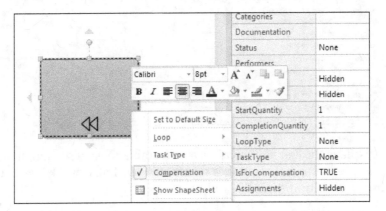

In the above example, you can see that the **Compensation** right-mouse menu option is checked, and the **IsForCompensation Shape Data** value is TRUE. These values are linked, and the **Task** shape itself displays the two triangles at the bottom edge.

The custom right-mouse menu options are defined in the **Actions** section of the shape's **ShapeSheet**, and one of the cells, **Checked**, holds a formula to determine if a tick should be displayed or not. In this case, the `Actions.Compensation.Checked` cell contains the following formula, which is merely a cell reference:

```
=Prop.BpmnIsForCompensation
```

`Prop` is the prefix used for all cells in the **Shape Data** section because this section used to be known as **Custom Properties**. The `Prop.BpmnIsForCompensation` row is defined as a **Boolean** (True/False) **Type**, so the returned value is going to be 1 or 0 (`True` or `False`).

Thus, if you were to build a validation rule that required a **Task** to be for **Compensation**, then you would have to check this value.

You will often need to branch expressions using the following:

```
IF(logical_expression, value_if_true, value_if_false)
```

You can nest expressions inside each other.

You will often need to use the logical expression evaluators like the following:

- AND(logical_expression1, logical_expression2
  [, opt_logical_expression3][,...] [, opt_logical_expressionN])
- OR(logical_expression1, logical_expression2
  [, opt_logical_expression3][,...] [, opt_logical_expressionN])

You may also need to reverse a Boolean value using NOT(logical_expression).

These are the main evaluators and there are no looping functions available. Now let's look at each relevant ShapeSheet section.

What are the important sections for rules validation?

When validating documents, there are some sections that are more important and more regularly used than others. Therefore, we will look at just a few of the sections in detail.

The User-defined Cells section

The **User-defined Cells** section is used to store hidden variables (because they are never displayed in the UI unless you open the ShapeSheet) and perform calculations. There are just two columns in this section. The first, **Value**, is normally where the real work is done, and the second, **Prompt**, is often used as a description of the row.

 You can make **Shape Data** rows invisible too (by setting the **Invisible** cell to True), but usually you do not need the overhead of all the other cells in the row, so a **User-defined Cell** is more efficient.

Microsoft will often use specially named **User-defined Cell** rows to hold specific information. For example, the **Task** shape has a row named, User.msvShapeCategories, which is used to specify the category or categories that it belongs to. The **Task** shape belongs, not surprisingly, to the Task category, but it could have belonged to multiple categories by having them expressed as a semi-colon separated list.

What category is a Shape?

Visio 2010 introduced the new function HASCATEGORY(category) in order to support structured diagrams.

In the BPMN diagrams, the **Task** shape has the `Task` category, so the following formula will return `TRUE` for the **Task** shape:

```
=HASCATEGORY("Task")
```

But the following will return `FALSE` because the string is case-sensitive:

```
=HASCATEGORY("task")
```

Therefore, it is important to know what the exact spelling and case is for the values in the `User.msvShapeCategories` cells.

Consequently, I have written the following VBA macro, `ListStencilShapeCategories`, to list all of the categories used in the docked stencils, and then to optionally list the stencil title, master name, and a count of the number of categories that the master belongs to.

 I am also using the **Dictionary** object in the following code, so you will need to ensure that the **Microsoft Scripting Runtime** library (`C:\Windows\system32\scrun.dll`) is ticked in the **References** dialog opened from the **Tools** menu in the Visual Basic user interface.

```
Public Sub ListStencilShapeCategories()
'List the categories used in the docked stencils
    If Not Visio.ActiveWindow.Type = _
        Visio.VisWinTypes.visDrawing Then
        Exit Sub
    End If
Dim aryStencils() As String
    Visio.ActiveWindow.DockedStencils aryStencils
Dim stenCounter As Integer
Dim sten As Visio.Document
Dim mst As Visio.Master
Dim shp As Visio.Shape
Dim categories() As String
Dim catCounter As Integer
Dim category As String
Dim colMasters As Collection
Dim dicCategories As Dictionary
    Set dicCategories = New Dictionary
    'Loop thru the stencils
    For stenCounter = 0 To UBound(aryStencils)
        'Do not read the document stencil
        If Len(aryStencils(stenCounter)) > 0 Then
```

```vb
        Set sten = _
            Visio.Documents(aryStencils(stenCounter))
        'Loop thru each master in the stencil
        For Each mst In sten.Masters
            Set shp = mst.Shapes.Item(1)
            'Check that the Category cell exists
            If shp.CellExists("User.msvShapeCategories", _
                VisExistsFlags.visExistsAnywhere) Then
                'The default List Separator is ;
                categories = _
                  Split(shp.Cells( _
                    "User.msvShapeCategories").ResultStrU(""), ";")
                For catCounter = 0 To UBound(categories)
                    If dicCategories.Exists( _
                      categories(catCounter)) Then
                        Set colMasters = _
                        dicCategories.Item(categories(catCounter))
                        colMasters.Add sten.Title & " - " & _
                          mst.Name & _
                            " (" & UBound(categories) + 1 & ")"
                        Set dicCategories.Item( _
                          categories(catCounter)) = _
                            colMasters
                    Else
                        Set colMasters = New Collection
                        colMasters.Add sten.Title & " - " & _
                          mst.Name & _
                            " (" & UBound(categories) + 1 & ")"
                        dicCategories.Add _
                            categories(catCounter), colMasters
                    End If
                Next catCounter
            End If
        Next
    End If
Next

Dim msg As String
    msg = "There are " & UBound(dicCategories.Keys) + 1 & _
        " categories in the " & _
        UBound(aryStencils) + 1 & " docked stencils:" & vbCrLf
    For catCounter = 0 To UBound(dicCategories.Keys)
        Set colMasters = _
            dicCategories.Item(dicCategories.Keys(catCounter))
```

```
            msg = msg & vbCrLf & dicCategories.Keys(catCounter) & " - " &
_
                colMasters.Count & " masters"
        Next catCounter
        msg = msg & vbCrLf & vbCrLf & "Do you want to view the details?"
    Dim ret As Integer
    Dim mstCounter As Integer
        ret = MsgBox(msg, vbInformation + vbYesNo, _
            "ListStencilShapeCategories")
        If Not ret = vbYes Then
            Exit Sub
        End If


        'Display the masters for each category
        For catCounter = 0 To UBound(dicCategories.Keys)
            Set colMasters = _
                dicCategories.Item(dicCategories.Keys(catCounter))
            msg = colMasters.Count & _
                " masters that have the Category : " & _
                dicCategories.Keys(catCounter) & vbCrLf
            For mstCounter = 1 To colMasters.Count
                msg = msg & vbCrLf & colMasters.Item(mstCounter)
            Next mstCounter
            msg = msg & vbCrLf & vbCrLf & _
                "Do you want to continue to view the next category?"
            ret = MsgBox(msg, vbInformation + vbYesNo, _
                "ListStencilShapeCategories")
            If Not ret = vbYes Then
                Exit For
            End If
        Next catCounter
    End Sub
```

If you run this macro with, say, a blank document created from the **BPMN Diagram (Metric)** template, then you will be presented with a list of all of the categories found in the docked stencils as shown in the following screenshot:

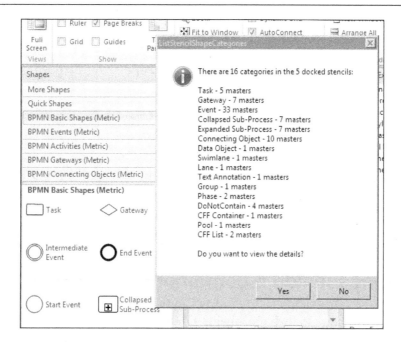

If you continue to view the details of the listed categories, then you will be presented with a dialog listing the stencil, master, and category count in brackets:

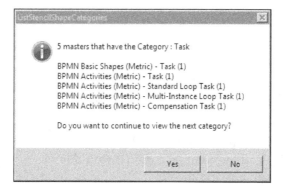

This is essential information for building validation rules that use category.

 Shapes that have the category **DoNotContain** cannot be added to a container.

What structure type is a Shape?

Visio 2010 structured diagrams use another specifically named **User-defined Cell**, User.msvStructureType, to define the **Structure Type** of the shape.

I will spare you the VBA code for the ListStencilStructureTypes method in this text because it is very similar to the ListStencilShapeCategories method shown previously, but we can discover that there are three different Structure Types in the BPMN stencils. They are:

- **Container**: There are 12 masters in all, including **Expanded Sub-Process**, **Pool/Lane**, and **Group**
- **Callout**: There is only one master, **Text Annotation**
- **List**: There are two masters, **Swimlane List** and **Phase List**

Is the shape inside a container?

The formula, =CONTAINERCOUNT(), returns 1 in the examples because the **Document** shape is inside the container shape labeled **Drafting**. If there are nested containers, then the function will return the total number of containers that the shape is within.

If the shape is inside a container, then you can use the new =CONTAINERSHEETREF(index[, category]) function to get a reference to the container shape, and thus to any of the cells inside it. As there can be multiple containers, the index, which is one-based (the first index number is 1, not 0), specifies which one to return. The category argument is optional.

How many shapes are inside a Container shape?

Perhaps surprisingly, the CONTAINERMEMBERCOUNT() returns 9 in this example, because it includes the three flowchart shapes, the three callouts, and the three connectors between the flowchart shapes, even though the last three are 1-D shapes. If either end of a connector is outside of the container, then it would not be counted. Also, note that the lines between the callouts and the flowchart shapes are part of the callout shape, and thus do not count either. It can be seen in the following screenshot:

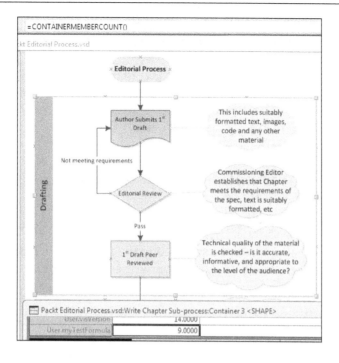

Where is the shape in the List?

In this example, I have used the **List box** and **List box item** shapes from **Controls** stencil in the **Software and Database | Wireframe Diagram** template, to construct a partial **Visio Type Library** object model. I have added two **User-defined Cells** to the **ShapeSheet** of the **List box item** so that the item contains the index of its position in the **List box** and the text of the **List box** shape.

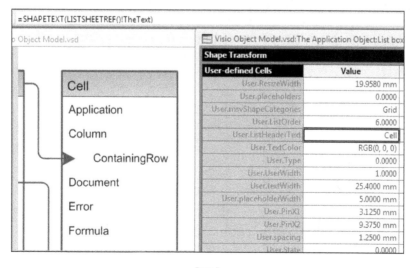

This is achieved by using the following formula in the `User.ListOrder.Value` cell:

```
=LISTORDER()
```

The `ListSheetRef()` function will return the containing list box shape (if there is one), and then its cells and properties can be referenced by following this with an exclamation mark. Therefore, the formula to return the text of the container list box in the `User.ListHeaderText.Value` cell is:

```
=SHAPETEXT(LISTSHEETREF()!TheText)
```

However, this formula will display `=#REF!` if the list item is not within a list box, so a more complete formula would be:

```
=IF(LISTORDER()=-1,"n/a",SHAPETEXT(LISTSHEETREF()!TheText))
```

Alternatively, these values could be surfaced to the UI as **Shape Data** rows, in which case you would protect them from being overwritten by using the `GUARD()` function.

```
=GUARD(IF(LISTORDER()=-1,"n/a",SHAPETEXT(LISTSHEETREF()!TheText)))
```

In either case, having these values available on the **List box item** makes reports and rule validation much easier.

How many shapes are in a List shape?

A **List** shape can contain the function `LISTMEMBERCOUNT()` in order to get the number of list item shapes within it.

Are there any Callouts attached to a shape?

In the following examples, I have added a new row to the **User-defined Cells** section, named `myTestFormula`, of the first **Document** shape in my example **Packt Editorial Process** diagram. I have entered the function `CALLOUTCOUNT()` into the **Value** cell of this row, and you can see that the result is displayed as `1.0000`.

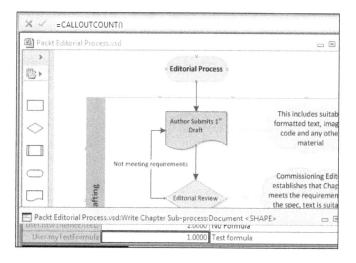

This is because there is a single Callout shape connected to this shape.

Which shape is a Callout connected to?

When a **Callout** shape is connected to another shape you can get at any of the cells in that target shape by use of the `CALLOUTTARGETREF()` function.

In the following example, I have used a formula to return the text of the target shape. The following formula uses the `ShapeText()` function to return the text of the associated **Callout** shape:

```
=SHAPETEXT(CALLOUTTARGETREF()!TheText)
```

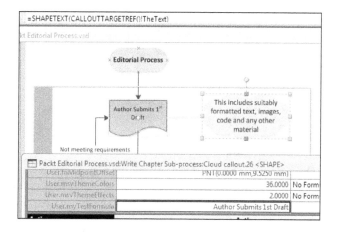

For example, this could be surfaced in the UI as a **Shape Data** row, thus making reporting easier.

The Shape Data section

The **Value** cell stores the actual values, and because it is the default cell in the row, it can be retrieved in a ShapeSheet formula as `Prop.Cost`, for example, rather than `Prop.Cost.Value`. Other cells have to be referenced explicitly, as say, `Prop.Cost.Invisible`, for example.

The ShapeSheet developer cannot move **Shape Data** rows up or down, but the display order can be modified by entering text into the `SortKey` cells. The Visio UI will sort the **Shape Data** rows according to the text sort order of the values in these cells.

The visibility of a **Shape Data** row is controlled by the Boolean result of the formula in the **Invisible** cell.

There are eight different types in **Shape Data** rows, almost all of which are data types. So, it is important to understand how to handle their values in any rule validation.

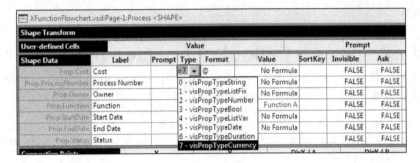

Each type is defined by an enumerator `visPropTypes`, which has the following values:

- String
- Fixed list
- Number
- Boolean
- Variable list
- Date or time
- Duration
- Currency

The default **Type** is `0`, so if the **Type** has not been set then it is assumed to be `String`.

Each row in the **Shape Data** section can be named, and has a **Label** that is displayed in the UI. If a row is not specifically named, then it will be automatically named `Row_1`, `Row_2`, and so on.

If your Visio diagrams have been used with **Data | Link Data to Shapes**, then you need to know that this feature will attempt to link the data by matching the text in the **Shape Data** row's **Label** cell with the column header, or the field name of the external data first and it is case-sensitive. If the target shape does not already have a **Shape Data** row, then Visio will automatically create a row named after the **Label** text, but with a _VisDM_ prefix, and any spaces or special characters removed.

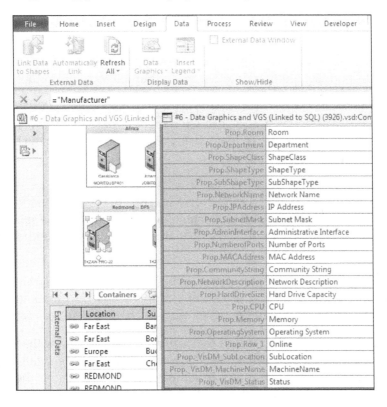

Therefore, you may need to match values based on the **Label** rather than the row **Name**, if your solution uses **Link Data to Shapes**.

 The older **Database Wizard** feature does use the row **Name** to perform its matching.

The String type

String data is just text that has been entered into a **Shape Data** row. It may have been imported from elsewhere, for example using the **Link Data to Shapes** feature, or it may just have been entered manually. In either case, if your validation rules are using text values to match, then you may be wise to ensure that the case is consistent by using the LOWER() or UPPER() functions, which will force the text to be in lowercase or uppercase respectively. Alternatively, use case sensitivity on the string matching functions below.

The **Format** cell may contain a pattern that modifies the display of the string to be in lowercase or uppercase, but that does not mean that the **Value** is in these cases.

You can use the STRSAME(string1,string2[,opt_ignore_case]) and STRSAMEEX (string1,string2,localeID,flag) functions to compare two strings, though you may need to use TRIM(string) to remove any accidental spaces at the beginning and end of the string.

Visio also provides a few functions to get specific parts of a string. LEFT(string[,num_of_chars]) and RIGHT(string[,num_of_chars]) functions will return the specified number of characters (default is 1) from the start or end of a string. The MID(string,start_num,num_of_chars) function will extract characters from within a string.

You can get the starting position of a string within another by using the FIND(find_text,within_text[,opt_start_num][,opt_ignore_case]) function. You may also need to use LEN(string) to get the number of characters in a text string.

Be aware that there are some solutions that will automatically enter the string values, and there are others that may contain special formulae to retrieve a value. For example, the **Cross-functional Flowchart** template in Visio 2010 gets the value of the Prop.Function **Shape Data** row of a shape from the text that has been entered into the **Swimlane** that it is within.

 The display of the **Value** cell can be toggled between **Formulas** and **Values** from the first two buttons on the **View** group of the **ShapeSheet Tools** tab, or by using the right-mouse menu of the ShapeSheet window.

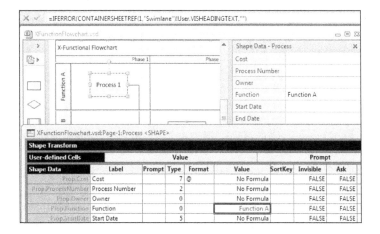

This is done with the following formula in the **Value** cell:

```
=IFERROR(CONTAINERSHEETREF(1,"Swimlane")!User.VISHEADINGTEXT,"")
```

What this means is that if the shape is surrounded by a container with the category **Swimlane** then return the value in the `User.visHeadingText` cell, otherwise just return an empty string.

Therefore, the `Prop.Function.Value` will be `""` if the **Process** shape is not inside a Swimlane shape, otherwise it will be the value of the text in the container Swimlane shape

The Fixed List type

If a **Shape Data** row is set to a `Fixed List` **Type**, then the value must exist in the drop-down list.

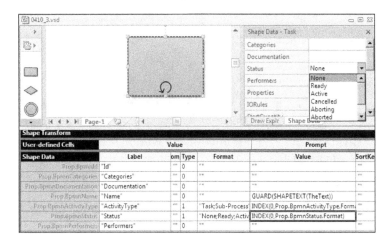

Recent versions of Visio will automatically create a formula in the **Value** cell that returns the string value at a specific zero-based index in this list. For example look at the following value:

```
=INDEX(2,Prop.BpmnStatus.Format)
```

It will return the third item from the semi-colon separated list in the `Prop.BpmnStatus.Format` cell, which contains the formula:

```
="None;Ready;Active;Cancelled;Aborting;Aborted;Completing;Completed"
```

Thus, the value is `Active`.

If you were using rules based on a **Fixed List** value, then it might be better to use the index rather than the string value, since this could be mistyped, or even translated into a different language. Therefore, you could get the index position using the `LOOKUP()` function as follows:

```
=LOOKUP(Prop.BpmnStatus,Prop.BpmnStatus.Format)
```

The Number type

Visio stores numbers as double precision numeral, but the **Format** cell may be used to modify the display in the UI.

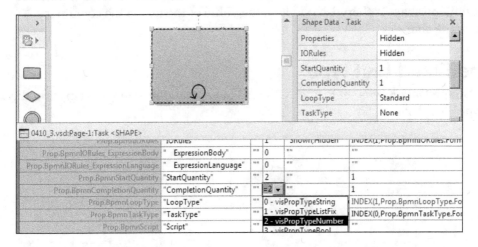

However, Visio also provides some functions to enable rounding and calculations. Commonly used functions are:

- `ROUND(number,numberofdigit)`, `INT(number)`
- `INTUP(number)` to round a number to a given precision, or to round down or up to the next integer

- `FLOOR(number[, opt_multiple])`, which rounds a number towards zero, to the next integer, or the next instance of the optional multiple
- `CEILING(number[, opt_multiple])`, which rounds a zero away from zero.

The `MODULUS(number, divisor)` function can also be useful if you need to formulate a rule that requires specific values to be entered, for example.

`ABS(number)` function returns the absolute value, and `SIGN(number[, opt_fuzz])` returns a value that represents the sign of a number.

Since Visio is a graphics system, there are a large number of functions for dealing with points, lines, and angles, that are not really relevant for rules validation.

You can simply compare number values using the *equals sign* (=), and you can add values using `number1+number2`, or `SUM(number1[, opt_number2] [, opt_number3] [, ...] [, opt_number14])`. Multiplication and division of values is simple, using `number1*number2` and `number1/number2`.

You can get the maximum or minimum value of a series of values with `MAX(number1 ,number2,...,numberN)` or `MIN(number1,number2,...,numberN)`.

The Boolean type

Often referred to as True/False or Yes/No type, the **Boolean** type returns `FALSE` (zero) or `TRUE` (non-zero). Visio actually stores `TRUE` as `1` internally, but some other programming languages use `-1`, so you may need to use the `ABS()` function to get the absolute value, depending on your circumstances.

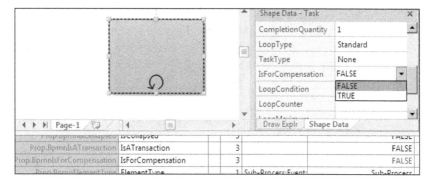

The Variable List type

A **Variable List** type is similar to the **Fixed List** mentioned earlier, but it is usually not appropriate to retrieve the index position of the selected value because Visio will automatically add values to the list if the user enters a value that is not present already. As can be seen in the following example, this even means that the same word can be repeated in the list if the case is different.

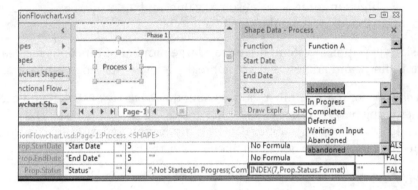

Also, the list is only extended for this particular shape instance, and other process shapes in the diagram will have their own variable list.

So, a **Variable List** may seem like a flexible feature for the user, but it is a nightmare for data validation, and the resultant text value should be treated just like the **String** type above.

The Date type

Visio provides a Date Picker for the user if the **Type** is set as Date for a **Shape Data** row. However, a custom solution may use either a date or a time picker, since a DATETIME(double) value is actually stored.

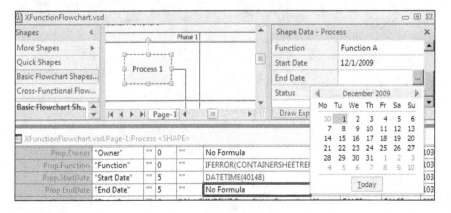

The display format of the date time value can be modified using the **Format** cell, but any rules validation should use the double precision number value. This will avoid any problems with the optional positioning of day and months in a date string. The UK, for example, always use DD/MM/YY, but the US uses MM/DD/YY.

There are a number of functions that enable you to get to specific integer parts of a date time value. They are:

- `DAY(datetime[, opt_lcid])`
- `MONTH(datetime[, opt_lcid])`
- `YEAR(datetime[, opt_lcid])`
- `HOUR(datetime[, opt_lcid])`
- `MINUTE (datetime[, opt_lcid])`
- `SECOND(datetime[, opt_lcid])`

There are also a couple of functions to return the integer value of the day in the week or in the year, namely, `WEEKDAY (datetime[, opt_lcid])` and `DAYOFYEAR(datetime[, opt_lcid])`.

If you need to convert text to dates or times then you can use the `DATETIME(datetime|expression[, opt_lcid])`, `DATEVALUE(datetime|expression[, opt_lcid])`, or `TIMEVALUE(datetime|expression[, opt_lcid])` functions.

However, if you have the integer parts of a date or time, then use the `DATE(year,month,day)` or `TIME(hour,minute,second)` functions.

 Visio use the System date, therefore the earliest date that can be stored is 30th December 1899.

Since date time is stored as double precision numbers internally, you can check if they are equal (=), before (<), or after (>) easily enough, but you may wish to check one date time against another within a duration range. For example, you may want to verify that `Prop.EndDate` is greater than the `Prop.StartDate` plus the `Prop.Duration`. This could be expressed as:

```
= Prop.EndDate<(Prop.StartDate+Prop.Duration)
```

This will return `True` or `False`.

Similarly, you could test if the `Prop.EndDate` is within the next 12 weeks by using the following:

```
=Prop.EndDate<(Now()+12 ew.)
```

You can use any of the duration units in such formulae.

The Duration type

Visio can store Duration values expressed as elapsed day (`ed.`), hour (`eh.`), minute (`em.`), second (`es.`), or week (`ew.`). They are all stored internally as days and fractions of days.

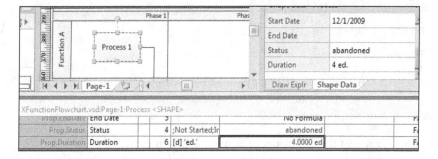

The **Format** cell may have been used to modify the presentation in the UI. The **Visio Developer SDK** contains a page called **About Format Pictures** in the documentation, where you can review all of the different format pictures.

The Currency type

The last **Type** is **Currency**, the display of which defaults to the system settings, although it is stored as a double precision number.

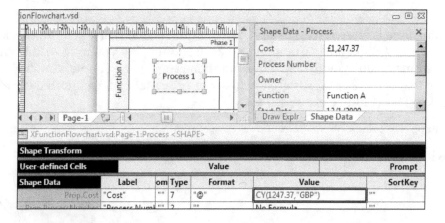

The **Format** cell may be used to modify the appearance of the value in the UI. See the Visio Developer SDK for more information.

Generally, you would treat Currency in a similar manner to Number **Type** described earlier.

The Hyperlinks section

A shape in Visio can have multiple hyperlinks but one row has a reserved name, Hyperlink.msvSubprocess, to provide a link to a subprocess page.

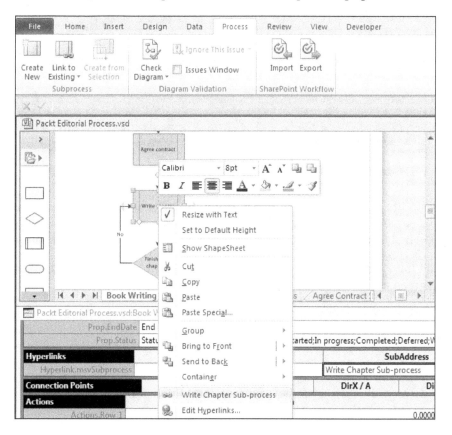

So, you can test if a shape has a subprocess reference with the following formula:

```
=NOT(ISERR(INT(INDEX(0,"Hyperlink.msvSubprocess.NewWindow"))))
```

You cannot easily test a page to check if it is a subprocess, or where it is used in a main process, because a subprocess may be part of many parent processes.

Layer Membership

Shape **Layer Membership** is more complicated than you might think. The ShapeSheet of the page stores the **Layers** for that page, and, as you can see from the following screenshot, an individual shape's ShapeSheet merely stores a list of indexes of the page's **Layers**.

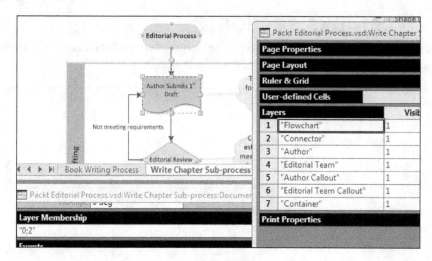

Layers with the same name may have a different index number on different pages within the same document. Therefore, you cannot create a rule that tests for a layer by index. The layer settings in the page control whether a layer is visible or printable.

You could have a rule that insists that all relevant shapes must be assigned to a layer, which is given as:

```
=NOT(STRSAME(LayerMember,""))
```

Or a rule that states that it must be on one layer only:

```
=NOT(AND(STRSAME(LayerMember,""),FIND(";",LayerMember,1)))
```

You can then check if the assigned layer is currently visible:

```
=INT(INDEX(0,"ThePage!Layers.Visible["&INDEX(0,LayerMember)+1&"]"))
```

Notice how you can refer to the ShapeSheet of the page using the `ThePage!` syntax. You can similarly refer to the ShapeSheet of the document using the `TheDoc!` syntax.

Summary

In this chapter we have explored a lot of the ShapeSheet functions that can be used in validation tests, and we have focused on the ShapeSheet sections that are probably most relevant for creating validation rules.

You may have noticed that there are no functions for checking connectivity in this chapter. Well, they are part of the new quasi-ShapeSheet functions that can only be used with the Validation API, so we will examine those later.

In the next chapter, we will examine the new **Validation Rules API** and you will understand why it is important to understand both the Visio object model and **ShapeSheet** functions, if you want to be able to analyze existing rules or create your own.

4
Understanding the Validation API

The **Validation API** is new in Visio 2010 Premium edition, and provides the opportunity to create diagramming rules. These rules can help eliminate common errors and enable companies to enforce diagramming standards.

In the first chapter, we had an overview of the user interface of the **Diagram Validation** group on the **Process** tab, and a quick look at the elements in XML format. In this chapter we will explore the objects, collections, and methods in the Validation API.

Overview of the Validation objects

The Validation object model is accessed from the Visio Document object. The Validation object is only available if the code is running in Visio Premium edition, so you should check the edition, as described previously in *Chapter 2*.

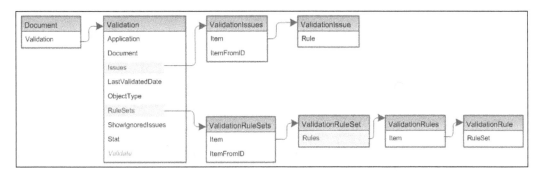

The Validation object contains two collections, Issues and RuleSets, which leads you to the main areas of the API.

The `ShowIgnoredIssues` property merely dictates whether or not the **Issues** window displays ignored issues. If the user selects to show ignored issues, then they are shown as grayed out.

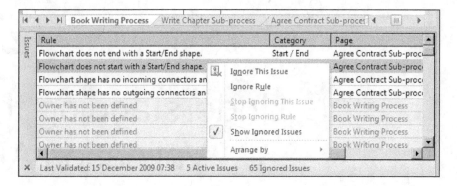

The following `DebugPrintValidation` macro will display the detail of the validation object, but notice that you have to delve into the `Issues`, `Issue`, and `Rule` objects to retrieve the count of ignored issues, as displayed in the UI. In fact, an issue can be ignored individually, or by virtue of its rule being marked as ignored.

```
Public Sub DebugPrintValidation()
Debug.Print "DebugPrintValidation"
Dim ignoredIssues As Integer
    With Visio.ActiveDocument.Validation
        ignoredIssues = getIgnoredIssueCount(.issues)
        Debug.Print , "ActiveDocument.Name", .Document.Name
        Debug.Print , "Total Issues", .issues.Count
        Debug.Print , "Active Issues", _
            .issues.Count - ignoredIssues
        Debug.Print , "Ignored Issues", ignoredIssues
        Debug.Print , "LastValidatedDate", .LastValidatedDate
        Debug.Print , "RuleSets.Count", .RuleSets.Count
        Debug.Print , "ShowIgnoredIssues", .ShowIgnoredIssues
        Debug.Print , "Stat", .Stat
    End With
End Sub

Private Function getIgnoredIssueCount(ByVal issues As
ValidationIssues) As Integer
Dim i As Integer
Dim issue As ValidationIssue
    For Each issue In issues
        i = i + (Abs(issue.Ignored = True) Or Abs(issue.rule.Ignored =
True))
```

```
    Next
    getIgnoredIssueCount = i
End Function
```

The above code will give an output like this:

DebugPrintValidation	
ActiveDocument.Name	Packt Editorial Process.vsd
Total Issues	70
Active Issues	5
Ignored Issues	65
LastValidatedDate	15/12/2009 07:38:47
RuleSets.Count	2
ShowIgnoredIssues	True
Stat	0

The Validate method

You cannot `Validate` a document unless you have at least one rule set in it. The `Validate([ruleSet as RuleSet] [, flags as visValidationFlags])` method has two optional parameters — the `RuleSet` to use and `flags` to indicate whether the **Issues** window should be opened.

`Validate` will check the rule set, if specified (or all enabled rule sets if none are specified), and clear any existing issues before creating any new issues found. The `LastValidatedDate` will be set so that you can check when a document was validated.

Can custom rules code be validated?

You do not have to add all rules within a rule set. You can have custom validation code for difficult tasks like checking cyclic routes in process flows, and then run your code whenever the `Validate()` method is called.

The `Document` object has a `RuleSetValidated` event that will fire for every rule set after validation. It is done as follows:

```
Private Sub Document_RuleSetValidated(ByVal RuleSet As
IVValidationRuleSet)
    Debug.Print "Document_RuleSetValidated for" & RuleSet.Name, Now()
End Sub
```

It is not worth checking the `Validation` object for number of issues until after all rule sets have been processed, because it does not get updated incrementally during `Validate()`.

The above code is in Visual Basic for Applications, which provides a `Document` object `WithEvents` in the `ThisDocument` class. In general, it is not considered good coding practice to use `WithEvents` because it can unintentionally create a very chatty application that wastes processing time raising unnecessary events. It is far better to use the `AddAdvise (EventCode As Integer, SinkIUnkOrIDisp, IIDSink As String, TargetArgs As String)` method to create events as required.

You can now add whatever code you want to for a rule set, and then run the code after the rule set has been validated. You can then add any issues to the `Validation.Issues` collection using `ValidationRule.AddIssue ([TargetPage As Page] [,TargetShape As Shape])` method.

The ValidationRuleSets collection

Validation Rules are grouped within `ValidationRuleSets`. The UI provides the ability to import a rule set from another open Visio document, but the programmer can use the `Add (NameU as String)` or `AddCopy (RuleSet as ValidationRuleSet [, NameU])` methods to create a new one.

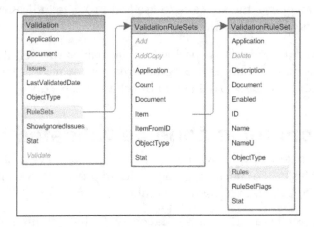

You can retrieve a rule set by its `index` position in the collection, using `ValidationRuleSets.Item(index)`, or by its `ID` using `ValidationRuleSets.ItemFromID(ID)`. Once you have retrieved a rule set, you can read its `Name` (which can be edited to be a localized version), `NameU`, `Description` (which is displayed as the tooltip in the UI), or check if the `RuleSets` is enabled for validation.

The `RuleSetFlags` value determines if the rule set is visible in the **Rules to Check** drop-down in the UI.

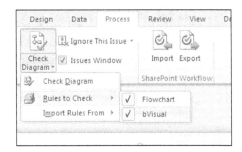

The default value is 0 (VisRuleSetFlags.visRuleSetDefault), but you could change it to 1 (VisRuleSetFlags.visRuleSetHidden) if you do not want it to appear in the **Rules to Check** menu.

The following macro, EnumerateRuleSets, displays a list of the rule sets in the active document:

```
Public Sub EnumerateRuleSets()
Dim doc As Visio.Document
Dim ruleSet As Visio.ValidationRuleSet
    Set doc = Visio.ActiveDocument
    Debug.Print "EnumerateRuleSets : Count = _
      " & doc.Validation.RuleSets.Count
    Debug.Print , "ID", "Enabled", "RuleSetFlags", _
        "Name", "Description"
    For Each ruleSet In doc.Validation.RuleSets
        With ruleSet
            Debug.Print , .ID, .Enabled, ._
                RuleSetFlags, .NameU, , .Description
        End With
    Next
End Sub
```

This will produce an output similar to the following:

EnumerateRuleSets : Count = 2				
ID	Enabled	RuleSetFlags	Name	Description
1	True	0	Flowchart	Verify that Flowchart shapes are connected properly.
2	True	0	bVisual	Sample RuleSet

How do I add or update a rule set?

Well, you can always copy a rule set from another document in the UI, but you can also create a new one in code, or update an existing one. This can be done as follows:

```
Public Sub AddOrUpdateRuleSet()
Dim ruleSet As Visio.ValidationRuleSet
Dim ruleSetNameU As String
    ruleSetNameU = "bVisual"
    'Check if the rule set exists already
    Set ruleSet = _
        getRuleSet(Visio.ActiveDocument, ruleSetNameU)
    If ruleSet Is Nothing Then
        'Create the new rule set
        Set ruleSet = _
            Visio.ActiveDocument.Validation.RuleSets.Add(ruleSetNameU)
    End If
    ruleSet.Name = "Be Visual"
    ruleSet.Description = "Example Rule Set"
    ruleSet.Enabled = True
    ruleSet.RuleSetFlags = visRuleSetDefault

End Sub
Private Function getRuleSet(ByVal doc As Visio.Document, _
    ByVal nameU As String) As Visio.ValidationRuleSet
Dim retVal As Visio.ValidationRuleSet
Dim ruleSet As Visio.ValidationRuleSet
    Set retVal = Nothing
    For Each ruleSet In doc.Validation.RuleSets
        If UCase(ruleSet.nameU) = UCase(nameU) Then
            Set retVal = ruleSet
            Exit For
        End If
    Next
    Set getRuleSet = retVal
End Function
```

Notice how the tooltip and displayed name are updated in the UI:

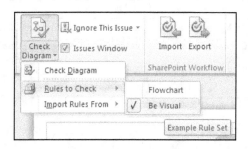

Of course, you can also delete a rule set which is done as follows:

```
Public Sub DeleteRuleSet()
Dim ruleSetNameU As String
    ruleSetNameU = "bVisual"
    'Check if the rule set exists already
    If Not getRuleSet(Visio.ActiveDocument, ruleSetNameU) Is Nothing
Then
        'Delete the rule set
        Visio.ActiveDocument.Validation.RuleSets(ruleSetNameU).Delete
    End If
End Sub
```

 You can use the `NameU` or `Index` of a rule set to retrieve it from the `Validation.RuleSets` collection.

The ValidationRules collection

Once you have a rule set you can review, amend, or add to the rules within it. You can add a rule using the `ValidationRules.AddRule(NameU as string)` method. Note that the `NameU` is really for use in code, since it is the **Description** property that is displayed in UI. The `NameU` must be unique within the `Rules` collection of the parent `ValidationRuleSet`.

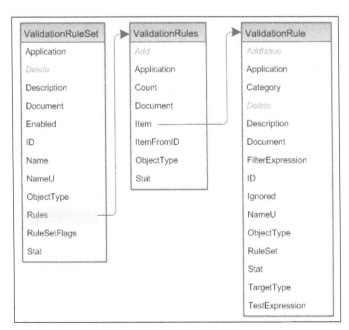

You can retrieve a rule by its `index` position in the collection, using `ValidationRules.Item(index)`, or by its ID using `ValidationRules.ItemFromID(ID)`. Once you have retrieved a `ValidationRule` you can read its `NameU` and `Description`, or check if the rule set is ignored for validation.

```
Public Sub EnumerateRules()
Dim doc As Visio.Document
Dim ruleSet As Visio.ValidationRuleSet
Dim rule As Visio.ValidationRule
    Set doc = Visio.ActiveDocument

    For Each ruleSet In doc.Validation.RuleSets
        If ruleSet.Enabled Then
            Debug.Print "EnumerateRules for RuleSet : " & _
                ruleSet.nameU & " : Count = " & _
                ruleSet.Rules.Count
            Debug.Print "ID", "Ignored", "Category", _
                "NameU", "Description", _
                "TargetType" & vbCrLf, _
                "FilterExpression", "TestExpression"
            For Each rule In ruleSet.Rules
                With rule
                    Debug.Print .ID, .Ignored, .category, _
                        .nameU, .Description, _
                        .TargetType & vbCrLf, _
                        .FilterExpression, _
                        .TestExpression
                End With
            Next
        End If    Next
End Sub
```

The output from this looks as follows: (note that I have wrapped lines within columns for clarity)

EnumerateRules for RuleSet : Flowchart : Count = 11					
ID	Ignored	Category	NameU	Description	TargetType
	FilterExpression			TestExpression	
1	False	Connectivity	Unglued Connector	Connector is not glued at both ends.	0
	ROLE()=1			AND(AGGCOUNT(GLUEDSHAPES(4)) = 1, AGGCOUNT(GLUEDSHAPES(5)) = 1)	

EnumerateRules for RuleSet : Flowchart : Count = 11

2	False	Start / End	StartWithout Terminator	Flowchart shape has no incoming connectors and is not a Start/End shape.	0
	AND(OR(HASCATEGORY("Flowchart"),ON LAYER("Flowchart")),NOT(OR(HASCATE GORY("Start/End"),STRSAME(LEFT(MAS TERNAME(750),9),"Start/End"),STRSA ME(LEFT(MASTERNAME(750),10),"Termi nator"))))			AGGCOUNT(GLUEDSHAPES(1)) > 0		
3	False	Start / End	EndWithout Terminator	Flowchart shape has no outgoing connectors and is not a Start/End shape.	0
	AND(OR(HASCATEGORY("Flowchart"),ON LAYER("Flowchart")),NOT(OR(HASCATE GORY("Start/End"),STRSAME(LEFT(MAS TERNAME(750),9),"Start/End"),STRSA ME(LEFT(MASTERNAME(750),10),"Termi nator"))))			AGGCOUNT(GLUEDSHAPES(2)) > 0		

At last, we are starting to see how the validation logic of each rule works, and you can see why the last chapter was about understanding the **ShapeSheet** functionality.

You should always set a value for the Category of a rule, because the UI can optionally group by Category, which helps the user fix any issues arising.

The TargetType can be one of three values of the VisRuleTargets enumerator, which defines the scope of the rule. They are:

- VisRuleTargets.visRuleTargetShape (0)
- VisRuleTargets.visRuleTargetPage (1)
- VisRuleTargets.visRuleTargetDocument (2)

You can create an issue for a rule using the AddIssue([TargetPage as Page] [,TargetShape as Shape]) method, but you should ensure that the relevant optional arguments are set. The TargetType of the rule determines which optional arguments should be set. For example, if the TargetType = 0 then you should include both the TargetPage and TargetShape parameters. If the TargetType = 1 then you should only set the TargetPage parameter, and if the TargetType = 2 then do not set any parameter. This is important as it controls the behavior when you select an issue in the **Issues** window.

The Ignored flag can be set in the UI or by the developer in code.

The Filter Expression is evaluated against each of the potential targets, as defined by the TargetType property. If the Filter Expression returns True then the Test Expression is evaluated, but if it returns False (or if there is invalid syntax), then the target is skipped. The Test Expression is then evaluated, and if it returns True then the target is deemed to comply with the rule. If it returns False (or if there is invalid syntax), then a ValidationIssue is added to the Validation.Issues collection.

Lastly, you can remove a rule from a rule set with the Rule.Delete() method.

How do I add or update a rule?

Later, we will go into FilterExpression and TestExpression in great detail, but for now, we are going to create a simple rule that checks that there are no blank pages in our document. To do this, I have added a rule called NoShapesInPage to the bVisual rule set in the following code:

```
Public Sub AddOrUpdateRule()
Dim ruleSet As Visio.ValidationRuleSet
Dim rule As Visio.ValidationRule
Dim ruleNameU As String
    ruleNameU = "NoShapesInPage"
    Set ruleSet = getRuleSet(Visio.ActiveDocument, "bVisual")
    If ruleSet Is Nothing Then
        Exit Sub
    End If
    Set rule = getRule(ruleSet, ruleNameU)
    If rule Is Nothing Then
        Set rule = ruleSet.Rules.Add(ruleNameU)
    End If
    rule.Category = "Shapes"
    rule.Description = _
        "A page must contain at least one shape"
    rule.TargetType = visRuleTargetPage
    rule.FilterExpression = ""
    rule.TestExpression = "AggCount(ShapesOnPage())>0"

End Sub

Private Function getRule(ByVal ruleSet As Visio.ValidationRuleSet, _
    ByVal nameU As String) As Visio.ValidationRule
Dim retVal As Visio.ValidationRule
```

```
Dim rule As Visio.ValidationRule
    Set retVal = Nothing
    For Each rule In ruleSet.Rules
        If UCase(rule.nameU) = UCase(nameU) Then
            Set retVal = rule
            Exit For
        End If
    Next
    Set getRule = retVal
End Function
```

Notice that I have set the target to the page, and the Test Expression is
`"AggCount(ShapesOnPage())>0"`, which will evaluate to `True` if there are any
shapes on the page.

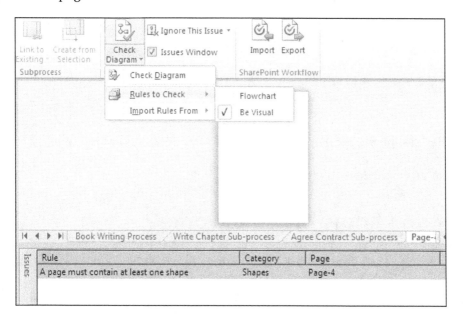

Since a document must usually have at least one page, this rule would
also ensure that there are shapes in the document. The only exception
would be if a document only contains background pages, because rules
are not validated for background pages.

Another example might be a rule that every flowchart shape has some text. If
we assume that every flowchart shape is on the `Flowchart` layer, then we could
construct a Filter Expression that tests for this. This will ensure that only relevant
shapes are processed with a Test Expression that checks for the existence of text.

```
Public Sub AddOrUpdateRuleA()
Dim ruleSet As Visio.ValidationRuleSet
Dim rule As Visio.ValidationRule
Dim ruleNameU As String
    ruleNameU = "FlowchartShapesMustHaveText"
    Set ruleSet = getRuleSet(Visio.ActiveDocument, "bVisual")
    If ruleSet Is Nothing Then
        Exit Sub
    End If
    Set rule = getRule(ruleSet, ruleNameU)
    If rule Is Nothing Then
        Set rule = ruleSet.Rules.Add(ruleNameU)
    End If
    rule.Category = "Shapes"
    rule.Description = _
        "Every Flowchart Shapes must have some text"
    rule.TargetType = visRuleTargetShape
    rule.FilterExpression = "ONLAYER(""Flowchart"")"
    rule.TestExpression = _
        "NOT(STRSAME(SHAPETEXT(TheText), """"))"
End Sub
```

This rule uses the ShapeSheet function `SHAPETEXT(shapename!TheText[,flag])` combined with the `STRSAME("string1", "string2"[, ignoreCase])` function to check for an empty text string.

How do I know my rule works?

This is not a simple question because you do not get any error syntax checking when you are writing the **Filter** and **Test Expressions** for rules. The Filter Expression has to return True if the page or shape is to be checked against the Test Expression. Therefore, I simply toggle the formula in Test Expression between `True` and `False` (or `1` and `0`), whilst observing if the expected page or shapes raise an issue or not by validating the document.

Once you are content that the Filter Expression is working, you can move on to verifying the Test Expression. This should also return a Boolean value, and should return `False` in order to raise an issue. Therefore, I reverse the logic by wrapping the formula with `NOT(...)`. This should result in the raising of an issue where there is a match. As before, I toggle the logic and observe if this causes the expected issues to be alternately raised or not.

If there is no change in the issues raised, at either stage when the logic is toggled, then there must be a syntax error in the Filter or Test Expression.

You will learn more about writing these expressions in *Chapter 7*.

 Validation rules that target the document are only reevaluated when the entire document changes. Since this occurs infrequently, there may be cases where an issue that targets the document remains in the document after it has been fixed by the user—a user may fix an issue and still see it in the **Issues** window after validation is run. For this reason, Microsoft recommends that you only use validation rules that target the document when you are using a custom solution to manage validation issues. When you manage the validation issues in code, you will be able to reevaluate the validation rule at your discretion.

ValidationIssues

The `ValidationIssues` collection stores the issues created by the `Validation. Validate([RuleSet as ValidationRuleSet] [, Flags as ValidationFlags])` method and by the `RuleSet.AddIssue([TargetPage as Page] [,TargetShape as Shape])` method. It can be reset using the `Clear()` method, which will also zero the `LastValidatedDate` of the parent `Validation` object.

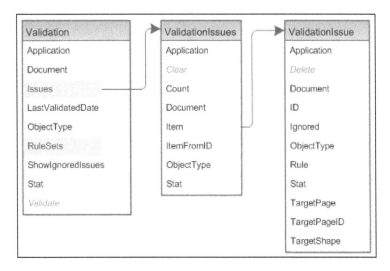

Most issues are automatically created by the `Validate()` method, but you can write code to add issues whenever the user clicks **Check Diagram** against a particular rule set. You would do this by listening to the `RuleSetValidated(RuleSet as ValidationRuleSet)` event of the `Application`, `Documents`, or `Document` object. This technique is used by the **Microsoft SharePoint Workflow** template in Visio 2010.

You can enumerate the current issues in a document, and check which rule has been transgressed.

```
Public Sub EnumerateIssues()
Dim issue As Visio.ValidationIssue
Dim shpName As String
Dim doc As Visio.Document
    Set doc = Visio.ActiveDocument

    Debug.Print "EnumerateIssues : Count = " &
     doc.Validation.Issues.Count
    Debug.Print , "ID", "Ignored", "Rule.NameU", "TargetPage.Name",
     "TargetShape.Name"
    For Each issue In doc.Validation.Issues
        If issue.targetShape Is Nothing Then
            shpName = ""
        Else
            shpName = issue.targetShape.Name
        End If
        Debug.Print , issue.ID, issue.Ignored, issue.Rule.NameU,
         issue.TargetPage.Name, shpName
    Next
End Sub
```

The `EnumerateIssues()` macro will produce an output similar to this:

EnumerateIssues : Count = 5				
ID	Ignored	Rule.NameU	TargetPage. Name	TargetShape. Name
6	False	NoStartTerminator	Agree Contract Sub-process	
7	False	NoEndTerminator	Agree Contract Sub-process	
8	False	StartWithoutTerminator	Agree Contract Sub-process	Process.9
9	False	EndWithoutTerminator	Agree Contract Sub-process	Process.9
10	False	UnconnectedShape	Agree Contract Sub-process	Process.9

The first two entries do not have a target shape because the rule applies to a page.

Compare the listing above with that seen in the following screenshot:

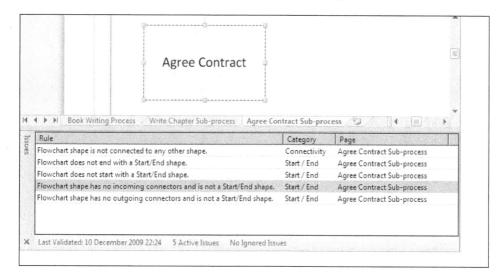

Firstly, you can tell that this is a multi-page document because the **Page** column is not displayed if there is only one foreground page.

Secondly, you cannot see which shape (if any) is the target of the issue. The user can see the shape in the page when an issue is selected because Visio automatically selects it. However, it is impossible to see how many issues a particular shape has.

You can retrieve an issue by its `index` position in the collection, using `ValidationIssues.Item(index)`, or by its ID using `ValidationIssues.ItemFromID(ID)`. Once you have retrieved an issue, you can access the rule that was broken, and if applicable, the page and shape involved.

Which issue is selected in the Issues window?

The **Issues** window is a built-in sub-window of the active window in Visio. If you were to write some code to enumerate through the sub-windows of the active window, then you can see that there are a number of built-in windows, which may or may not be visible.

```
Public Sub EnumerateWindows()
Dim win As Visio.Window
    Debug.Print "EnumerateWindows : Count = _
        " & Application.ActiveWindow.Windows.Count
    Debug.Print , "ID", "Type", "Visible", "Caption"
    For Each win In Application.ActiveWindow.Windows
        Debug.Print , win.ID, win.Type, _
            win.Visible, win.Caption
    Next win
End Sub
```

The `EnumerateWindows()` macro will produce a listing similar to the following:

EnumerateWindows : Count = 9			
ID	Type	Visible	Caption
1658	10	False	Shape Data
1653	10	False	Pan & Zoom
1670	10	False	Size & Position
1669	10	False	Shapes
2263	10	True	Issues
1721	10	False	
2044	10	False	
1354	67	False	Document Stencil
1354	47	False	Basic Flowchart Shapes (Metric)

Here you can see that there are different types of windows, and they all have a unique ID. In fact, the `Type = 10` is the constant `visWinTypes.visAnchorBarAddon`, and the `ID = 2263` is the constant `visWinTypes.visWinIDValidationIssues`.

Knowing this, you can write some code to get more information about the selected issue by using the following code:

```
Public Sub DebugPrintIssue()
Dim issue As Visio.ValidationIssue
    Set issue = GetSelectedIssue
    If issue Is Nothing Then
        Exit Sub
    End If
    Debug.Print "DebugPrintIssue : " & issue.ID
    With issue
        Debug.Print , "Ignored", .Ignored
        Debug.Print , "RuleSet.Name", .rule.ruleSet.Name
        Debug.Print , "Rule.ID", .rule.ID
```

```vb
            Debug.Print , "Rule.NameU", .rule.nameU
            Debug.Print , "Rule.Description", .rule.Description
            Debug.Print , "Rule.Category", .rule.Category
            Debug.Print , "Rule.FilterExpression", _
                .rule.FilterExpression
            Debug.Print , "Rule.TestExpression", .rule.TestExpression
            Debug.Print , "TargetPageID", .TargetPageID
            If Not .TargetPage Is Nothing Then
                Debug.Print , "TargetPage.Name", .TargetPage.Name
            End If
            If Not .targetShape Is Nothing Then
                Debug.Print , "TargetShape.ID", .targetShape.ID
                Debug.Print , "TargetShape.Name", _
                    .targetShape.Name
            End If
        End With
End Sub

Private Function GetSelectedIssue() As ValidationIssue
Dim issue As Visio.ValidationIssue
Dim win As Visio.Window
    Set win = _
        Application.ActiveWindow.Windows.ItemFromID(_
        VisWinTypes.visWinIDValidationIssues)
    If win.Visible = False Then
        Set issue = Nothing
    Else
        Set issue = win.SelectedValidationIssue
    End If
    Set GetSelectedIssue = issue
End Function
```

So, with the fourth issue selected in the above listing, the **Immediate Window** displayed the following:

```
DebugPrintIssue : 8
        Ignored                 False
        RuleSet.Name            Flowchart
        Rule.ID                 2
        Rule.NameU              StartWithoutTerminator
        Rule.Description        Flowchart shape has no incoming
                                connectors and is not a Start/End shape.
        Rule.Category           Start / End
        TargetPageID            5
        TargetPage.Name         Agree Contract Sub-process
        TargetShape.ID          1
        TargetShape.Name        Process.9
```

There are times when you need to react to the user selecting an issue in the UI. In this case, you can listen to the SelectionChanged event of the ActiveWindow in the Visio Application.

The following code can be added to the ThisDocument class in the **VBA Editor**. Notice that the **Issues** window itself, like all of the add-on windows, does not have a selection changed event. Instead, you must listen to the SelectionChanged event of the parent window, which fires whenever the shape selection changes. When a user clicks an issue in the **Issues** window, then all shapes in the drawing window are deselected. If the issue is not a document issue, then the target page is activated in the drawing window, and if there is a target shape, then this is selected in the drawing window The following code snippet, from the ThisDocument class, is not perfect because it has to listen for the SelectionChanged event of the drawing window object in order to retrieve the selected item in the **Issues** window, if it is open. This event only fires if the user selects an issue for a different shape or page in the **Issues** window. It does not detect a change of selection if the user subsequently selects another item in the **Issues** window that belongs to the same shape or page as the previously selected item. In the following code, the RuleSetValidated event for the Document object will be enabled because VBA automatically creates the Document object WithEvents in the ThisDocument class, however the StartListening() method is required to initialize the WithEvents Window object for the drawing window itself.

```
Option Explicit
Private WithEvents mWin As Visio.Window
Public Sub StartListening()
```

```
        Set mWin = Application.ActiveWindow
    End Sub

    Private Sub Document_RuleSetValidated(_
        ByVal RuleSet As IVValidationRuleSet)
        Debug.Print "Document_RuleSetValidated for " & _
            RuleSet.Name, Now()
    End Sub

    Private Sub mWin_SelectionChanged(ByVal Window As IVWindow)
        Dim winIssues As Window
        Set winIssues = _
            Window.Windows.ItemFromID(_
            VisWinTypes.visWinIDValidationIssues)

        If Not winIssues.SelectedValidationIssue Is Nothing Then
            Debug.Print "mWin_SelectionChanged", _
                "Issue = " & _
                winIssues.SelectedValidationIssue.Rule.Description
        Else
            Debug.Print "mWin_SelectionChanged", "No Issue"
        End If

    End Sub
```

How do I toggle the Issues window visibility?

In the last section, you listed all of the current windows using the
EnumerateWindows() method, and you could see that the ID of the **Issues**
window is **2263**. This is, in fact, the value of the constant Visio.VisWinTypes.
visWinIDValidationIssues. You can use this constant to toggle the visibility
of the **Issues** window in the UI with the following method:

```
    Public Sub ToggleIssuesWindowVisibility()
    Dim win As Visio.Window
        Set win = ActiveWindow.Windows.ItemFromID( _
            Visio.VisWinTypes.visWinIDValidationIssues)
        win.Visible = Not win.Visible
    End Sub
```

Note that the **Issues** window is automatically made visible whenever the document
is validated.

Which issues are caused by a particular shape?

A shape does not have a collection of issues directly associated with it. You will need to retrieve the relevant issues from the `Document.Validation.ValidationIssues` collection as follows:

```
Public Sub EnumerateShapeIssues()
If Application.ActiveWindow.Selection.Count = 0 Then
    Exit Sub
End If
Dim shp As Visio.Shape
Dim issue As Visio.ValidationIssue
    Set shp = Application.ActiveWindow.Selection.PrimaryItem
    Debug.Print "EnumerateShapeIssues : " & shp.Name
    Debug.Print , "ID", "Ignored", "Rule.NameU"
    For Each issue In shp.Document.Validation.Issues
        If issue.targetShape Is shp Then
            Debug.Print , issue.ID, _
                issue.Ignored, issue.Rule.NameU
        End If
    Next
End Sub
```

This will produce an output similar to this:

EnumerateShapeIssues	:	Process.9
ID	Ignored	Rule.NameU
8	False	StartWithoutTerminator
9	False	EndWithoutTerminator
10	False	UnconnectedShape

How do I clear issues in code?

When you are writing rules, and then validating them in code, you will soon realize Visio does not automatically clear all of the issues previously created. Nor does Visio necessarily re-validate the same rule on an existing shape. It assumes that, by default, the rules have not changed. Therefore, if the diagram has not been changed, then it is not necessary to re-validate the shapes against the rules. So, it may be necessary to force Visio to re-validate by removing all existing issues. Fortunately this can be done simply as follows:

```
Public Sub ClearAllIssues()
    Visio.ActiveDocument.Validation.Issues.Clear
End Sub
```

How do I validate in code?

I mentioned the Validate() method of the Validation API earlier, and you can use this method without any parameters if you just want to validate the document against all enabled rule sets. I suggest that you clear all the issues first, so that you can be sure that any rule amendments are re-validated, as in the following code.

```
Public Sub ValidateAll()
    Visio.ActiveDocument.Validation.Issues.Clear
    Visio.ActiveDocument.Validation.Validate
End Sub
```

How do I retrieve an existing issue in code?

There will be times when you will need to test if a particular document, page, or shape has already raised an issue for a specific rule. The following method, getIssue(), will retrieve an existing issue, if there is one, otherwise it will return Nothing. You should pass in the rule object, and then the targetPage object (or Nothing), and targetShape (or Nothing), as appropriate for the TargetType of the rule.

```
Private Function getIssue(_
    ByVal rule As Visio.ValidationRule,_
    ByVal targetPage As Visio.Page, _
    ByVal targetShape As Visio.Shape) As Visio.ValidationIssue
Dim retVal As Visio.ValidationIssue
Dim issue As Visio.ValidationIssue
    Set retVal = Nothing
    For Each issue In Visio.ActiveDocument.Validation.Issues
        If issue.rule Is rule Then
            If rule.TargetType = visRuleTargetShape And _
                    Not targetShape Is Nothing Then
                If targetShape Is issue.targetShape Then
                    Set retVal = issue
                    Exit For
                End If
            ElseIf rule.TargetType = visRuleTargetPage And _
                    Not targetPage Is Nothing Then
                If targetPage Is issue.targetPage Then
                    Set retVal = issue
                    Exit For
```

```
                         End If
                ElseIf rule.TargetType = _
                    visRuleTargetDocument Then
                         Set retVal = issue
                         Exit For
                End If

            End If
        Next
        Set getIssue = retVal
End Function
```

How do I add an issue in code?

There are times when Filter Expression and Test Expression cannot adequately define the rule you want to check; then it is easier to write a bit of code. One such example could be ensuring that every page in the document is of portrait orientation. This involves iterating through all of the foreground pages in the document to check if the height is greater than the width. In a real solution, I would probably check that the ratio is correct too. To do this, we'll first have to add an empty rule with a macro that utilizes the getRuleSet() and getRule() methods created earlier. This is done as follows:

```
Public Sub AddOrUpdateRuleB()
Dim ruleSet As Visio.ValidationRuleSet
Dim rule As Visio.ValidationRule
Dim ruleNameU As String
    ruleNameU = "PagesMustBePortraitOrientation"
    Set ruleSet = getRuleSet(Visio.ActiveDocument, "bVisual")
    If ruleSet Is Nothing Then
        Exit Sub
    End If
    Set rule = getRule(ruleSet, ruleNameU)
    If rule Is Nothing Then
        Set rule = ruleSet.Rules.Add(ruleNameU)
    End If
    rule.Category = "Pages"
    rule.Description = _
        "Every page must be portrait orientation"
    rule.TargetType = visRuleTargetDocument
    rule.FilterExpression = ""
    rule.TestExpression = ""
End Sub
```

Now that we have a rule, we need to create some custom validation code, and utilize the getIssue() method from earlier. So, if getIssue() does indeed return something, then I first delete this using the ValidationIssue.Delete() method, in order to ensure that a new ID is generated when the ValidationRule.AddIssue() method is called.

```
Public Sub CheckAllPagesArePortrait( _
    ByVal ruleSet As Visio.ValidationRuleSet)
Dim isPortrait As Boolean
Dim pageHeight As Double
Dim pageWidth As Double
Dim pag As Visio.Page
Dim issue As Visio.ValidationIssue
Dim rule As Visio.ValidationRule
    Set rule = _
        getRule(ruleSet, "PagesMustBePortraitOrientation")
    If rule Is Nothing Then
        Exit Sub
    End If
    For Each pag In ruleSet.Document.Pages
        If pag.Type = visTypeForeground Then
            pageHeight = pag.PageSheet.CellsSRC( _
                Visio.VisSectionIndices.visSectionObject, _
                Visio.VisRowIndices.visRowPage, _
                Visio.VisCellIndices.visPageHeight).ResultIU
            pageWidth = pag.PageSheet.CellsSRC( _
                Visio.VisSectionIndices.visSectionObject, _
                Visio.VisRowIndices.visRowPage, _
                Visio.VisCellIndices.visPageWidth).ResultIU
            isPortrait = pageHeight > pageWidth
            If isPortrait = False Then
                Set issue = getIssue(rule, pag, Nothing)
                If Not issue Is Nothing Then
                    issue.Delete
                End If
                Set issue = rule.AddIssue(pag)
            End If
        End If
    Next
End Sub
```

So, all we need now is to call the `CheckAllPagesArePortrait()` method when the rule set is validated, as we saw earlier using the `Document_RuleSetValidated` event:

```
Private Sub Document_RuleSetValidated(ByVal ruleSet As
   IVValidationRuleSet)
      If ruleSet.nameU = "bVisual" Then
          CheckAllPagesArePortrait ruleSet
      End If
End Sub
```

This will ensure that our custom validation code is run, and any pages that are not portrait orientation create an issue for that rule. These issues will then appear in the **Issues** window in the UI.

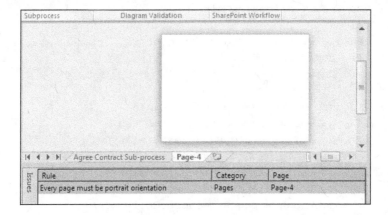

Although I have shown you how to add issues in code using a custom validation rule, I would encourage you to write your own rules using the Filter Expression and Test Expression formulae as often as possible. This is because you can expose these rules to public scrutiny more easily, and they can be copied from one rule set to another.

Summary

In this chapter, we have examined the **Validation API**, and seen how we can review or create rule sets and rules. We have also seen how rules can be validated to create issues automatically, or how issues can be created in code as the result of custom validation code.

In the next chapter, we are going to start building a Visio VSTO 2010 add-in that we can use to analyze existing rules, or create new ones more easily. We are also going to switch from VBA to using C# in Visual Studio 2010, so that you can have a proper development tool to use.

5
Developing a Validation API Interface

Microsoft Visio 2010 does not provide a user interface to the **Validation API** that rules developers can use, so this chapter is devoted to building a useful tool to enable the tasks to be performed easily. The tool will enable you to review and amend existing rules, to create new rules, and to even perform tests on rules.

Don't worry if you are not a C# coder, because the completed tool is available from the companion website `http://www.visiorules.com`. However, I will lead you through the development of this tool in this chapter because it introduces you to using C#, rather than VBA that was used in the previous chapters.

This chapter will also describe how to use this tool, so it should be worth reading through, even if you are not a C# coder. It will cover the following topics:

- The architecture of the tool—a VSTO add-in with a WPF UI
- The `ThisAddin` class—listening for Visio application events and checking the Visio edition
- Creating the `ViewModel`—wrapping the Validation API objects to enable automatic updating of the UI of the new tool
- Modifying the Fluent UI using callbacks in the ribbon
- Creating the **Rules Explorer** window—the tree view, detail panels, and the new ribbon buttons
- Displaying the rule for a selected issue
- Displaying the issues for the current selection

The architecture of the tool

This tool is developed using Microsoft Visual Studio 2010, using C# and .NET Framework 4. This means that it can be developed as a Visio 2010 Add-in using VSTO 2010. This will make deployment simple using **ClickOnce**, because once it has been installed it will periodically check to see if there is an updated version available.

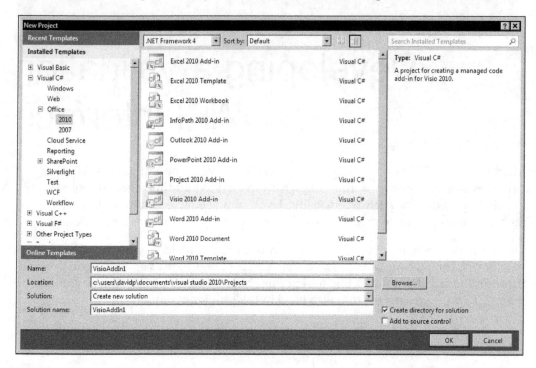

I have called the project ValidationExplorer, and it will be extended in later chapters to provide enhanced capabilities.

I decided to use **Windows Presentation Foundation (WPF)** to create the UI elements wherever possible because it has become my preference over the last few years. Visio is a COM application, therefore the WPF elements have to be hosted within a WinForm control. The effort is worth it though, because of the superior data-binding and UI element flexibility.

Programming in WPF promotes the adoption of a data-driven model, rather than the event-driven model more common in WinForm applications. A programming guide pattern called **Model View ViewModel** (**MVVM**) has evolved over the last couple of years for working with WPF and Silverlight, which should be followed where possible. However, as this is only a small application and it is hosted inside a COM application, I have not adopted all of its patterns, but I have tried to follow the spirit. The most important part of this model form is the binding of the UI elements to views of the data. This is particularly important for XAML-based coding, because XAML can be so verbose that trying to follow programming logic within it is a thankless and almost impossible task. It is far easier to separate the design of the UI, which is described in XAML, from the current state of the interface. For example, I have added `IsSelected` and `IsExpanded` properties to the classes bound to the main tree view. These properties are merely bound (both ways) to the state of the interface. This means that the code can set the values of the object properties, and the UI will respond automatically. There is no need to iterate through the tree view nodes in the UI, or indeed to find the tree view node by its key to select it. The magic of data binding *just does it*.

 The XAML binding capability is reminiscent of the Visio ShapeSheet formula capability. Perhaps that is why I like it so much!

The Visio add-in template will create the `ThisAddin` class automatically because this is the main hook into your project when the host application starts.

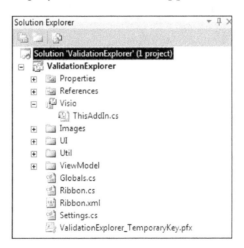

The **data layer** is provided by the Visio objects and in particular, by the new **Validation** objects described in the earlier chapters.

The **UI layer** comprises of WinForms controls as hosts for XAML User Controls, or just XAML Windows, and are created in the UI folder.

The business logic or **view model layer** consists of classes and collections that can be bound to the UI, and are created in the ViewModel folder.

ThisAddin class

The ThisAddin_Startup() event is a good place to test for the correct Visio version and edition, along with checking that the Visio application events are indeed enabled, otherwise this add-in will not work properly anyway.

```
private void ThisAddIn_Startup(object sender, System.EventArgs e)
{
    try
    {
        veApplication.VisioApplication = this.Application;
        /* check prereq's */
        // check for Visio >= 2010 and Edition >= PRO
        if (!this.IsVisio14PremiumInstalled)
        {
            MessageBox.Show(
                "This add-in requires the Premium edition of Visio
                    2010", "Visio Premium edition required",
                MessageBoxButton.OK, MessageBoxImage.Exclamation);
            return;
        }
        // events must be enabled
        if (!Convert.ToBoolean(Globals.ThisAddIn.Application.
            EventsEnabled))
// -1 is TRUE, 0 is FALSE, typically anything other than 0 is TRUE
        {
            if (MessageBox.Show(
                    "Event are currently disabled, this add-in
                    requires events to be enabled.  Would you
                    like to enable events now?",
                    "Rules Tools", MessageBoxButton.OKCancel,
                    MessageBoxImage.Information,
                    MessageBoxResult.OK) == MessageBoxResult.OK)
            {
                Globals.ThisAddIn.Application.EventsEnabled =
                Convert.ToInt16(true); // convert to short from
                TRUE which ends up being 1
            }
        }
```

```
        // init locals
        this.documents = new Dictionary<int, ViewModel.VEDocument>();
        // connect to events
        VisioEvents_Connect();
    }
    catch (COMException ex)
    {
        throw ex;
    }
    catch (Exception ex)
    {
        throw ex;
    }
}
```

Listening for application events

We need to listen for the creation, opening, or closing of any documents so that our VEDocuments collection can be maintained. Therefore, the following VisioEvents_ Connect() method is called by the ThisAddIn_Startup event.

```
private void VisioEvents_Connect()
{
    Globals.ThisAddIn.Application.DocumentOpened +=
        new Visio.EApplication_DocumentOpenedEventHandler(
            VisioApplication_DocumentOpened);
    Globals.ThisAddIn.Application.DocumentCreated +=
        new Visio.EApplication_DocumentCreatedEventHandler(
            VisioApplication_DocumentCreated);
    Globals.ThisAddIn.Application.BeforeDocumentClose +=
        new Visio.EApplication_BeforeDocumentCloseEventHandler(
            VisioApplication_BeforeDocumentClose);
    //Listen for selection changes
    Globals.ThisAddIn.Application.SelectionChanged +=
        new Visio.EApplication_SelectionChangedEventHandler(
            Window_SelectionChanged);
}
```

The last event listens to the SelectionChanged event, because this is required later to ascertain the currently selected issue in the **Issues** window.

> The SelectionChanged event will only fire when an issue pertaining to a different shape or page from the previous one is selected. Unfortunately, there is no selection changed event for the **Issues** window.

There is also a `VisioEvents_Disconnect()` method called by the `ThisAddIn_Shutdown()` event.

Checking for Visio Premium edition

In an earlier chapter, I showed you how to test for the Visio edition in VBA; here is the equivalent as a C# method:

```csharp
internal bool IsVisio14PremiumInstalled
{
    get
    {
        bool retVal = false;
        // the installed version of Visio has to be 14 or > and the
          edition has to be PRO or >
        if (this.Application.TypelibMinorVersion >= 14)
        {
            // CurrentEdition tells us that their Editions is Premium
            if (this.Application.CurrentEdition ==
              Visio.VisEdition.visEditionPremium)
            {
                retVal = true;
            }
        }
        return retVal;
    }
}
```

Creating the ViewModel

I created new classes to mirror the relevant parts of the **Visio Type Library** objects, and all of the **Validation API** objects and collections. I prefixed these wrapper classes with VE for `ValidationExplorer`, which is the project name.

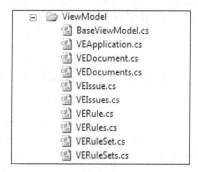

When you select a folder in the **Solution Explorer**, then select **Project**, **Add Class**, and so on, Visual Studio will automatically append the folder name to the namespace of the class.

As the Visio objects are COM objects, you cannot bind to them directly because XAML really needs to bind to dependency objects that can notify the UI of any changes that take place.

Therefore, I created a `BaseViewModel` abstract class that implements the `System.ComponentModel.INotifyPropertyChanged` interface, which will notify the client when property values are changed.

All of my wrapper object classes implement this base class. The wrapper collections implement the `System.Collections.ObjectModel.ObservableCollection<T>` class because this will provide notifications when items are added, removed, or when the whole list is refreshed. The class diagram from Visual Studio 2010 shows how all of the view model classes are related.

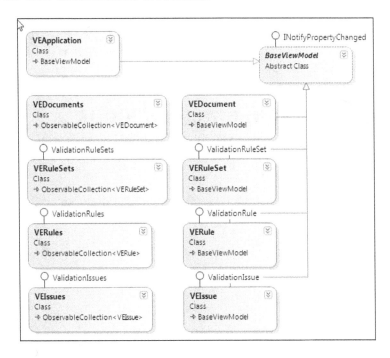

Each of the classes also implements the corresponding Visio class, and the **Validation** objects are explicitly implemented so that individual properties can be enhanced, if required.

Creating the BaseViewModel class

The `BaseViewModel` class merely implements the `INotifyPropertyChanged`
interface explicitly.

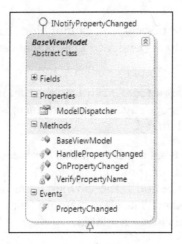

Each of the classes that implement this base class will have the important
`OnPropertyChanged` method available. It is this that ensures that the data bound
UI is kept automatically synchronized.

Viewing the documents collection

I created the `VEApplication` class to be the top level of our mirror hierarchy. This
contains the `ObservableCollection` called `VEDocuments`, which in turn provides
access to each `VEDocument`.

The following class diagram displays the properties and methods of the
`VEApplication`, `VEDocuments`, and `VEDocument` classes:

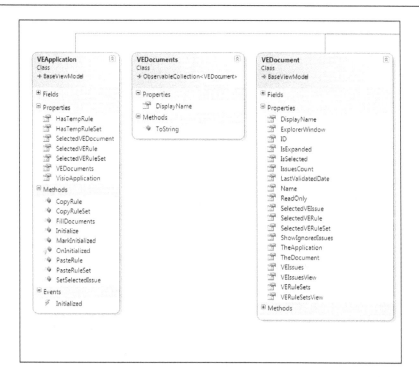

The `FillDocuments` method in the `VEApplication` class creates the collection of `VEDocuments` from the open list of Visio documents. This is only used on the initialization because, once created, documents will be added or removed from the collection in response to the relevant events (`VisioApplication_DocumentCreated`, `VisioApplication_DocumentOpened`, and `VisioApplication_BeforeDocumentClose`). The following method thus iterates through the open Visio documents and creates a new `VEDocument` object for each relevant Visio Document:

```
public void FillDocuments()
{
    this.VEDocuments.Clear();
    if (visioApplication == null) return;
    foreach (Visio.Document doc in visioApplication.Documents)
    {
        //Only add drawings and templates to the collection
        if (doc.Type == Visio.VisDocumentTypes.visTypeDrawing
        || doc.Type == Visio.VisDocumentTypes.visTypeTemplate)
        {
            this.VEDocuments.Add(new VEDocument(this, doc));
            VEDocument ved = this.VEDocuments.Single(dc => dc.ID ==
                doc.ID);
            ved.IsExpanded = true;
```

```
                    //Set the Selected Document
            if (visioApplication.ActiveDocument.ID == doc.ID)
                {
                    this.SelectedVEDocument = ved;
                }
            }
        }
    }
    OnPropertyChanged("VEDocuments");
}
```

 Note that stencil documents are filtered out by testing the type of the document.

One of the coolest bits of C# is the terseness of the **Lambda** expressions in **LINQ** statements. For example, the above code contains the following line:

```
VEDocument ved = this.VEDocuments.Single(dc => dc.ID == doc.ID);
```

This is such a simple way to select a specific element from a collection.

The VEDocument class contains the properties and methods for controlling the extra forms in the add-in, and I have surfaced the methods for adding, copying, pasting, and deleting rule sets, rules, and issues because it is the entry point to these collections.

The following class diagram displays the methods of the VEDocuments class:

Viewing the ValidationRuleSets collection

Each VEDocument object contains an ObservableCollection called VERuleSets, which in turn provides access to each VERuleset object.

The VERuleSets and VERuleSet classes implement Visio.ValidationRuleSets and Visio.ValidationRuleSet respectively, which means that all of the properties and methods for them are available to the developer. However, special attention must be made to ensuring that the notifiable properties are updated whenever the underlying properties are changed. Similarly, it is necessary to create custom methods to add and delete objects from the collections so that the observable collections are kept synchronized.

The following class diagram displays the properties and methods of the VERuleSets and VERuleSet classes:

Viewing the ValidationRules collection

Each VERuleSet object contains an ObservableCollection called VERules, which in turn, provides access to each VERule.

The VERules and VERule classes implement Visio.ValidationRules and Visio.ValidationRule respectively, which means that all of the properties and methods of them are available to the developer.

The following class diagram displays the properties and methods of the VERules and VERule classes:

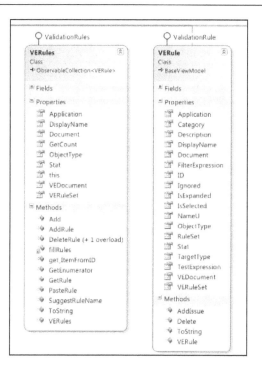

The constructor for the VERules class takes the Visio.ValidationRules and the VERuleSet object to create the collection of VERule objects:

```
public class VERules : ObservableCollection<VERule>, Visio.
ValidationRules
{
    public ICollectionView VERulesView;
    private Visio.ValidationRules rules;
    public VERules(Visio.ValidationRules rles, VERuleSet verset)
    {
        rules = rles;
        veRuleSet = verset;
        veDocument = verset.VEDocument;
        fillRules();
        //Set the default views
        this.VERulesView = CollectionViewSource.GetDefaultView(this);
        //Group by Category, sort by Description
        this.VERulesView.GroupDescriptions.Add(new
          PropertyGroupDescription("Category"));
        this.VERulesView.SortDescriptions.Add(new
          SortDescription("Description", ListSortDirection.Ascending));
        OnPropertyChanged(new PropertyChangedEventArgs("GetCount"));
        this.VERuleSet.RaisePropertyChanged("DisplayName");
    }
```

Viewing the ValidationIssues collection

I wanted to be able to view the issues for a page, or a selection of shapes, grouped by each shape. Therefore, I decided to create the `VEIssues` collection of `VEIssue` objects.

These objects need to be created when the document is first opened, and then re-created whenever the document is validated. Similar to the `VEApplication` class, there is a call to the `VisioEvents_Connect()` method in the constructor, and a call to the `VisioEvents_Disconnect()` method in the destructor.

```
private void VisioEvents_Connect()
{
    if (this.document != null)
    {
        this.document.RuleSetValidated += new
          Visio.EDocument_RuleSetValidatedEventHandler(
          Document_RuleSetValidated);
    }
}
private void VisioEvents_Disconnect()
{
    this.document.RuleSetValidated -= new
      Visio.EDocument_RuleSetValidatedEventHandler(
      Document_RuleSetValidated);
}
private void Document_RuleSetValidated(Visio.ValidationRuleSet rset)
{
    OnRuleSetValidated(rset);
}
private void OnRuleSetValidated(Visio.ValidationRuleSet rset)
{
    //Refresh the issues
    this.RefreshIssues();
}
public void RefreshIssues()
{
    this.LastValidatedDate = document.Validation.LastValidatedDate;
    OnPropertyChanged("LastValidatedDate");
    this.ShowIgnoredIssues = document.Validation.ShowIgnoredIssues;
    OnPropertyChanged("ShowIgnoredIssues");
    this.VEIssues.FillIssues();
}
```

The `VEDocument.RefreshIssues()` method calls the `VEIssues.FillIssues()` method as follows:

```
public void FillIssues()
{
    try
```

```
        {
            this.Clear();
            foreach (Visio.ValidationIssue iss in issues)
            {
                this.Add(new VEIssue(iss, veDocument));
            }
        }
        catch (Exception)
        {
            throw;
        }
    }
```

The following class diagram displays the properties and methods of the `VEIssues` and `VEIssue` classes:

Fortunately, for this add-in, we can listen to the event `Visio.EDocument_RuleSet ValidatedEventHandler(Document_RuleSetValidated)` because the validation objects are all created at this time. I will describe how this is used later in this chapter.

Modifying the Visio Fluent UI

The Fluent UI is new in Visio 2010 so, at last, Visio is sharing the same UI objects as the big three in Office (Word, Excel, and PowerPoint). This means that there are a lot more relevant resources available on the Web for developers to refer to. Before Microsoft bought Visio in 1999, the Visio application had its own **UIObject API**, which provided a programming model for menus, toolbars, the status bar, and accelerator keys. One of the first changes to be made, after the Microsoft acquisition, was the adoption of the Microsoft Office **CommandBars API** in Visio. This meant that developers could start using the same UI objects as other Office developers. But then the big three Office applications got the new Ribbon in the 2007 version. This is now improved and commonly called the Fluent UI, so even though the legacy UI objects may still be available in the Visio type library, it is recommended that developers get to grips with the Ribbon object.

One of the good things about the Fluent UI is the ability to describe the modifications that you want in an XML file. You can even modify built-in ribbon tabs in this XML file, which is fortunate because the new **Process** tab has plenty of unused space at the right-hand side. So, I created a `Ribbon.xml` file that described a new group, labeled **Rules Tools**, with a large button to open the main **Rules Explorer** window. The next five smaller buttons are only usable when the **Rules Explorer** window is open, so they are disabled until then. The last button can be pressed any time because it displays the issues for the selection or page (if nothing is selected). I have also reproduced the **Selection Issues** button on the right-mouse menu of a shape or page.

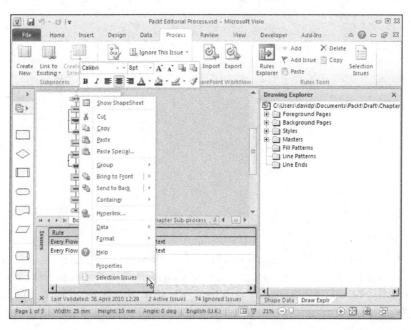

I cannot pretend that I took the months of usability research that Microsoft would have done for the optimum size and appearance of the buttons in the **Rules Tools** group, but I have tried to put an order to them. Also, I should thank Chris Hopkins of Microsoft for his excellent article about extending the Visio Ribbon at: http://blogs.msdn.com/chhopkin/archive/2009/11/20/ribbon-extensibility-for-visio-solutions-in-visio-2010.aspx.

This is an abbreviation of the Ribbon.xml file that creates this modification to the UI:

```xml
<?xml version="1.0" encoding="UTF-8"?>
<customUI
  xmlns="http://schemas.microsoft.com/office/2009/07/customui"
  onLoad="Ribbon_Load">
  <ribbon>
    <tabs>
      <tab idMso="TabProcess" >
        <group id="RulesTools"
               label="Rules Tools">
          <button id="buttonValidationExplorerWindow"
                  imageMso="ReviewReviewingPaneVertical"
                  size="large"
                  onAction="OnAction"
                  getEnabled="GetEnabled"
                  getLabel="GetLabel"
                  getSupertip="GetSupertip"
                  getVisible="GetVisible"
                  />
          <separator/>
          <button id="buttonRuleAdd"
                  getImage="GetImage"
                  onAction="OnAction"
                  getEnabled="GetEnabled"
                  getLabel="GetLabel"
                  getSupertip="GetSupertip"
                  getVisible="GetVisible"
                  />
           <!--etcà
          <button id="buttonIssues"
                  size="large"
                  getImage="GetImage"
                  onAction="OnAction"
                  getEnabled="GetEnabled"
                  getLabel="GetLabel"
```

```
                                getSupertip="GetSupertip"
                                getVisible="GetVisible"
                                />
                </group>
             </tab>
          </tabs>
      </ribbon>
      <contextMenus>
          <contextMenu idMso="ContextMenuShape1D"   >
             <button id="buttonIssues1D"
                            getImage="GetImage"
                            onAction="OnAction"
                            getEnabled="GetEnabled"
                            getLabel="GetLabel"
                            getSupertip="GetSupertip"
                            getVisible="GetVisible"
                            />
          </contextMenu>
          <contextMenu idMso="ContextMenuShape" >
             <button id="buttonIssues2D"
                            getImage="GetImage"
                            onAction="OnAction"
                            getEnabled="GetEnabled"
                            getLabel="GetLabel"
                            getSupertip="GetSupertip"
                            getVisible="GetVisible"
                            />
          </contextMenu>
          <contextMenu idMso="ContextMenuDrawingPage" >
             <button id="buttonIssuesPage"
                            getImage="GetImage"
                            onAction="OnAction"
                            getEnabled="GetEnabled"
                            getLabel="GetLabel"
                            getSupertip="GetSupertip"
                            getVisible="GetVisible"
                            />
          </contextMenu>
       </contextMenus>
   </customUI>
```

The `idMso="TabProcess"` attribute is the important bit to know, because `TabProcess` is the `control.id` of the new **Process** tab in Visio 2010. If you do not use the `idMso` attribute, then you need to use the `id` attribute to create your own unique identifier.

The `Ribbon.xml` has effectively got code behind in a class called `Ribbon.cs`, and this class contains the callbacks specified in the `getImage`, `onAction`, `getEnabled`, `getLabel`, `getSupertip`, and `getVisibile` methods. These neat methods enable you to centralize the custom images, text, and actions, in addition to defining when each control is enabled.

For example, the following snippet is an extract from the `Ribbon` class which returns the label for each of the buttons:

```
public string GetLabel(Microsoft.Office.Core.IRibbonControl control)
{
    string retVal = ""; // default
    switch (control.Id)
    {
        case "buttonValidationExplorerWindow":
        {
            return "Rules Explorer";
        }
        case "buttonRuleAdd":
        {
            return "Add...";
        }
//etc
        case "buttonIssues":
        {
            return "Selection Issues";
        }
    }
    return "";
}
```

Similar calls return the image for each button.

```
public System.Drawing.Bitmap GetImage(
    Microsoft.Office.Core.IRibbonControl control)
{
    switch (control.Id)
    {
        case "buttonRuleAdd":
        {
            return GetResourceImage("base_plus_sign_32.png");
        }
//etc
    }
    // we should not get here for these buttons
    return null;
}
```

The above function calls the `GetResourceImage()` method to extract `Resource` images from the `Images` folder.

```
private System.Drawing.Bitmap GetResourceImage(string image)
{
    // build up a relative path to the image.
    System.Uri imageLocation = new
        System.Uri("/ValidationExplorer;component/Images/" + image,
        System.UriKind.Relative);
    // Use the helper methods on WPF's application
    // class to create an image.
    using (Stream resourceStream =
        System.Windows.Application.GetResourceStream(
        imageLocation).Stream)
    {
        return new System.Drawing.Bitmap(resourceStream);
    }
}
```

The overall effect is a pleasing extension to the built-in **Process** tab, which can be seen in the following screenshot:

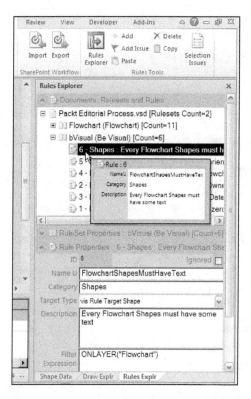

Creating the Rules Explorer window

The **Rules Explorer** Window is a Visio anchor window, for which there are many examples available, including some in the Microsoft Visio SDK. The resultant window is a sub-window of the document window, just like a number of other built-in windows like the **Drawing Explorer**, **Shape Data** window, and of course, the new **Issues** window. These windows can float free, anchored to an edge of the drawing window, or merged with other sub-windows.

The following screenshot of Visual Studio shows that the `FormExplorer` class merely acts as a host for the `UserControlExplorer` control.

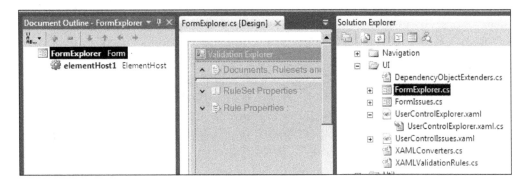

The `UserControlExplorer` is the WPF control that contains all of the goodies, and contains some code behind.

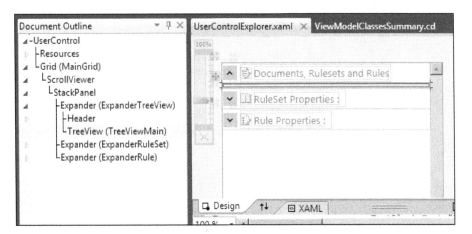

The **Document Outline** shows that very little is defined directly within the `TreeViewMain` element because it calls on templates defined in the `Resources`.

Self-describing tree views

I wanted the tree view to display the open documents, their rule sets, and the rules within them. This is achieved by creating three `HierarchicalDataTemplate` definitions—`DocumentTemplate`, `RuleSetTemplate`, and `RuleTemplate`.

```
<TreeView Grid.Row="0" Name="TreeViewMain"
    Background="White"
    ItemsSource="{Binding Path=VEDocuments}"
    ItemTemplate="{StaticResource ResourceKey=DocumentTemplate}"
    SelectedItemChanged="TreeViewMain_SelectedItemChanged"
    />
```

The `ResourceKey` property of the `ItemTemplate` attribute specifies the `HierarchicalDataTemplate` that is defined in the `ResourceDictionary` of the `UserControl`.

```
<HierarchicalDataTemplate x:Key="DocumentTemplate"
                    DataType="{x:Type localVM:VEDocument}"
                    ItemsSource="{Binding Path=VERuleSetsView}"
                    ItemTemplate="{StaticResource
                    ResourceKey=RuleSetTemplate}"
                    >
    <StackPanel Orientation="Horizontal"
            ToolTip="{StaticResource
                ResourceKey=DocumentToolTip}">
        <Image Source="..\Images\Page.png"
                Style="{StaticResource
                ResourceKey=ImageStyle}"/>
        <TextBlock Text="{Binding Path=DisplayName}"
                Style="{StaticResource
                    ResourceKey=TreeItemStyle}" />
    </StackPanel>
</HierarchicalDataTemplate>
```

Thus, the `HierarchicalDataTemplate` for each `DataType` specifies the template for its child items.

Informative tooltips

WPF enables a developer to create larger and more interesting tooltips than those usually created with WinForms applications.

Each of the tree view items has a tooltip defined in XAML in order to display the most important details for them.

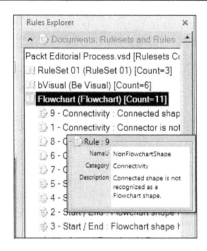

The `RuleToolTip` is defined in the `UserControlExplorer.xaml` file:

```xml
<ToolTip x:Key="RuleToolTip">
    <Border Style="{StaticResource ResourceKey=ToolTipBorderStyle}">
        <GroupBox >
            <GroupBox.Header>
                <StackPanel Orientation="Horizontal">
                    <Image Source="..\Images\IssueTracking_32x32.png"
                        Style="{StaticResource
                            ResourceKey=ImageStyle}" />
                    <TextBlock Text="Rule : " />
                    <TextBlock Text="{Binding Path=ID}" />
                </StackPanel>
            </GroupBox.Header>
            <Grid Style="{DynamicResource
              ResourceKey=ToolTipGridStyle}">
                <Grid.ColumnDefinitions>
                    <ColumnDefinition Width="60" />
                    <ColumnDefinition Width="120" />
                </Grid.ColumnDefinitions>
                <Grid.RowDefinitions>
                    <RowDefinition Height="18" />
                    <RowDefinition Height="18" />
                    <RowDefinition Height="54" />
                </Grid.RowDefinitions>

                <TextBlock Text="NameU"
                        Style="{StaticResource
                          ResourceKey=ToolTipLabelStyle}"
                        Grid.Row="0" Grid.Column="0" />
```

```
                    <TextBlock Text="{Binding Path=NameU}"
                            Style="{StaticResource
                                ResourceKey=ToolTipTextBlockStyle}"
                            Grid.Row="0" Grid.Column="1" />

                    <TextBlock Text="Category"
                            Style="{StaticResource
                                ResourceKey=ToolTipLabelStyle}"
                            Grid.Row="1" Grid.Column="0" />
                    <TextBlock Text="{Binding Path=Category}"
                            Style="{StaticResource
                                ResourceKey=ToolTipTextBlockStyle}"
                            Grid.Row="1" Grid.Column="1" />

                    <TextBlock Text="Description"
                            Style="{DynamicResource
                                ResourceKey=ToolTipLabelStyle}"
                            Grid.Row="2" Grid.Column="0" />
                    <TextBlock Text="{Binding Path=Description}"
                            Style="{StaticResource
                                ResourceKey=ToolTipTextBlockStyle}"
                            Grid.Row="2" Grid.Column="1"
                            TextWrapping="Wrap"/>
                </Grid>
            </GroupBox>
        </Border>
    </ToolTip>
```

Linked detail panels

I wanted the relevant detail panel to be displayed whenever a rule set or a rule is selected in the tree view.

Editing rule set properties

You can edit a rule set by selecting the rule set tree view item. This enables and expands the **RuleSet Properties** panel, thus providing access to the **Enabled**, **NameU**, **Name**, **Flags**, and **Description** properties. Remember that the **NameU** is the internal unique identifier, whilst the **Name** can be localized, if desired.

The **Flags** property is selected from a combo box, which contains the humanized version of the `Visio.VisRuleSetFlags` enumerator.

 I borrowed the code for this from Tom F Wright's CodeProject article: `http://www.codeproject.com/KB/WPF/enumlistconverter.aspx`.

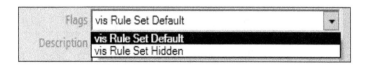

This technique requires a `Resources` reference in the XAML:

```
<UserControl.Resources>
  <localUI:VisRuleSetFlagsListConverter
    x:Key="VisRuleSetFlagsListConverter"/>
```

This `Converter` is then specified in the `ItemSource` and `SelectedIndex` of the `ComboBox` element:

```
<TextBlock Text="Flags"
   Style="{DynamicResource ResourceKey=LabelStyle}"
   Grid.Row="3" Grid.Column="0" />
      <ComboBox ItemsSource="{Binding Source={StaticResource
         ResourceKey=VisRuleSetFlagsListConverter}}"
         SelectedIndex="{Binding Path=Flags, Mode=TwoWay,
         Converter={StaticResource
         ResourceKey=VisRuleSetFlagsListConverter}}"
         Grid.Row="3" Grid.Column="1" Grid.ColumnSpan="3" />
```

Editing rule properties

Whenever the user selects a rule in the tree view of the **Rules Explorer** window, the **Rule Properties** expander is automatically expanded, thus providing easy access to the properties for viewing or editing.

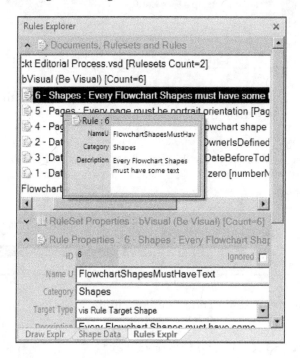

The expander for the **Documents, Rulesets and Rules** tree view (and **RuleSet Properties**) can be collapsed, and the vertical scrollbar positioned, to allow full access to the **Rule Properties** panel.

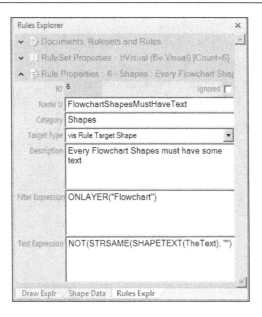

The XAML data binding and the underlying `VERule` object ensures that the `Visio.ValidationRule` object is automatically updated, but of course, the Visio document must be saved eventually to preserve these changes.

Handling special key strokes

The user can type normal characters into the text boxes in the detail panels, but there are some special key combinations that will act upon the drawing page rather than the add-in window, unless they are handled. In particular, a rules developer will want to use *Delete*, *Ctrl+C*, *Ctrl+X*, and *Ctrl+V* keys to delete, copy, cut, and paste. Other useful keys are *Ctrl+A*, *Ctrl+Z*, and *Ctrl+Y* to select all, undo, and redo.

 See the following MSDN article for more information about the `OnMessageKeystrokeForAddon` event: `http://msdn.microsoft.com/en-us/library/ms427669.aspx`.

Firstly, the `ThisAddin.VisioEvents_Connect()` method was enhanced to add the `OnKeystrokeMessageForAddon` event, which is as follows:

```
//Listen for key strokes for addon
Globals.ThisAddIn.Application.OnKeystrokeMessageForAddon +=
    new Visio.EApplication_OnKeystrokeMessageForAddonEventHandler(
    VisioApplication_MessageForAddon);
```

Next, the `VisioApplication_MessageForAddon()` event was written to handle each of the anticipated keystrokes in order to action upon the currently active text box.

```csharp
public System.Windows.Controls.TextBox CurrrentTextBox = null;
private bool VisioApplication_MessageForAddon(
  Microsoft.Office.Interop.Visio.MSGWrap msg)
{
    if (CurrrentTextBox == null) return false;
    if ((int)msg.wParam == (int)System.Windows.Forms.Keys.Delete)
    {
        if (CurrrentTextBox.SelectionLength > 0)
        {
            CurrrentTextBox.Text.Remove(
              CurrrentTextBox.SelectionStart,
              CurrrentTextBox.SelectionLength);
            CurrrentTextBox.SelectedText = "";
        }
      return true;
    }
    else if (System.Windows.Input.Keyboard.IsKeyDown(
      System.Windows.Input.Key.LeftCtrl) == true ||
        System.Windows.Input.Keyboard.IsKeyDown(
          System.Windows.Input.Key.RightCtrl) == true)
    {
        if ((int)msg.wParam == (int)System.Windows.Forms.Keys.A)
        {
            CurrrentTextBox.SelectionStart = 0;
            CurrrentTextBox.SelectionLength =
              CurrrentTextBox.Text.Length;
            CurrrentTextBox.SelectedText = CurrrentTextBox.Text;
            return true;
        }
        else if ((int)msg.wParam == (int)System.Windows.Forms.Keys.C)
        {
            Clipboard.SetText(CurrrentTextBox.SelectedText);
            return true;
        }
        else if ((int)msg.wParam == (int)System.Windows.Forms.Keys.X)
        {
            Clipboard.SetText(CurrrentTextBox.SelectedText);
            if (CurrrentTextBox.SelectionLength > 0)
            {
                CurrrentTextBox.Text =
                  CurrrentTextBox.Text.Remove(
                  CurrrentTextBox.SelectionStart,
```

```
                    CurrrentTextBox.SelectionLength);
                CurrrentTextBox.SelectedText = "";
            }
            return true;
        }
        else if ((int)msg.wParam == (int)System.Windows.Forms.Keys.V)
        {
            if (Clipboard.ContainsText() == false) return false;
            CurrrentTextBox.SelectedText = Clipboard.GetText();
            return true;
        }
        else if ((int)msg.wParam == (int)System.Windows.Forms.Keys.Z)
        {
            CurrrentTextBox.Undo();
            return true;
        }
        else if ((int)msg.wParam == (int)System.Windows.Forms.Keys.Y)
        {
            CurrrentTextBox.Redo();
            return true;
        }
        else return false;
    }
    return false;
}
```

The GotFocus event was then added to the textbox controls in the UserControlExplorer.xaml that is used for editing text, as in the following example:

```
<TextBox Text="{Binding Path=NameU, Mode=TwoWay}"
    GotFocus="TextBox_GotFocus"
    LostFocus="TextBox_LostFocus"
    Style="{DynamicResource ResourceKey=TBStyle}"
    Grid.Row="1" Grid.Column="1" Grid.ColumnSpan="3" />
```

The TextBox_GotFocus() event handler was added to the code in the UserControlExplorer.xaml.cs class as follows:

```
private void TextBox_GotFocus(object sender, RoutedEventArgs e)
{
    if (sender is System.Windows.Controls.TextBox)
    {
        Globals.ThisAddIn.CurrrentTextBox =
            (System.Windows.Controls.TextBox)sender;
    }
```

```
            else
            {
                Globals.ThisAddIn.CurrrentTextBox = null;
            }
        }
```

The Explorer actions

The smaller action buttons are available when the **Rules Explorer** window is open.

The `Ribbon` class contains a method to test if this **Explorer Window** is open for the active document:

```
    public static bool IsExplorerWindowOpen(Visio.Document document)
    {
        //Check if the explorer window is open
        if (document != null)
        {
            foreach (Visio.Window win in document.Application.Windows)
            {
                if (win.Document == document)
                {
                    foreach (Visio.Window subWin in win.Windows)
                    {
                        if (subWin.Caption == Globals.AnchorBarTitle)
                        {
                            return subWin.Visible;
                        }
                    }
                }
            }
        }
        return false;
    }
```

The particular actions that the buttons perform depend upon the type of item selected in the tree view. Therefore, I added a couple of methods to the `Ribbon` class that test if a `VERuleSet` or `VERule` is selected in the tree view.

```
    public static bool IsRuleSetSelected(Visio.Document document)
    {
        if (document != null)
        {
            //Get the VEDocument
            ViewModel.VEDocument ved =
```

```
            Globals.ThisAddIn.VEApp.VEDocuments.Single(
              doc => doc.ID == document.ID);
          //Test if SelectedRuleSet is null
          return ved.SelectedVERuleSet != null;
      }
      return false;
  }


  public static bool IsRuleSelected(Visio.Document document)
  {
      if (document != null)
      {
        //Get the VEDocument
        ViewModel.VEDocument ved =
          Globals.ThisAddIn.VEApp.VEDocuments.Single(
          doc => doc.ID == document.ID);
         //Test if SelectedRule is null
         return ved.SelectedVERule != null;
      }
      return false;
  }
```

Of course, something needs to set the SelectedVERuleSet and SelectedVERule
properties of the active VEDocument instance. This is done in the TreeViewMain_
SelectedItemChanged() event in the code in the UserControlExplorer.xaml file.
This event is also used to set the DataContext of the expanders for the **RuleSet** and
Rule Properties panels.

The Add button

The **Add** button action will add a rule set if a document is selected in the tree view, but it will add a rule if a rule set is selected in the tree view. Then, the new item itself is automatically selected in the tree view.

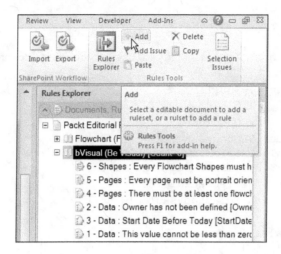

The `OnAction(Office.IRibbonControl control)` callback defines the case for the `buttonRuleAdd` button. It tests if a `VEDocument` or `VERuleSet` is selected, and then calls the relevant method in the `VEDocument` object.

```
case "buttonRuleAdd":
    {
        //Only enable if a ruleset or rule is selected
        bool isWinOpen = Ribbon.IsExplorerWindowOpen(
          Globals.ThisAddIn.Application.ActiveDocument);
        if (isWinOpen)
        {
            if (Ribbon.IsRuleSetSelected(
              Globals.ThisAddIn.Application.ActiveDocument))
            {
                Globals.ThisAddIn.VEApp.SelectedVEDocument.AddRule();
            }
            else if (!Ribbon.IsRuleSelected(
              Globals.ThisAddIn.Application.ActiveDocument))
            {
             Globals.ThisAddIn.VEApp.SelectedVEDocument.AddRuleSet();
            }
            else
            {
                System.Windows.MessageBox.Show(
```

```
                    this.GetSupertip(control),
                       this.GetLabel(control),
                       System.Windows.MessageBoxButton.OK,
                       System.Windows.MessageBoxImage.Information);
                }
            }
            else
            {
                System.Windows.MessageBox.Show(this.GetSupertip(control),
                    this.GetLabel(control),
                    System.Windows.MessageBoxButton.OK,
                    System.Windows.MessageBoxImage.Information) ;
            }
            break;
        }
```

For example, the AddRule() method ensures that a unique new name is proposed, and then passed through to the AddRule() method of the VERuleSet object.

```
public void AddRule()
{
    try
    {
        if (this.SelectedVERuleSet != null)
        {
            //Add a rule
            string newName =
                this.SelectedVERuleSet.VERules.SuggestRuleName();
            VERule ver =
                this.selectedVERuleSet.VERules.AddRule(newName);
            this.selectedVERuleSet.SelectedVERule = ver;
            this.selectedVERule =
                this.selectedVERuleSet.SelectedVERule;
        }
    }
    catch (Exception)
    {
        throw;
    }
}
```

```
public VERule AddRule(string NameU)
{
    Visio.ValidationRule rul = rules.Add(NameU);
    this.Add(new VERule(rul, veRuleSet));
    OnPropertyChanged(new PropertyChangedEventArgs("GetCount"));
    this.VERuleSet.RaisePropertyChanged("DisplayName");
    return this.Single(ver => ver.NameU == NameU);
}
```

Notice that this method creates a new Visio.ValidationRule first, then adds this to the VERules ObservableCollection. It then calls the OnPropertyChanged() method to ensure that the UI display of the VERules is updated.

The AddRuleSet() method is similar to the AddRule() method.

The Add Issue button

The **Add Issue** button action will simply add an issue to a rule.

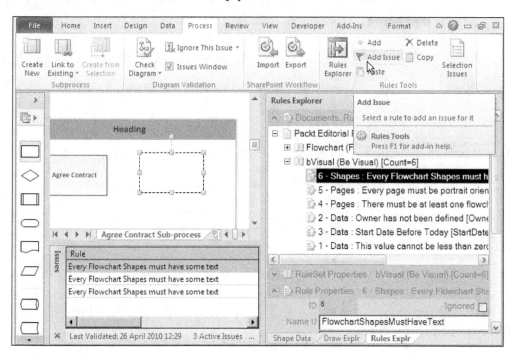

The AddRuleIssue() method in the VEDocument class establishes the TargetType of the rule, then adds the issue to the relevant item or items.

```csharp
public void AddRuleIssue()
{
    try
    {
        if (this.SelectedVERule != null)
        {
            //Add an issue for the rule
            if (this.selectedVERule.TargetType ==
              Visio.VisRuleTargets.visRuleTargetDocument)
            {
                Visio.ValidationIssue iss=
                    this.selectedVERule.AddIssue();
                this.VEIssues.AddIssue(iss);
            }
            else if (this.selectedVERule.TargetType ==
              Visio.VisRuleTargets.visRuleTargetDocument)
            {
                Visio.ValidationIssue iss =
                    this.selectedVERule.AddIssue(
                    document.Application.ActivePage);
                this.VEIssues.AddIssue(iss);
            }
            else
            {
                foreach (Visio.Shape shp in
                  document.Application.ActiveWindow.Selection)
                {
                    Visio.ValidationIssue iss =
                        this.selectedVERule.AddIssue(
                        document.Application.ActivePage,shp);
                    this.VEIssues.AddIssue(iss);
                }
            }
        }
    }
    catch (Exception)
    {
        throw;
    }
}
```

The Paste button

The **Paste** button action will paste a previously copied rule set or rule to the selected document or rule set respectively.

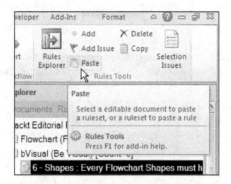

The `VEApplication.PasteRule()` method establishes that a `VERuleSet` item is selected, and that there is a temporary `VERule` object copied. It then calls the `VERules.PasteRule()` method.

```
public void PasteRule()
{
    if (this.SelectedVERuleSet != null && tempRule != null)
    {
        VERule newVer =
            this.SelectedVERuleSet.VERules.PasteRule(tempRule);
        this.SelectedVEDocument.SelectedVERule = newVer;
    }
}
```

The `VERules.PasteRule()` method checks if a new unique name is required before creating a new rule, and cloning the properties:

```
public VERule PasteRule(VERule sourceRule)
{
    VERule newVer = null;
    if (this.Count(ver => ver.NameU == sourceRule.NameU) == 0)
    {
        //Use same name
        newVer = this.AddRule(sourceRule.NameU);
    }
    else
    {
        //Get a new name
        string newName = this.SuggestRuleName();
```

```
        newVer = this.AddRule(newName);
    }
    //Set all of the Visio Validation properties
    newVer.Ignored = sourceRule.Ignored;
    newVer.Category = sourceRule.Category;
    newVer.Description = sourceRule.Description;
    newVer.FilterExpression = sourceRule.FilterExpression;
    newVer.TestExpression = sourceRule.TestExpression;
    newVer.TargetType = sourceRule.TargetType;
    OnPropertyChanged(new PropertyChangedEventArgs("GetCount"));
    this.VERuleSet.RaisePropertyChanged("DisplayName");
    return newVer;
}
```

The Copy button

The **Copy** action will take a copy of the selected rule set or rule, so that it is available for the **Paste** action.

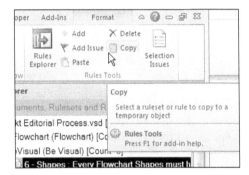

The `VEApplication.CopyRule()` method simply copies the `SelectedVERule` object to a temporary object, and then ensures that the `HasTempRule` property is notified.

```
public void CopyRule()
{
    tempRule = this.SelectedVERule;
    OnPropertyChanged("HasTempRule");
}
```

There is a similar `VEApplication.CopyRuleSet()` method, which is called if the user has a `VERuleSet` object selected in the **Validation Explorer** tree view, rather than a `VERule` object.

The Delete button

The **Delete** action enables the user to delete the selected rule set or rule.

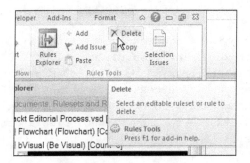

The `VERules.DeleteRule()` method ensures that the `Visio.ValidationRules` collection and the `VERules ObservableCollection` are kept synchronized.

```
public void DeleteRule(VERule ver)
{
    Visio.ValidationRule rul = this.rules[ver.NameU];
    this.Remove(ver);
    rul.Delete();
    OnPropertyChanged(new PropertyChangedEventArgs("GetCount"));
    this.VERuleSet.RaisePropertyChanged("DisplayName");
}
```

There is a similar `VERuleSets.DeleteRuleSet()` method, which is called if the user has a `VERuleSet` object selected in the **Validation Explorer** tree view, rather than a `VERule` object.

Displaying the rule for a selected issue

The built-in **Issues** window, which is opened from the **Diagram Validation** group on the **Process** tab, provides an existing method for a user to select an issue. Therefore we can synchronize the selected rule in the **Rules Explorer** whenever an issue is selected. This enables the rules developer to analyze the expressions used.

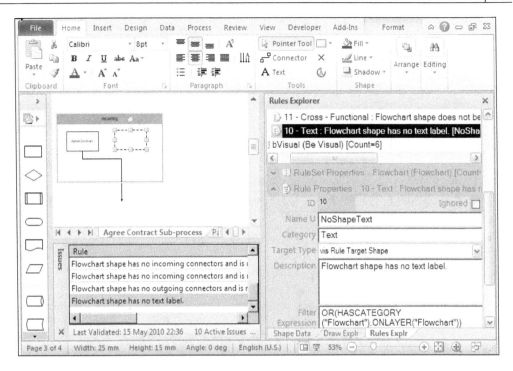

Actually, the **Issues** window does not cause any events at all, but it does select the target shape or page whenever an issue is selected in the window.

Thus, we can use the `Application.Window_SelectionChanged()` event to test if the **Issues** window is open. If it is, then the selected issue ID is sent into the `veApplication.SetSelectedIssue()` method.

```
private void Window_SelectionChanged(Visio.Window Window)
{
    //Check the selected Issue
    Visio.Window winIssues = Window.Windows.get_ItemFromID(
      (short)Visio.VisWinTypes.visWinIDValidationIssues);
    if (winIssues.Visible == false)
    {
        selectedIssueID = -1;
        veApplication.SetSelectedIssue(Window.Document.ID, null);
    }
    else
    {
        if (winIssues.SelectedValidationIssue != null)
        {
            selectedIssueID = winIssues.SelectedValidationIssue.ID;
            veApplication.SetSelectedIssue(Window.Document.ID,
```

```
                     selectedIssueID);
        }
        else
        {
            selectedIssueID = -1;
            veApplication.SetSelectedIssue(Window.Document.ID, null);
        }
    }
}
```

The `VEApplication.SetSelectedIssue()` method then gets the correct `VEDocument` object, and passes the `issue` ID through to it via the `selectedVEDocument.SetSelectedIssue(issue)` method.

```
public void SetSelectedIssue(int? docid, int? issue)
{
    if (docid.HasValue && this.VEDocuments.Count() > 0)
    {
        selectedVEDocument = this.VEDocuments.Single(doc => doc.ID ==
        docid);
        selectedVEDocument.SetSelectedIssue(issue);
    }
    else
    {
        selectedVEDocument = null;
    }
}
```

Finally, the `VEDocument` object sets the `SelectedVEIssue` property by selecting it from the `VEIssues` collection. This sets the `IsSelected` property of all `VERuleSet` and `VERule` objects before setting the `IsSelected` property of `VERuleSet` and `VERule` of the selected issue to `true`.

```
public void SetSelectedIssue(int? iss)
{
    if (iss.HasValue)
    {
        this.SelectedVEIssue = this.VEIssues.Single(
          issu => issu.ID == iss);
        selectedVEIssue.IsSelected = true;
        var results = from rls in this.VERuleSets select rls;
        foreach (VERuleSet rls in results)
        {
            rls.IsSelected = false;
            rls.UnSelect();
        }
```

```
        this.SelectedVERuleSet = this.VERuleSets.Single(
          rs => rs.ID == selectedVEIssue.Rule.RuleSet.ID);
        selectedVERuleSet.IsSelected = true;
        this.SelectedVERule = selectedVERuleSet.VERules.Single(
          rl => rl.ID == selectedVEIssue.Rule.ID);
        selectedVERule.IsSelected = true;
    }
    else
    {
        this.SelectedVEIssue = null;
        this.SelectedVERuleSet = null;
        this.SelectedVERule = null;
    }
}
```

Now, because the `IsSelected` property of the tree view items are bound to the `IsSelected` property of the underlying objects, the UI instantly reacts and displays the details of the rule for the selected issue in the **Issues** window.

For example, the `UserControlExplorer.xaml` file contains the `HierarchicalDataTemplate` for the rule. This definition does not contain any binding for the `TreeViewItem` because it merely describes the UI elements for the item. In order to set the binding for the item, and to vary the colors when it is selected, you can define a `Style` with the `TargetType="{x:Type TreeViewItem}"` attribute. This style will automatically be applied to each `TreeViewItem` as follows:

```xml
<Style TargetType="{x:Type TreeViewItem}">
    <Setter Property="Background" Value="Transparent" />
    <Setter Property="Foreground" Value="Black" />
    <Setter Property="IsExpanded" Value="{Binding Path=IsExpanded}" />
    <Setter Property="IsSelected" Value="{Binding Path=IsSelected}" />
    <Style.Triggers>
        <DataTrigger Binding="{Binding Path=IsSelected}"
          Value="True">
            <Setter Property="Background" Value="Black" />
            <Setter Property="Foreground" Value="White" />
        </DataTrigger>
    </Style.Triggers>
</Style>

<HierarchicalDataTemplate x:Key="RuleTemplate"
                          DataType="{x:Type localVM:VERule}"  >
    <StackPanel Orientation="Horizontal"
              ToolTip="{StaticResource ResourceKey=RuleToolTip}">
        <Image Source="..\Images\IssueTracking_32x32.png"
              Style="{StaticResource ResourceKey=ImageStyle}" />
```

```
<TextBlock Text="{Binding Path=DisplayName}"
           Style="{StaticResource ResourceKey=TreeItemStyle}" />
    </StackPanel>
</HierarchicalDataTemplate>
```

Displaying the issues for the current selection

The **Selection Issues** button opens a dialog that contains just the issues for the selected page or shapes. If there are multiple issues on the page, or on a shape, then they are grouped together for clarity.

I have already expressed a preference to use WPF where possible. However, the VSTO template, which is a Windows Forms project, hides the WPF window item type from selection if you try to add one. You are only offered the **User Control (WPF)** to add in the WPF category of installed templates. Fortunately, you can select this option and then make some simple changes to the code to turn a **User Control (WPF)** into a **Window (WPF)**. In this case, I added a new **UserControl (WPF)** named WindowIssues. I then edited the XAML of the WindowIssues.xaml file.

From:

```
<UserControl x:Class="ValidationExplorer.UI.WindowIssues"
...etc
</UserControl>
```

To:

```
<Window x:Class="ValidationExplorer.UI.WindowIssues"
...etc
</Window>
```

Similarly, I edited the WindowIssues.xaml.cs and changed the following line:

From:

```
public partial class WindowIssues : UserControl
```

To:

```
public partial class WindowIssues : Window
```

The WindowIssues class is now a true WPF window that can be edited to display the issues for the selection.

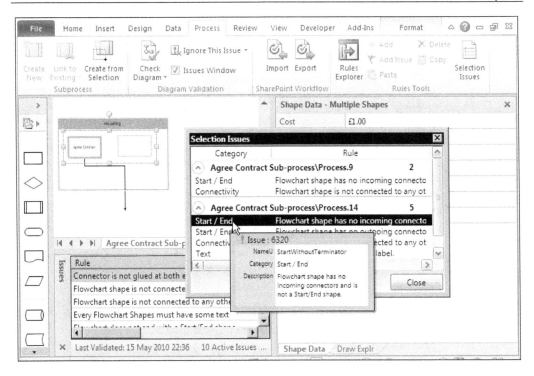

The `ThisAddin` class has a method to open the selected issues dialog.

```
public void OnActionOpenSelectionIssues()
{
    ViewModel.VEDocument document = this.documents[Globals.ThisAddIn.
Application.ActiveDocument.ID];
    if (document != null)
    {
        // this is our document so call open window
        document.OpenSelectionIssues();
    }
}
```

The `OpenSelectionIssues()` method is quite simple, because the list view in the `WindowIssues.xaml` file is based on a filtered view of the current document `VEIssues` observable collection.

```
public void OpenSelectionIssues()
{
    Globals.ThisAddIn.VEApp.SelectedVEDocument = this;
    UI.WindowIssues frm = new UI.WindowIssues();
    frm.ShowDialog();
}
```

The `WindowIssues.xaml` file defines the list view, complete with its grouping.

First, you need to include an extra namespace:

```
xmlns:dat="clr-namespace:System.Windows.Data;
  assembly=PresentationFramework"
```

Next, you can use this namespaces to define the `CollectionViewSource` grouping, as follows:

```
<CollectionViewSource Source="{Binding Path=VEIssues}"
x:Key="listingDataView"
        Filter="CollectionViewSource_Filter">
    <CollectionViewSource.GroupDescriptions>
        <dat:PropertyGroupDescription PropertyName="TargetName" />
    </CollectionViewSource.GroupDescriptions>
</CollectionViewSource>
```

You can then reference this collection view source in the `ListView`.

```
<ListView Name="ListViewMain"
        SelectionChanged="ListViewMain_SelectionChanged"
        ItemsSource="{Binding Source={StaticResource
          ResourceKey=listingDataView}}">
```

Next, you can define the `ListView.GroupStyle` binding to the Name of the group:

```
<ListView.GroupStyle>
    <GroupStyle>
        <GroupStyle.ContainerStyle>
            <Style TargetType="{x:Type GroupItem}">
                <Setter Property="Margin" Value="0,0,0,5"/>
                <Setter Property="Template">
                    <Setter.Value>
                        <ControlTemplate TargetType="{x:Type
                          GroupItem}">
                            <Expander IsExpanded="True"
                              BorderBrush="#FFA4B97F"
                              BorderThickness="0,0,0,1">
                                <Expander.Header>
                                    <DockPanel>
                                        <TextBlock FontWeight="Bold"
                                          Text="{Binding Path=Name}"
                                          Margin="5,0,0,0"
                                          Width="300"/>
                                        <TextBlock FontWeight="Bold"
                                          Text="{Binding
                                          Path=ItemCount}"/>
```

```
                </DockPanel>
              </Expander.Header>
              <Expander.Content>
                  <ItemsPresenter />
              </Expander.Content>
            </Expander>
          </ControlTemplate>
        </Setter.Value>
      </Setter>
    </Style>
  </GroupStyle.ContainerStyle>
</GroupStyle>
</ListView.GroupStyle>
```

Lastly, the `ListView.View` can be defined binding to the properties of the `VEIssue` objects:

```
<ListView.View>
    <GridView>
        <GridViewColumn Width="120" Header="Category"
          DisplayMemberBinding="{Binding Path=Rule.Category}"/>
        <GridViewColumn Width="240" Header="Rule"
          DisplayMemberBinding="{Binding Path=Rule.Description}"/>
        <GridViewColumn Width="120" Header="NameU"
          DisplayMemberBinding="{Binding Path=Rule.NameU}"/>
        <GridViewColumn Width="60" Header="IsIgnored"
           DisplayMemberBinding="{Binding Path=IsIgnored}"/>
        <GridViewColumn Width="120" Header="RuleSet Name"
          DisplayMemberBinding="{Binding Path=Rule.RuleSet.Name}"/>
        <GridViewColumn Width="240" Header="RuleSet Description"
          DisplayMemberBinding="{Binding
          Path=Rule.RuleSet.Description}"/>
    </GridView>
</ListView.View>
```

The constructor in the code sets the `DataContext` for `UserControlIssues`:

```
public WindowIssues()
{
    InitializeComponent();
    if (Globals.ThisAddIn.VEApp.SelectedVEDocument != null)
    {
        this.DataContext =
            Globals.ThisAddIn.VEApp.SelectedVEDocument;
    }
}
```

The `CollectionViewSource_Filter()` method is called in the XAML definition of the `CollectionViewSource` and is defined as follows:

```
private void CollectionViewSource_Filter(object sender,
  FilterEventArgs e)
{
    ViewModel.VEIssue issue = e.Item as ViewModel.VEIssue;
    bool ignore = (issue.IsIgnored == true
        && Globals.ThisAddIn.Application.ActiveDocument.Validation.
        ShowIgnoredIssues == false);
    if (ignore == true) {e.Accepted = false; return; }

    if (Globals.ThisAddIn.Application.ActiveWindow.Selection.Count
    == 0)
    {
        //Check for the active page
        if (issue.TargetPage ==
          Globals.ThisAddIn.Application.ActivePage
              && issue.TargetShape == null)
            e.Accepted = true;
        else e.Accepted = false;
    }
    else
    {
        //Check for the Target Shape in the active selection
        foreach (Visio.Shape shp in
          Globals.ThisAddIn.Application.ActiveWindow.Selection)
        {
            if (issue.TargetPage ==
              Globals.ThisAddIn.Application.ActivePage
                  && issue.TargetShape != null)
            {
                if (shp == issue.TargetShape)
                {
                    e.Accepted = true;
                    break;
                }
                else { e.Accepted = false; }
            }
            else e.Accepted = false;
        }
    }
}
```

Summary

In this chapter we started to develop a Visio 2010 Add-In that enables the rules developer to analyze what rules have been transgressed to cause any particular issue. We have provided an interface that allows the rules developer to add, copy, paste, modify, and delete rule sets and rules.

In the next chapter, we are going to extend the add-in to provide an export of rules to XML, and to a report so that the rules can be reviewed. We will provide an import of rule sets from the XML files that we created. Finally, we will also create annotations for issues in Visio so that the diagrams can be viewed with corresponding issues to assist the rules developer in analyzing the reason for failing validation.

6
Reviewing Validation Rules and Issues

In the last chapter, we created a tool to allow us to review and edit rules in Microsoft Visio 2010 Premium. In this chapter, we will extend this tool to provide an import/ export routine of rules to an XML file or to an HTML report, and enables us to add issues as annotations in Visio diagrams. These features will allow rules to be stored, restored, printed out, and pondered over, along with the issues that they may create in a diagram. This should provide confidence that the data diagrams have been created with a rigor that can be relied upon.

This chapter will cover:

- Further extensions to the Fluent UI ribbon
- Annotating the diagram with issues
- Exporting rule sets to XML
- Importing rule sets from XML
- Creating rule set reports

Extensions to our ribbon

Our **Rules Tools** group in the **Process** tab of the Visio ribbon needs to be extended to include our new features. The features can be viewed in the following screenshot:

There are four new buttons required. They are:

- **Annotate**
- **Report**
- **Export**
- **Import**

These are added to `Ribbon.xml` and the relevant callbacks are added to the `Ribbon` class.

The **Annotate** button is enabled for all diagrams, but the other buttons are only enabled when the **Rules Explorer** window is open, and I have arranged them on the dropdown menu of a split button.

The `OnAction` event of the **Annotate** button checks whether the active page type is a `visTypeForeground`. This is because a user may inadvertently be on a reviewer (`visTypeMarkup`) or background (`visTypeBackground`) page when the button is clicked. This is explained further in the next section.

```
case "buttonAnnotate":
    Globals.ThisAddIn.OnActionAnnotateIssues();
    break;
```

The `ThisAddin` class has the following method:

```
public void OnActionAnnotateIssues()
{
    ViewModel.VEDocument document =
      this.documents[Globals.ThisAddIn.Application.ActiveDocument.ID];
    if (document != null)
    {
        // this is our document so call open window
        document.OpenAnnotateIssues();
    }
}
```

The `VEDocument` class has the `OpenAnnotateIssues()` method that checks the page type, and whether the user is in markup mode or not (this is done by checking if the value of a specific cell in the document's ShapeSheet):

```
public void OpenAnnotateIssues()
{
    Globals.ThisAddIn.VEApp.SelectedVEDocument = this;
    //Toggle the annotation
    if (Globals.ThisAddIn.VEApp.VisioApplication.ActivePage.Type ==
      Visio.VisPageTypes.visTypeForeground)
```

```
        if (this.document.DocumentSheet.get_CellsSRC(
          (short)Visio.VisSectionIndices.visSectionObject,
          (short)Visio.VisRowIndices.visRowDoc,
          (short)Visio.VisCellIndices.visDocViewMarkup).ResultIU ==0)
        { this.DisplayIssueMarkup(); }
        else
        { this.HideIssueMarkup(); }
    else
        this.HideIssueMarkup();
}
```

Both the **Export RuleSets** and **RuleSets Report** button will output a single rule set if a rule or rule set item is selected in the **Rules Explorer** window, or all of the rule sets if a document item is selected. The export method is as follows:

```
Globals.ThisAddIn.VEApp.SelectedVEDocument.ExportDocument(true, true);
```

And the report method is called as follows:

```
Globals.ThisAddIn.VEApp.SelectedVEDocument.ReportDocument(true,
false);
```

The two arguments passed through are used to decide whether to include rule sets and issues in the action. Actually, whilst I have provided exporting rule sets and issues to XML, I have not included a report for issues currently. Therefore, the second argument for `ReportDocument` is `false`. Perhaps, you would like to create a XSL report for issues.

The action for the **Import RuleSets** button simply checks that a document has been selected in the **Rules Explorer** before asking for a confirmation of the rule sets in the selected XML document.

```
if (Globals.ThisAddIn.VEApp.SelectedVEDocument != null)
{
    if (System.Windows.MessageBox.Show("Do you want to import the
      rule sets to " +
    Globals.ThisAddIn.VEApp.SelectedVEDocument.DisplayName + "?",
        this.GetLabel(control),
        System.Windows.MessageBoxButton.YesNo,
        System.Windows.MessageBoxImage.Question,
        System.Windows.MessageBoxResult.Yes) ==
          System.Windows.MessageBoxResult.Yes)
    {
        Globals.ThisAddIn.VEApp.SelectedVEDocument.ImportRuleSets();
    }
}
```

Annotating Visio diagrams with issues

One useful feature of Visio is the ability to add reviewers' notes and scribbles via the **Review** tab. You can add comments, which are automatically numbered against the current user, but they are not associated with any particular shape, except by juxtaposition. This means that a reviewer's comment does not move if you move the shape that it relates.

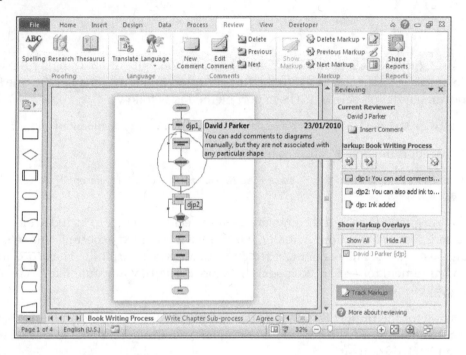

The comments are assigned to the current user, which you can set using the **File | Options** dialog.

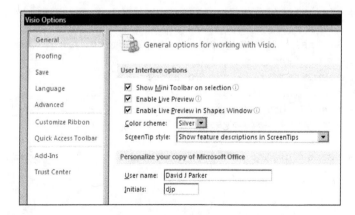

In fact, these comments are not added to the current page unless you switch on **Track Markup**, and they are not even normal shapes. They are actually stored as annotation rows in the ShapeSheet of the page and are not printable. When you switch on **Track Markup**, a new special page is created as an overlay over the existing page. This new page is of type Visio.VisPageTypes.visTypeMarkup, and is named after the foreground page that it is associated with, but with a suffix of the user's initials. The idea is that a drawing can be passed from user to user, with each adding their own distinct markup page, without affecting the original drawing.

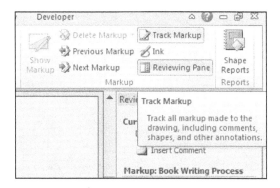

When you add a comment, it gets added as a row in the **Annotation** section of the ShapeSheet of the page.

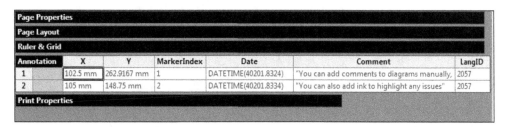

You can see that each comment has an **X** and **Y** value for its location in the page, an index, and a datetime stamp.

Both the **Track Markup** and **Show Markup** buttons automatically reveal the **Reviewing** pane to the right of the diagram. The visibility of this pane can be toggled with the **Reviewing Pane** button. With **Track Markup** off but with **Show Markup** on, the user can see the tabs of all the associated markup pages.

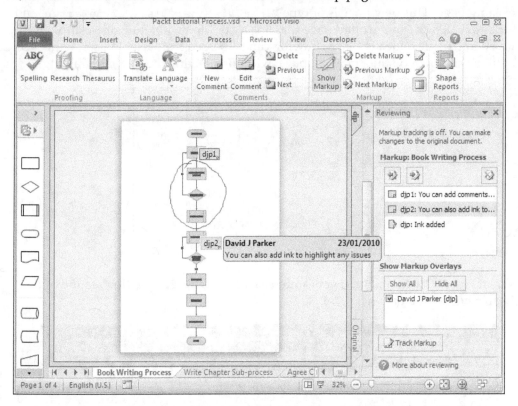

You can double-click on a comment in the diagram, or in the **Reviewing** pane to display the details of the comment.

So I decided to use this **Review** feature to add current issues as comments for the page and each affected shape. However, I did not want these notes to be confused with any notes that the current user may wish to create, so I decided to create a dummy user, Validation Explorer, with the initials vex, in order to keep them separate. Of course, I do not expect anyone to manually add this dummy user; it will be added automatically. The only trace that it exists will be an entry in the **Reviewer** section of the ShapeSheet of the document, because this is where Visio automatically creates an entry when **Track Markup** is switched on.

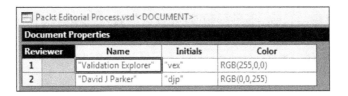

Saving the current user settings

There are two application **Settings** to provide the strings for the dummy user.

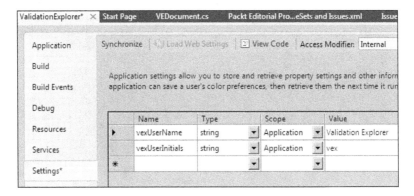

I then added two private strings to store the current user's settings.

```
private string theUserName = "";
private string theUserInitials = "";
```

These variables are set during the constructor of the `VEDocument` class:

```
this.theUserName = veApplication.VisioApplication.Settings.UserName;
this.theUserInitials =
  veApplication.VisioApplication.Settings.UserInitials;
```

They will be required in order to set the user details back again.

Displaying the issue markup page

The **Annotate** button adds the issues to the Reviewer Comments automatically for the page and each shape that has issues.

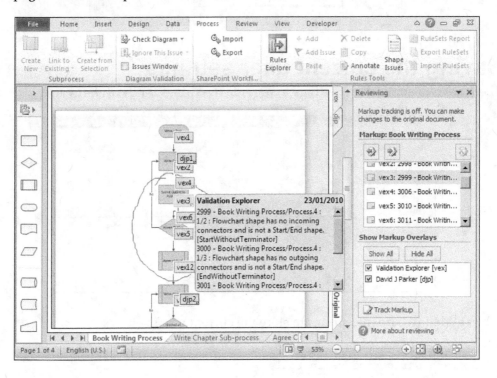

After checking that the active page is not already a markup page, this method collects all of the issues that are not ignored in the current page, and groups them by the page or shape. See the `var pagIssues = from issu in this.VEIssues ...` statement below to see how cool `Linq` is. It then transfers these objects into a `Dictionary` because experimentation found that the `pagIssues` collection is emptied as soon as the active page is changed. This is because I have elsewhere setup a `ViewCollection` on the `VEIssues` collection that automatically filters by the active page.

The Visio application settings are then changed to the dummy user before **Track Markup** and **View Markup** are switched on. This automatically changes the active page to the markup page.

The comments are then added to the markup page, and finally, **Track Markup** is switched off, but **View Markup** is left on so that the user can see the comments.

```
public void DisplayIssueMarkup()
{
```

```
try
{
  //Check the page type
  Visio.Page pag =
    (Visio.Page)veApplication.VisioApplication.ActiveWindow.Page;
  if (pag.Type == Visio.VisPageTypes.visTypeMarkup) return;

  //Group the issues for this page by target
  var pagIssues = from issu in this.VEIssues
     where issu.IsIgnored == false && issu.TargetPageID == pag.ID
     group issu by issu.Target into g
     select new { Target = g.Key, Issues = g };

  //Transfer into a dictionary otherwise it will be empty when the
  page changes
  Dictionary<object, List<VEIssue>> dicIssues = new
    Dictionary<object, List<VEIssue>>();
    foreach (var v in pagIssues)
    {
        List<VEIssue> lst = new List<VEIssue>();
        foreach (var i in v.Issues)
        {
            lst.Add(i);
        }
        dicIssues.Add(v.Target, lst);
    }
  //Set the dummy user settings
  veApplication.VisioApplication.Settings.UserName =
    Properties.Settings.Default.vexUserName;
  veApplication.VisioApplication.Settings.UserInitials =
    Properties.Settings.Default.vexUserInitials;
  //Turn on Track Markup
  //this will use the User settings to either create a new
  markup page or go to a previously created one
  this.document.DocumentSheet.get_CellsSRC(
    (short)Visio.VisSectionIndices.visSectionObject,
    (short)Visio.VisRowIndices.visRowDoc,
    (short)Visio.VisCellIndices.visDocAddMarkup).FormulaU =
    true.ToString();
  //Turn on View Markup
  this.document.DocumentSheet.get_CellsSRC(
    (short)Visio.VisSectionIndices.visSectionObject,
    (short)Visio.VisRowIndices.visRowDoc,
    (short)Visio.VisCellIndices.visDocViewMarkup).FormulaU =
    true.ToString();

  //Get the markup page
```

```
    pag =
      (Visio.Page)veApplication.VisioApplication.ActiveWindow.Page;
      if (pag.Type == Visio.VisPageTypes.visTypeMarkup)
      {
          int rvwrID = pag.ReviewerID;
          //Clear any existing annotations
          if (pag.PageSheet.get_SectionExists(
            (short)Visio.VisSectionIndices.visSectionAnnotation,
            (short)Visio.VisExistsFlags.visExistsAnywhere) != 0)
          {
            pag.PageSheet.DeleteSection(
              (short)Visio.VisSectionIndices.visSectionAnnotation);
          }
          //Add notes to the markup page
          foreach (var k in dicIssues.Keys)
          {
              Visio.Shape shp = null;
              string note = @"";
              List<VEIssue> lst = (List<VEIssue>)dicIssues[k];
              foreach (VEIssue i in lst)
              {
                  note += i.DisplayName + "\n";
              }
              if (k is Visio.Page)
              { addIssueNote(pag, null, rvwrID, note); }
              else if (k is Visio.Shape)
              { addIssueNote(pag, (Visio.Shape)k, rvwrID, note); }
          }
          //Turn off track markup
          this.document.DocumentSheet.get_CellsSRC(
            (short)Visio.VisSectionIndices.visSectionObject,
            (short)Visio.VisRowIndices.visRowDoc,
            (short)Visio.VisCellIndices.visDocAddMarkup).FormulaU =
            false.ToString();

      }
}
catch (Exception)
{
    throw;
}
//Set the Settings back to the current user
veApplication.VisioApplication.Settings.UserName =
  this.theUserName;
```

```
    veApplication.VisioApplication.Settings.UserInitials =
      this.theUserInitials;
}
```

Add in the issue comments

The issue comments are added to the markup page as follows:

```
private void addIssueNote(Visio.Page pag, Visio.Shape shp,
  int rvwrID, string msg)
{
    //Get the last row number in the Annotations section of the
ShapeSheet of the page
    int intAnnotationRow = pag.PageSheet.AddRow(
      (short)Visio.VisSectionIndices.visSectionAnnotation,
      (short)Visio.VisRowIndices.visRowLast, 0);
    if (shp != null)
    {
        //Add the comment
        pag.PageSheet.get_CellsSRC(
          (short)Visio.VisSectionIndices.visSectionAnnotation,
          (short)intAnnotationRow,
          (short)Visio.VisCellIndices.visAnnotationX).FormulaU =
          "=GUARD(Pages[" + shp.ContainingPage.Name + "]!" +
          shp.NameID + "!PinX)";
        pag.PageSheet.get_CellsSRC(
          (short)Visio.VisSectionIndices.visSectionAnnotation,
          (short)intAnnotationRow,
          (short)Visio.VisCellIndices.visAnnotationY).FormulaU =
          "=GUARD(Pages[" + shp.ContainingPage.Name + "]!" +
          shp.NameID + "!PinY)";
    }
    else
    {
        //Add the comment at the centre of the page, but allow it to
        be re-positioned, if required
        pag.PageSheet.get_CellsSRC(
          (short)Visio.VisSectionIndices.visSectionAnnotation,
          (short)intAnnotationRow,
          (short)Visio.VisCellIndices.visAnnotationX).FormulaU =
          "=PageWidth*0.5";
        pag.PageSheet.get_CellsSRC(
          (short)Visio.VisSectionIndices.visSectionAnnotation,
          (short)intAnnotationRow,
          (short)Visio.VisCellIndices.visAnnotationY).FormulaU =
          "=PageHeight*0.5";
    }
    //Add the reviewer ID
    pag.PageSheet.get_CellsSRC(
      (short)Visio.VisSectionIndices.visSectionAnnotation,
```

```
      (short)intAnnotationRow,
      (short)Visio.VisCellIndices.visAnnotationReviewerID).FormulaU =
      rvwrID.ToString();
  //Add the index
  pag.PageSheet.get_CellsSRC(
      (short)Visio.VisSectionIndices.visSectionAnnotation,
      (short)intAnnotationRow,
     (short)Visio.VisCellIndices.visAnnotationMarkerIndex).FormulaU =
     (intAnnotationRow + 1).ToString();
  //Add timestamp
  pag.PageSheet.get_CellsSRC(
      (short)Visio.VisSectionIndices.visSectionAnnotation,
      (short)intAnnotationRow,
      (short)Visio.VisCellIndices.visAnnotationDate).FormulaU =
      "DATETIME(" + DateTime.Now.ToOADate() + ")";
  //Add the concatenated issues
  pag.PageSheet.get_CellsSRC(
      (short)Visio.VisSectionIndices.visSectionAnnotation,
      (short)intAnnotationRow,
      (short)Visio.VisCellIndices.visAnnotationComment).FormulaU =
      "\"" + msg + "\"";
}
```

Hiding the issue markup page

This is only called if the active page type is not a foreground page. It ensures that the active page is returned back to the foreground page by ensuring that **Track Markup** and **View Markup** are switched off. Finally, an attempt is made to hide the **Reviewing** pane by using the DoCmd() method on the Visio application object. This will only toggle the visibility though, but it is most probable that it is visible, so this will hide it most of the time.

```
public void HideIssueMarkup()
{
    try
    {
        //Ensure that the user Settings are correct
        veApplication.VisioApplication.Settings.UserName =
          this.theUserName;
        veApplication.VisioApplication.Settings.UserInitials =
          this.theUserInitials;
        //Turn off Add Markup
        this.document.DocumentSheet.get_CellsSRC(
            (short)Visio.VisSectionIndices.visSectionObject,
            (short)Visio.VisRowIndices.visRowDoc,
            (short)Visio.VisCellIndices.visDocAddMarkup).FormulaU =
            false.ToString();
        //Turn off View Markup
```

```
        this.document.DocumentSheet.get_CellsSRC(
            (short)Visio.VisSectionIndices.visSectionObject,
            (short)Visio.VisRowIndices.visRowDoc,
            (short)Visio.VisCellIndices.visDocViewMarkup).FormulaU =
            false.ToString();
        //Hide the Reviewing pane (probably)
        this.TheApplication.VisioApplication.DoCmd(
            (short)Visio.VisUICmds.visCmdTaskPaneReviewer);
    }
    catch (Exception)
    {
        throw;
    }
}
```

Exporting rule sets to XML

Even though there is an option to import a rule set from another Visio document, I know that some rules developers would like to export and import rule sets to XML. This allows rule sets to be stored, restored, and analyzed more easily.

I decided that the XML structure exported should mimic the Visio XML format, and thus use a part of the Visio XML schema. This means using the same namespaces, but it would mean that any XSL stylesheets developed for our export would also work for the standard Visio XML format (*.vdx and *.vtx files).

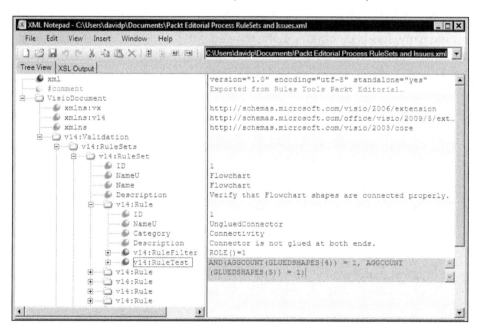

I decided to include the option to export the issues in a document too, because someone may have the need to use them in an external program. Having the issues available in XML format means that they could be displayed as a table, for example, so that they can be reviewed independently.

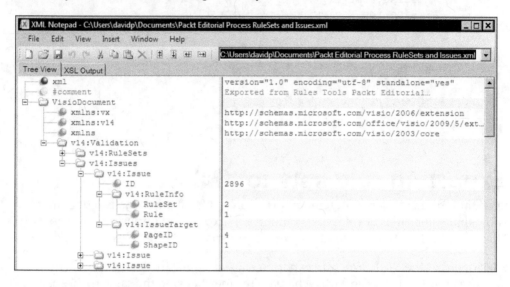

The `ExportDocument()` method first constructs a title for `SaveFile` dialog, depending upon the `include` options provided. The default name preferred for the XML file uses the drawing file name as a base.

Once a file name has been obtained, the `System.XMl.Linq.XDocument` object is created; saved and opened in the associated application.

```
public void ExportDocument(bool includeRulesets, bool includeIssues)
{
    try
    {
        //Set the title for the SaveFile dialog
        string title = "";
        if (includeRulesets) title += "RuleSets";
        if (includeRulesets && includeIssues) title += " and ";
        if (includeIssues) title += "Issues";
        string shortName = System.IO.Path.GetFileNameWithoutExtension(
            this.document.FullName);
        string fileName = System.IO.Path.Combine(this.document.Path,
            shortName + ".xml");
        Microsoft.Win32.SaveFileDialog dlg = new
            Microsoft.Win32.SaveFileDialog();
        dlg.Title = "Save " + title;
```

```
    dlg.InitialDirectory = System.Environment.GetFolderPath(
      System.Environment.SpecialFolder.MyDocuments);
    dlg.FileName = shortName + " " + title + ".xml";
    dlg.OverwritePrompt = true;
    dlg.DefaultExt = ".xml";
    dlg.Filter = "XML documents (.xml)|*.xml";
    if (dlg.ShowDialog() == true)
    {
        fileName = dlg.FileName;
    }
    else return;
    XDocument xDoc = getXDocument(includeRulesets,
      includeIssues);
    if (xDoc != null)
    {
        //Save the file
        xDoc.Save(fileName);
        //Open the file with the associated program
        System.Diagnostics.ProcessStartInfo startInfo =
          new System.Diagnostics.ProcessStartInfo(fileName);
        startInfo.WindowStyle =
          System.Diagnostics.ProcessWindowStyle.Normal;
        System.Diagnostics.Process.Start(startInfo);
    }
}
catch (Exception)
{
    throw;
}
}
```

Getting the XDocument object

The following method first creates the required XNamespace objects, then it creates a new XDocument object and retrieves the XElement objects for the VERules and/or VEIssues of the VEDocument.

```
private XDocument getXDocument(bool includeRulesets, bool
includeIssues)
{
    try
    {
        //v14:Validation
        //  v14:ValidationPoperties
        //      LastValidated
```

```
//        ShowIgnored
//    v14:RuleSets
//        v14:RuleSet
//           ID
//           NameU
//           Description
//           v14:Rule
//              ID
//              NameU
//              Category
//              Description
//              v14:RuleFilter
//              v14:RuleTest
//    v14:Issues
//        v14:Issue
//           ID
//           v14:IssueTarget
//              PageID
//              ShapeID
//           v14:RuleInfo
//              RuleSetID
//              RuleID
XNamespace xns =
   "http://schemas.microsoft.com/visio/2003/core";
XNamespace v14 =
"http://schemas.microsoft.com/office/visio/2009/5/extension";
XNamespace vx =
   "http://schemas.microsoft.com/visio/2006/extension";
XDocument xdoc = new XDocument(
   new XDeclaration("1.0", "utf-8", "yes"),
   new XComment("Exported from Rules Tools " +
   this.document.Name + " on " +
   System.DateTime.Now.ToUniversalTime().ToString()),
   new XElement(xns + "VisioDocument",
   new XAttribute(XNamespace.Xmlns + "vx", vx.NamespaceName),
   new XAttribute(XNamespace.Xmlns + "v14",
   v14.NamespaceName),
   new XElement(v14 + "Validation")));
XElement validNode = xdoc.Element(xns +
   "VisioDocument").Element(v14 + "Validation");
if (includeRulesets)
{
    if (this.SelectedVERuleSet == null)
    {
        validNode.Add(new XElement(v14 + "RuleSets",
```

```
                    from el in this.VERuleSets
                    select el.GetXElement(v14)
                    ));
              }
              else
              {
                    validNode.Add(new XElement(v14 + "RuleSets",
                    from el in this.VERuleSets
                    where (el.ID == this.selectedVERuleSet.ID)
                    select el.GetXElement(v14)
                    ));
              }
        }
        if (includeIssues)
        {
              validNode.Add(new XElement(v14 + "Issues",
              from el in this.VEIssues
              select el.GetXElement(v14)
              ));
        }
        return xdoc;
    }
    catch (Exception)
    {
    }
    return null;
}
```

Getting the VERuleSet XElement

The following method creates an XElement for the VERuleSet object, and then adds an XElement for each VERule in the VERules collection.

```
public XElement GetXElement(XNamespace v14)
{
    XElement retNode;
    try
    {
        retNode = new XElement(v14 + "RuleSet",
            new XAttribute("ID", this.ID),
            new XAttribute("NameU", this.NameU),
            new XAttribute("Name", this.Name),
            new XAttribute("Description", this.Description));
```

```
        retNode.Add(from ver in this.VERules select
          ver.GetXElement(v14));
    }
    catch (Exception)
    {
        throw;
    }
    return retNode;
}
```

Getting the VEIssue XElement

This method creates an XElement for the VEIssue object, and then adds an XElement
for the RuleInfo and IssueTarget.

```
public XElement GetXElement(XNamespace v14)
{
    XElement retNode;
    try
    {
        retNode = new XElement(v14 + "Issue",
          new XAttribute("ID", this.ID),
            new XElement(v14 + "RuleInfo",
            new XAttribute("RuleSet",this.Rule.RuleSet.ID),
            new XAttribute("Rule", this.Rule.ID)));
        if (this.Ignored)
        {
            retNode.Add(new XAttribute("Ignored", this.Ignored));
        }
        if (this.TargetPage != null || this.TargetShape != null)
        {
            XElement targetNode = new XElement(v14 + "IssueTarget");
            if (this.TargetPage != null)
                targetNode.Add(new XAttribute("PageID",
                  this.TargetPage.ID));
            if (this.TargetShape != null)
                targetNode.Add(new XAttribute("ShapeID",
                  this.TargetShape.ID));
            retNode.Add(targetNode);
        }
    }
    catch (Exception)
    {
        throw;
    }
    return retNode;
}
```

Importing rule sets from XML

This method first requests the user to select the XML file (it can be in the standard Visio XML file format too) that contains the rule or rule sets to import from. It then iterates through the rule set and rule elements to add them to the selected VEDocument.

If it encounters a rule set with the same name as an existing rule set in the selected VEDocument, then the user is prompted to overwrite or not.

Imported rule sets are immediately added to the **Rules Explorer** tree view.

```
public void ImportRuleSets()
{
    try
    {
        string title = "RuleSets";
        string shortName =
            System.IO.Path.GetFileNameWithoutExtension(
            this.document.FullName);
        string fileName = System.IO.Path.Combine(
            this.document.Path, shortName + ".xml");
        Microsoft.Win32.OpenFileDialog dlg = new
            Microsoft.Win32.OpenFileDialog();
        dlg.Title = "Import " + title;
        dlg.InitialDirectory = System.Environment.GetFolderPath(
            System.Environment.SpecialFolder.MyDocuments);
        dlg.DefaultExt = ".xml";
        dlg.Filter = "XML documents (.xml)|*.xml |Visio XML drawing
            (.vdx)|*.vdx|Visio XML template (.vtx)|*.vtx";
        if (dlg.ShowDialog() == true)
        {
            fileName = dlg.FileName;
        }
        else return;

        XDocument xdoc = XDocument.Load(fileName);
        XNamespace xns =
            "http://schemas.microsoft.com/visio/2003/core";
        XNamespace v14 =
        "http://schemas.microsoft.com/office/visio/2009/5/extension";
        XNamespace vx =
            "http://schemas.microsoft.com/visio/2006/extension";

        XElement docNode = xdoc.Element(xns + "VisioDocument");
```

```
    if (docNode == null) return;
    //Get the Validation element (abort if none found)
    XElement validNode = docNode.Element(v14 + "Validation");
    if (validNode == null) return;
    //Get the RuleSets element (abort if none found)
    XElement ruleSetsNode = validNode.Element(v14 + "RuleSets");
    if (ruleSetsNode == null) return;
    foreach (XElement ruleSetNode in ruleSetsNode.Elements(v14 +
      "RuleSet"))
    {
        //Get the NameU attribute
        string rsName = ruleSetNode.Attribute("NameU").Value;
        //Set the default response
        System.Windows.MessageBoxResult process =
          System.Windows.MessageBoxResult.Yes;
        //Check if the rule set exists already
        if (this.VERuleSets.Count(ver => ver.NameU == rsName) >0)
        {
            //Ask to replace an existing ruleset (or skip if
            declined)
            process = System.Windows.MessageBox.Show(
              "The rule set, " + rsName + ", exists
              already.\\nDo you wish to replace it?",
              "Import Ruleset",
              System.Windows.MessageBoxButton.YesNo,
              System.Windows.MessageBoxImage.Question,
              System.Windows.MessageBoxResult.Yes);
            if (process == System.Windows.MessageBoxResult.No)
break;
            this.VERuleSets[rsName].Delete();
        }
        else process = System.Windows.MessageBoxResult.Yes;
        //Add a new VERuleSet object to this VEDocument
        VERuleSet vrset = this.VERuleSets.AddRuleSet(rsName);
        //Set the properties of the VERuleSet from the attributes
        foreach (XAttribute xat in ruleSetNode.Attributes())
        {
            switch (xat.Name.LocalName)
            {
                case "Name":
                    vrset.Name = xat.Value;
                    break;
                case "Description":
                    vrset.Description = xat.Value;
                    break;
```

```
                case "RuleSetFlags":
                    vrset.RuleSetFlags =
                      (Visio.VisRuleSetFlags)Convert.ToInt32(
                      xat.Value);
                    break;
            }
        }
        //Set the remaining properties of the VERuleSet from the
        elements
        foreach (XElement xelm in ruleSetNode.Elements())
        {
            switch (xelm.Name.LocalName)
            {
                case "Rule":
                    string rName = xelm.Attribute("NameU").Value;
                    VERule vrle = vrset.VERules.AddRule(rName);
                    //Set the properties of the VERule from the
                    attributes
                    foreach (XAttribute xat in xelm.Attributes())
                    {
                        switch (xat.Name.LocalName)
                        {
                            case "Category":
                                vrle.Category = xat.Value;
                                break;
                            case "Description":
                                vrle.Description = xat.Value;
                                break;
                            case "TargetType":
                                vrle.TargetType =
                                (Visio.VisRuleTargets)Convert.ToInt32(
                                xat.Value);
                                break;
                        }
                    }
                    //Set the remaining properties of the VERule
                    from the elements
                    foreach (XElement xelmR in xelm.Elements())
                    {
                        switch (xelmR.Name.LocalName)
                        {
                            case "RuleFilter":
                                vrle.FilterExpression =
                                  xelmR.Value;
                                break;
```

```
                                 case "RuleTest":
                                     vrle.TestExpression =
                                         xelmR.Value;
                                     break;
                             }
                         }
                         break;
                 }
             }
         }
     }
     catch (Exception)
     {
         throw;
     }
 }
```

Creating rule set reports

It is a relatively simple operation to use `System.Xml.Xsl` and `System.Xml.XPath` to iterate through the elements in the `XDocument` created by the `getXDocument()` method. The result is an HTML page that can be displayed in any browser.

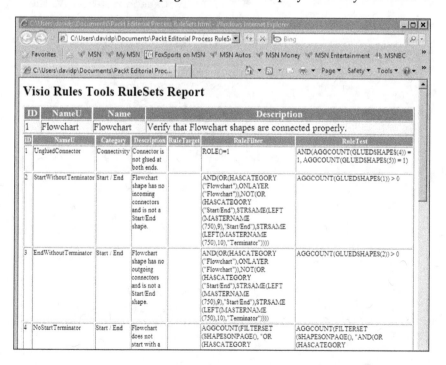

The ReportDocument() method prompts for the name of an HTML document to output to.

```csharp
public void ReportDocument(bool includeRulesets, bool includeIssues)
{
    try
    {
        string title = "";
        if (includeRulesets) title += "RuleSets";
        if (includeRulesets && includeIssues) title += " and ";
        if (includeIssues) title += "Issues";
        string shortName =
            System.IO.Path.GetFileNameWithoutExtension(
            this.document.FullName);
        string fileName = System.IO.Path.Combine(this.document.Path,
            shortName + ".html");
        Microsoft.Win32.SaveFileDialog dlg = new
            Microsoft.Win32.SaveFileDialog();
        dlg.Title = "Save " + title;
        dlg.InitialDirectory = System.Environment.GetFolderPath(
            System.Environment.SpecialFolder.MyDocuments);
        dlg.FileName = shortName + " " + title + ".html";
        dlg.OverwritePrompt = true;
        dlg.DefaultExt = ".html";
        dlg.Filter = "HTML documents (.html)|*.html";
        if (dlg.ShowDialog() == true)
        {
            fileName = dlg.FileName;
        }
        else return;
        XDocument xDoc = getXDocument(includeRulesets,
            includeIssues);
        if (xDoc == null)
        {
            return;
        }
        //Get the XSL Stylesheet
        string xslMarkup = getRuleSetXSL();
        // Load the style sheet.
        XslCompiledTransform xslt = new XslCompiledTransform();
        xslt.Load(System.Xml.XmlReader.Create(new
            StringReader(xslMarkup)));
        //Save the XDocument to a temporary file
        string tempFile = System.IO.Path.GetTempFileName();
        xDoc.Save(tempFile);
```

```
        // Execute the transform and output the results to html.
        xslt.Transform(tempFile, fileName);
        //Delete the temporary file
        System.IO.File.Delete(tempFile);

        //Open in web browser (associated program)
        System.Diagnostics.ProcessStartInfo startInfo = new
          System.Diagnostics.ProcessStartInfo(fileName);
        startInfo.WindowStyle =
          System.Diagnostics.ProcessWindowStyle.Normal;
        System.Diagnostics.Process.Start(startInfo);
    }
    catch (Exception)
    {
        throw;
    }
}
```

Getting the XSL stylesheet

The XSL template returned by this method can be saved as a file, say `RuleSets.xslt`, and can be used to transform the rule sets in any Visio document saved in XML format. The output will be a rule set report in HTML.

```
private string getRuleSetXSL()
{
    return @"<?xml version='1.0' encoding='UTF-8' ?>
      <xsl:stylesheet version='1.0'
        xmlns:xsl='http://www.w3.org/1999/XSL/Transform'
        xmlns:vx=
           'http://schemas.microsoft.com/visio/2006/extension'
        xmlns:v14=
           'http://schemas.microsoft.com/office/visio/2009/5/extension'
        xmlns='http://schemas.microsoft.com/visio/2003/core'>
<HTML>
  <BODY>
    <H1>Visio Rules Tools RuleSets Report</H1>
  </BODY>
</HTML>

<!--<xsl:template match='text()' />-->
<xsl:template match='/'>
  <xsl:apply-templates select='//*/*/*/v14:RuleSet' />
</xsl:template>

<xsl:template match='v14:RuleSet' >
  <HTML>
```

```
<BODY>
  <H1>Visio Rules Tools RuleSets Report</H1>
  <xsl:for-each select='.'>
    <TABLE width='100%'>
      <TR>
        <TABLE width='100%' frame='border'
          style='font-size:24px'>
          <TR style='background-color:teal;color:white;
            font-weight:bold'>
            <TH >ID</TH>
            <TH >NameU</TH>
            <TH >Name</TH>
            <TH >Description</TH>
          </TR>
          <TR style='background-color:azure'>
            <TD>
              <xsl:value-of select='@ID'/>
            </TD>
            <TD>
              <xsl:value-of select='@NameU'/>
            </TD>
            <TD>
              <xsl:value-of select='@Name'/>
            </TD>
            <TD >
              <xsl:value-of select='@Description'/>
            </TD>
          </TR>
        </TABLE>
      </TR>
      <TR>
        <TABLE width='100%' frame='border' >
          <TR style='font-weight:bold;
            background-color:gray;color:white;padding:4px'>
            <TH>ID</TH>
            <TH>NameU</TH>
            <TH>Category</TH>
            <TH>Description</TH>
            <TH>RuleTarget</TH>
            <TH>RuleFilter</TH>
            <TH>RuleTest</TH>
          </TR>
          <xsl:for-each select='v14:Rule'>
            <TR style='vertical-align:top'>
```

```
                    <TD >
                      <xsl:value-of select='@ID'/>
                    </TD>
                    <TD >
                      <xsl:value-of select='@NameU'/>
                    </TD>
                    <TD >
                      <xsl:value-of select='@Category'/>
                    </TD>
                    <TD >
                      <xsl:value-of select='@Description'/>
                    </TD>
                    <TD >
                      <xsl:value-of select='@RuleTarget'/>
                    </TD>
                    <TD >
                      <xsl:value-of select='v14:RuleFilter'/>
                    </TD>
                    <TD >
                      <xsl:value-of select='v14:RuleTest'/>
                    </TD>
                  </TR>
                </xsl:for-each>
              </TABLE>
            </TR>
          </TABLE>
        </xsl:for-each>
      </BODY>
    </HTML>
  </xsl:template>
</xsl:stylesheet>";
}
```

Save the main body of the `getRuleSetXSL()` into a `RuleSets.xslt` file, then use **XML Notepad** to open a Visio XML format document.

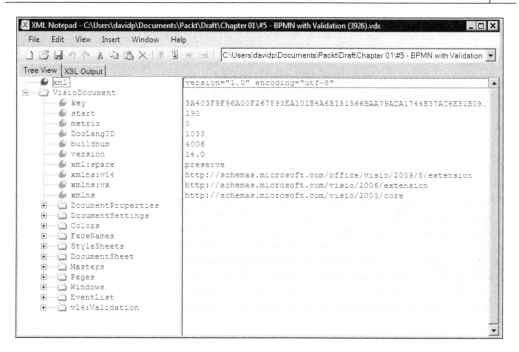

You can then enter the full path to the RuleSets.xslt file on the **XSL Output** tab in **XML Notepad**, and press **Transform**. The **Visio Rules Tools RuleSets Report** will then be displayed.

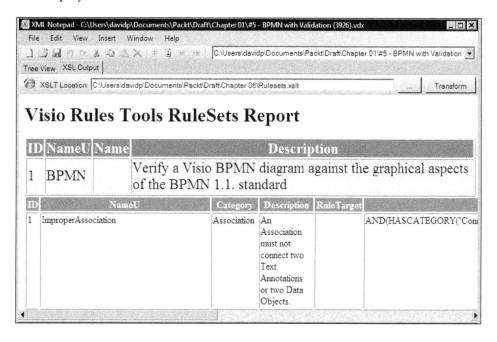

Alternatively add the following line as line 2 in any XML file that contains rule sets (edit the `href` path accordingly):

```
<?xml-stylesheet type="text/xsl" href="RuleSets.
xslt"?>
```

Open in your web browser to display the report!

Summary

In this chapter we extended the Rules Tools add-in to provide the capability to export and import rule sets to and from an XML file. We also transformed the rule set XML into an HTML report and we annotated pages with current issues. We now have a complete UI tool to create and test new rules.

In the next chapter, we are going to get deep into the new validation functions, and learn how to create test and filter expressions.

7
Creating Validation Rules

In the last chapter, we finished creating a tool to allow us to manipulate rules in Microsoft Visio 2010 Premium in the following ways:

- Review rules
- Edit rules
- Create rules
- Test rules
- Import rules
- Export rules

In this chapter, we will use this tool to create rules for structured diagramming. We will look at common ShapeSheet functions that will be useful for rules, and the new **Validation** functions.

We will also go through different scenarios for creating rules, especially with regard to **Filter** and **Test Expressions**.

Overview of the document validation process

The user can initiate the validation process by clicking the **Check Diagram** button on the **Process** tab. The process will clear any existing issues for any changed pages in the document before looping through any rule sets . A changed page, sometimes referred to as *dirty*, is one that has shapes on it that have been altered in some way since the last validation. After validation, the process will re-mark as ignored any issues that were previously marked as ignored.

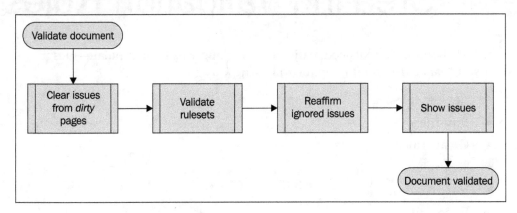

Any custom validation rules for a rule set should be executed in code whenever the relevant `RuleSetValidated` event is fired. Visio does not automatically clear all issues in the document when the user selects the **Process | Check Diagram** button. It only clears issues for pages that are **dirty**, that is those that have had shape changes since the last time it was validated.

 If you are writing code to validate your rule set, then you could just iterate through any existing issues to delete only those that are associated with your rule set because the `ValidationIssues.Clear()` method will remove all issues in the document.

After the rule sets are validated, Visio will check if the user has checked **Show Ignored Issues** option. If **Show Ignored Issues** is ticked, then issues for rules that have been marked as ignored will be displayed as grayed out in the **Issues** window.

- **Validating rule sets**: The validation process will loop through all of the rule sets in the document, and will continue to process the rule set if the **Enabled** property is `True`.

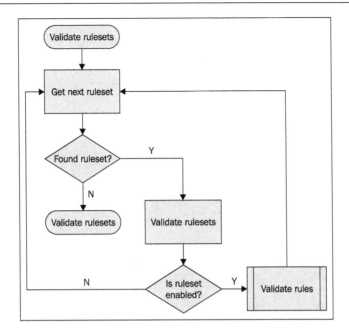

- **Validating rules**: If the rule set is enabled, then the process will loop through each of the rules in the rule set.

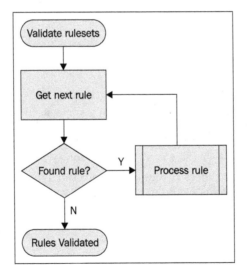

- **Processing a rule**: Rules are processed even if they are marked as ignored, though the ignored marker will be preserved. The validation process will retrieve the target object, which can be a document, page, or shape (the default).

Then, if the `FilterExpression` evaluates to `True`, the target will be passed through to the `TestExpression`. Note that Visio will not pass the target through if there is an error in the syntax of the `FilterExpression`.

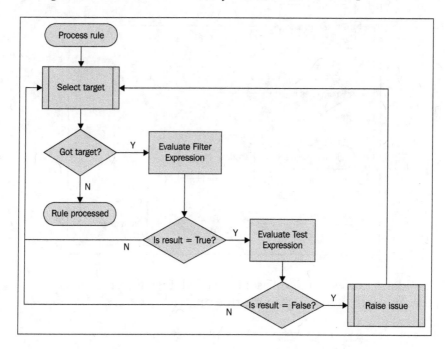

If the `TestExpression` evaluates to `False`, or there is a syntax error in the formula, then an issue is raised.

To check that the Filter Expression is syntactically correct, enter True in the Test Expression before validating, then enter False in the Filter Expression before validating again. If you do not get any issues on either pass then there is something wrong with your syntax.

Similarly, to check if your Test Expression is syntactically correct, you can alternately wrap your formula with NOT (...) to reverse its meaning.

Validation functions

The syntax for the Filter Expression and Test Expression formulae are the same as for ShapeSheet formulae. However, Visio 2010 includes some extra validation functions that are like ShapeSheet functions, but cannot be used in ShapeSheet formulae.

The following table is an extract from The Diagram Validation API blog that can be found at: `http://blogs.msdn.com/visio/archive/2010/01/07/the-diagram-validation-api.aspx`

It lists the special quasi-ShapeSheet functions that can be used in the Filter Expression and Test Expression formulae.

Function	Description
`Role()`	Returns an integer indicating the shape role: (Element = 0, Connector = 1, Container = 2, Callout = 4).
`OnLayer(LayerName)`	Returns a Boolean indicating whether the shape is a member of the specified layer. Returns a Boolean indicating whether layer exists on the page, if called on a page.
`ConnectedShapes(Direction)`	Returns the set of shapes, matching the `Direction` criteria, connected to the shape.
`GluedShapes(Direction)`	Returns the set of shapes, matching the `Direction` criteria, glued to the shape.
`ContainerMembers()`	Returns the set of shapes that are members of the container/list shape.
`ListMembers()`	Returns the set of shapes that are members of the list shape.
`Callouts()`	Returns the set of shapes that are callouts on the shape.
`ParentContainers()`	Returns the set of containers that the shape belongs to.
`ShapesOnPage()`	Returns the set of top-level shapes on page. If no page specifier precedes the function, the shape's containing page is assumed.
`AggCount(Set)`	Counts the number of shapes in a set.
`FilterSet(Set, FilterExpression)`	Returns the subset of shapes in a set that match an expression.
`OnBoundaryOf()`	Returns the set of containers such that the shape is on the boundary of these containers.

Useful ShapeSheet functions

This is a table of the ShapeSheet functions that are commonly used in Filter Expression and Test Expression formulae.

Function	Description
`AND(logical expression1,logical expression2,...,logical expressionN)`	Returns TRUE (1) if all of the logical expressions supplied are true. If any of the logical expressions are FALSE or 0, the AND function returns FALSE (0).
`OR(logicalexpression1,logicalexpression2,...,logicalexpressionN)`	Returns TRUE (1) if any of the logical expressions are TRUE.
`NOT(logicalexpression)`	Returns TRUE (1) if logicalexpression is FALSE. Otherwise, it returns FALSE (0)
`IF(logicalexpression,valueiftrue,valueiffalse)`	Returns valueiftrue if logicalexpression is TRUE. Otherwise, it returns valueiffalse.
`INDEX(index,"list"[,[delimiter][,[errorvalue]]])`	Returns the substring at the zero-based location index in the list delimited by delimiter. Or, it returns -1 if not found.
`LOOKUP("key","list"[,"delimiter"])`	Returns a zero-based index that indicates the location of the substring key in a list, or returns -1 if the target string contains the delimiter.
`HASCATEGORY(category)`	Returns TRUE if the specified string is found in the shape's category list.
`IS1D()`	Returns TRUE if the shape is 1-D (one-dimensional); returns FALSE if the shape is 2-D (two-dimensional).
`IFERROR(primary expression, alternate expression)`	Returns the evaluated result of a primary expression if it does not evaluate to an error. Otherwise, returns the evaluated result of an alternate expression.
`CALLOUTCOUNT()`	Returns the total number of callout shapes that are associated with the shape.
`CALLOUTTARGETREF()!`	Returns a sheet reference to the target shape of the callout shape.
`CONTAINERCOUNT()`	Returns the total number of containers that include the shape as a member (including nested relationships, that is, containers within containers).

Function	Description
CONTAINERSHEETREF(index[, category])	Returns a sheet reference to the specified container that contains the shape.
LISTMEMBERCOUNT()	Returns the number of member shapes in the list container shape.
LISTORDER()	Returns the 1-based position of the shape in the list.
LISTMEMBERCOUNT()	Returns a sheet reference to the list container shape that contains the shape.
<sheetref>!SHEETREF()	Returns a reference to the sheet (shape) that is specified in sheetref, or if there is no sheetref qualifier, to the current sheet. You can use this function in other functions that take a sheet reference token.
SHAPETEXT (shapename!TheText,flag)	Retrieves the text from a shape.
MASTERNAME (langID_opt)	Returns a sheet's master name as a string, or the string "<no master>" if the sheet doesn't have a master. The master name is in the form "<master name>:<shape name>",
LEFT(text, [,num_chars_opt])	Returns the first character or characters in a text string, based on the number of characters you specify.
LEN (text)	Returns the number of characters in a text string.
STRSAME ("string1", "string2", ignoreCase)	Determines whether strings are the same. It returns TRUE if they are the same, and FALSE if they aren't. To compare multi-byte strings or to do comparisons using case rules for a specific locale, use the STRSAMEEX function.
FIND (find_text, within_text , [start_num], [ignore_case])	Finds one text string contained within another, and returns the starting position of the text string you are seeking relative to its position in the text string that contains it.

All ShapeSheet functions are valid, but some are strongly discouraged because they cause an action to be performed rather than a value to be returned, and their impact cannot be predicted. The following list details the specific ShapeSheet functions that should not be used in Filter Expression and Test Expression formulae:

- `CallThis`
- `DoOleVerb`
- `DefaultEvent`
- `DoCmd`
- `GotoPage`
- `Help`
- `Hyperlink`
- `OpenFile`
- `OpenGroupWin`
- `OpenPage`
- `OpenSheetWin`
- `OpenTextWin`
- `PlaySound`
- `RunAddon`
- `RunAddonWArgs`
- `RunMacro`
- `SetF`

Filter and Test Expressions

You should use the Filter Expression to reduce the number of target shapes (or pages) to be tested. You can then use the Test Expression to apply to this reduced set in order to obtain a Boolean result.

A good way to understand how to write these expressions is to review the ones already created by Microsoft for the flowcharts and **Business Process Modeling Notation (BPMN)** templates. You can use **Rules Tools** add-in to review them interactively, or to create a report. For example, create a new flowchart diagram by going to **Flowchart | Cross-functional Flowchart**, and review the 11 rules already in the document in the **Flowchart** rule set.

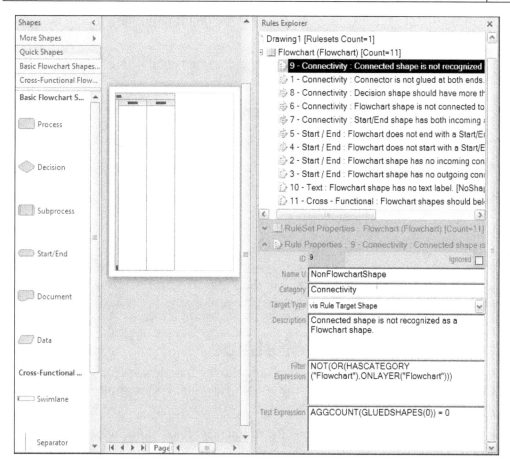

In fact, the same rule set is applied to the **Basic Flowchart** and **Six Sigma** diagrams too, so there are some rules that do not apply to all of them, such as the ones that involve swimlanes. These particular rules refer to containers, which do not exist unless the user manages to use a swimlane shape from the **Cross-functional Flowchart Shapes** stencil.

So, in order to test a few expressions, uncheck the **Enabled** property of the **Flowchart** rule set, and you can add a new rule set.

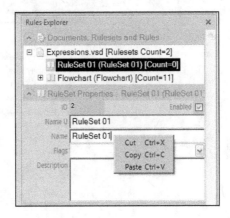

If you want to **Cut**, **Copy**, or **Paste** text in the **Rules Explorer** window, then you can use the right-mouse menu rather than the accelerator keys (*Ctrl+X, Ctrl+C, Ctrl+V*).

Checking the type of shape

You can test whether a shape is OneD or not with the function IS1D(), and you can test the type more specifically with the ROLE() function. For example, ROLE()=1 also returns True if the shape is a connector.

The ROLE() function matches against the following Visio.VisRoleSelectionTypes constant values:

- Default or element = 0 (this is not explicitly in the enum, but it is valid)
- visRoleSelConnector = 1
- visRoleSelContainer = 2
- visRoleSelCallout = 4

Let us create a test rule by selecting the **Add** button on the **Rules Tools** ribbon group. You can edit the **Category** and **Description** if you like, but be sure to enter ROLE()=0 in the **Filter Expression**, and False in the **Test Expression**, then select **Check Diagram**.

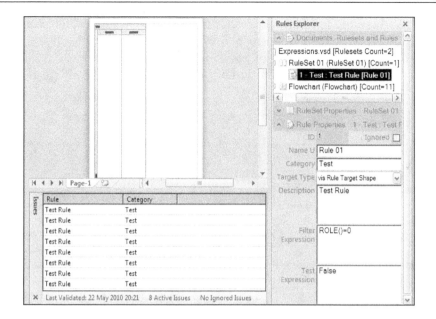

As you can see, there are **8 Active Issues**, so what is happening? Firstly, the **Test Expression** is obviously always going to return `False`, so there must be eight shapes being passed through to the **Test Expression** by the **Filter Expression**.

The **Drawing Explorer** window reveals that there are six shapes in the shapes collection of the page, and four of these shapes have two sub-shapes. So, there are actually 14 shapes in total, but only eight of them are returned by `ROLE()=0`. By the way, if you were to change the **Filter Expression** to `ROLE()=1` then there are no issues because there are no connectors on the drawing page yet!

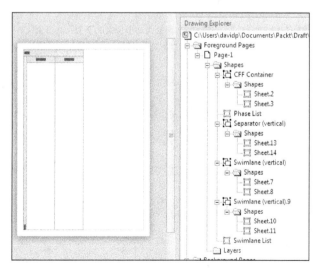

We can shed a bit more light on which shapes are raising issues by selecting the **Annotate** button on the **Rules Tools** ribbon group. You can double-click a row in the **Issues** window to select the shape or page that is causing that issue, but this does not give you an overview of the distribution of issues, nor does it simply display all of the issues for that shape.

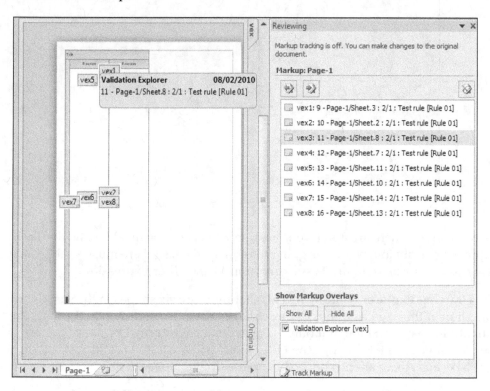

We can now see that the eight shapes raising issues are in fact all of the sub-shapes! This is probably not desirable in this particular case, so a real rule will need to have a more refined Filter Expression.

Checking the category of shape

Master shapes created for use in Visio 2010 may include the new, reserved user-defined cell, User.msvShapeCategories. This cell can contain the name of a single category, or multiple categories in a list separated by a semi-colon. Therefore, you can use the HASCATEGORY(category) function on instances of these shapes. For example, the following formula will return True if the shape has the Flowchart category:

```
HASCATEGORY("Flowchart")
```

However, the shapes to test may be instances of masters that do not contain this cell, so, you may have to use an alternative approach. You could use the MASTERNAME(lang_id) function to get the name of the master, if any. You should use lang_id = 750 to specify the universal language. Though often, users inadvertently create duplicate, or in fact multiple masters, through no fault of their own. In these cases, Visio automatically adds a .nn suffix to ensure uniqueness of name. Thus, you need to test that the first part of the name is a match by employing the STRSAME() and LEFT() functions too.

```
STRSAME(LEFT(MASTERNAME(750),10),"Terminator",0)
```

Rather than count the number of characters in the name, you could use the following formula:

```
STRSAME(LEFT(MASTERNAME(750),LEN("Terminator")),"Terminator",0)
```

 The MasterName() function actually returns both the name of the master and the shape in the master, with a colon separator. That is why you must use the LEFT() function.

If you look at the ShapeSheet of the outer shape labeled **Title** and one of the swimlane shapes labeled **Function**, then you will see that they have User.msvStructureType="Container", but User.msvShapeCategories is different.

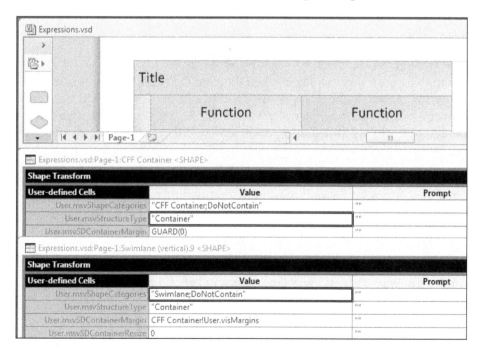

So, if you were to amend the **Filter Expression** to AND(ROLE()=2,HASCATEGORY("Swi
mlane")) then you will get two shapes raising issues.

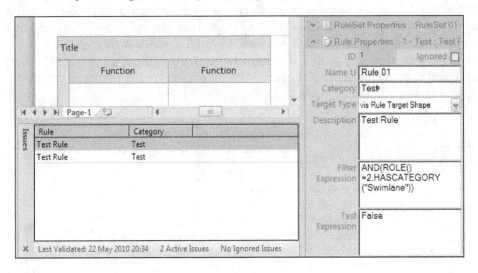

If you change the formula to AND(ROLE()=2,HASCATEGORY("CFF Container"))
then you will get just one issue.

You will only get one issue if you were to change the **Filter Expression** formula to:

```
STRSAME(LEFT(MASTERNAME(750),LEN("Phase List")),"Phase List",0)
```

Checking the layer of a shape

Some shapes are assigned to a layer when they are dragged from a stencil. This can
be because the master shape was pre-assigned to a layer, or because the user set an
active layer when the shape instance was created. A user can also change the layer
assignment interactively and shapes can belong to either no layer at all, one layer, or
multiple layers.

Knowing this, you should use the layer assignment of a shape with caution,
but sometimes it may be the only way of distinguishing a shape, as in the
following formula:

```
ONLAYER("Flowchart")
```

So, if you were to amend our **Test Rule** accordingly, and then drag-and-drop a
Start/End shape into the first swimlane, you will get one issue.

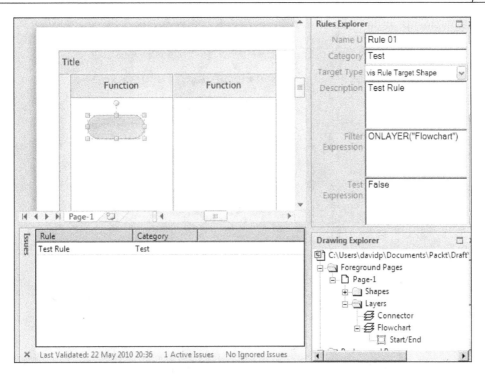

You can see in the **Drawing Explorer** window that the **Start/End** shape was pre-assigned to the **Flowchart** layer, and thus this layer was automatically created in the page when the master shape instance was dropped.

Checking if the page contains relevant shapes

Sometimes you may need to only continue testing the shapes on a page if that particular page contains specific shapes. In this case, you will need to get a collection of all of the shapes on the page using SHAPESONPAGE(), and then filter this set of shapes by matching their properties against an expression result using FILTERSET(). This expression must be passed through as a string, thus any quotation marks must be reaffirmed by doubling them within the expression. Finally, a **Boolean** result must be returned by checking the count of matching shapes using AGGCOUNT(). For example, the following formula returns True if the page contains any swimlane shapes:

```
AGGCOUNT(FILTERSET(SHAPESONPAGE(),"HASCATEGORY(""Swimlane"")"))>0
```

So, using this formula in our test rule reveals 10 active issues:

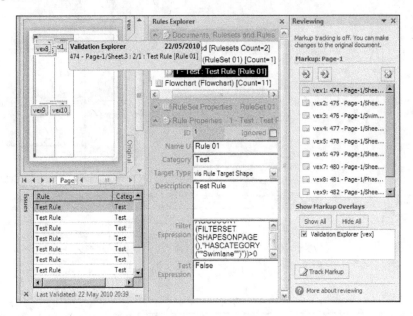

These issues are raised by all of the shapes, except for the top group shape of the container type shapes.

If you change the **Target Type** to vis Rule Target Page, then you will only get one issue raised for the page:

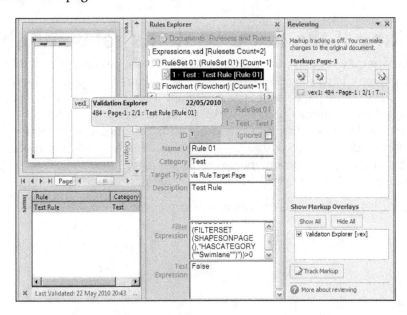

Of course, if you changed the **Target Type** to vis Rule Target Document, then there are no issues.

> The function ShapesOnPage() will cause Visio to check every shape on the page, and will take more time if there are lot of shape on the page. Therefore, you should use this function sparingly.

Checking for specific cell values

You may want to test for particular values in a cell. Initially, you may want to check only the shapes that actually have that cell present (remember that some sections in the ShapeSheet are optional). For example, all of the flowchart shapes contain at least seven **Shape Data** rows as shown in the following screenshot:

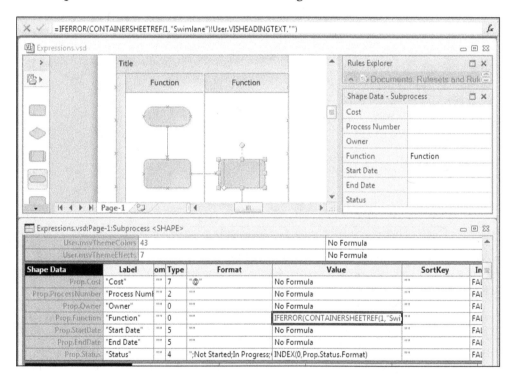

The connectors, swim-lanes, and so on do not have these **Shape Data** rows. So, we can filter for the shapes that contain the `Prop.Owner` cell by entering the following **Filter Expression**:

```
NOT(ISERROR((Prop.Owner)))
```

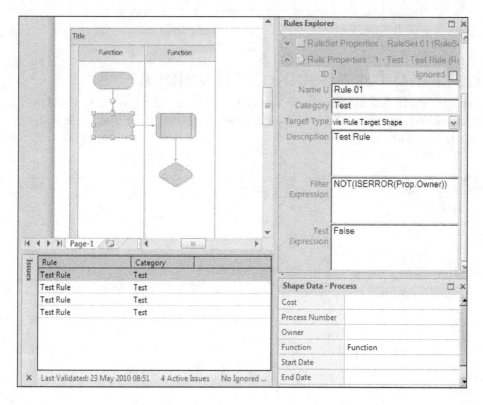

This formula works because the formula will return `True` if the `Prop.Owner` cell exists because it will not return an error when requesting its value. This reveals that there are four such shapes on this page.

Now that you have established which shapes contain the **Shape Data** cell, you can test for actual values. However, you must exercise a little caution. You may have thought that an empty value in a **Shape Data** row is always the same but it's not. This is similar to the **null** versus **empty string** value in databases. In Visio, a master shape instance will have default **Shape Data** values inherited from the master, and in the case of the flowchart shapes there is no formula in any of the **Shape Data** rows. As you can see, they do not display any values in the **Shape Data** window, except for the **Function** row. In fact, the **Function** row is updated by Visio automatically because it references the swimlane header text that it lies within.

If a user enters some text in the **Owner** row and later decides to delete it, then the underlying row has an **empty string** value, not a **null** value. So, if you want to ensure a value has been entered in a **Shape Data** row, then you need to check for the existence of a value using the `LOCALFORMULAEXISTS()` function. You also need to check that it is not an empty string, using the `STRSAME()` function. Consequently, the following formula will test if `Prop.Owner` contains a value:

```
OR(LOCALFORMULAEXISTS(Prop.Owner),NOT(STRSAME(Prop.Owner,"")))
```

If this is entered as the **Test Expression** and one of the flowchart shapes had a `Prop.Owner` value entered and then deleted, and if another flowchart shape has a value, then only three of the four shapes will raise an issue.

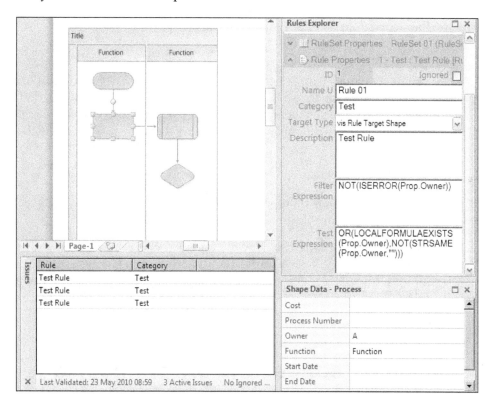

Of course, this will work for a text value too instead of the empty string.

If you want to check for numerical values, such as the `Prop.Cost` **Shape Data** row, then you will need to amend the **Test Expression**. If you want to find all shapes that have not had any user input then the following will suffice:

```
NOT(LOCALFORMULAEXISTS(Prop.Cost))
```

This is because numeric fields will reset to 0 if the user deletes an entry as it can never be an empty string.

Of course, you could test that the user has entered value greater than zero with the following **Test Expression**:

```
AND(LOCALFORMULAEXISTS(Prop.Cost),Prop.Cost>0)
```

Interestingly, dates do return back to no formula if the user deletes an entry. So, the following **Test Expression** is sufficient to check that an entry has been made:

```
LOCALFORMULAEXISTS(Prop.StartDate)
```

If you want to raise an issue for all shapes that do not have a Prop.StartDate value after today, then you could use the **Test Expression**:

```
Prop.StartDate>Now()
```

If your user can select values from a list, either fixed or variable, then you can use the INDEX() function with the STRSAME() function to test if the value is matched. For example, the **Flowchart** shapes have a Prop.Status list, therefore you could test if the value is equal to the fifth value using the following **Test Expression** (note that the array is zero-based):

```
STRSAME(Prop.Status,INDEX(4,Prop.Status.Format))
```

Testing the value at a particular index position in the list is preferable to using actual values because it will still work if the text has been localized.

Not all data is stored in the **Shape Data** rows. You may need to test whether an **Actions** row is checked or not. For example, the **BPMN** shapes have multiple options on their right-mouse menus and the ImproperAssociation rule has the following **Filter Expression**:

```
AND(HASCATEGORY("Connecting Object"),Actions.Association.Checked)
```

Checking that connectors are connected

One common structured diagramming error is leaving connectors unconnected at one or both ends. In these flowchart diagrams, you can filter for connectors using ROLE()=0, then check that there is one glued shape at either end of it, using the GLUEDSHAPES() function.

So, the following formula in the **Test Expression** will return False if there is a connection missing:

```
AND(AGGCOUNT(GLUEDSHAPES(4)) = 1, AGGCOUNT(GLUEDSHAPES(5)) = 1)
```

The GluedShapes(n) function has the following Visio.VisGluedShapesFlags constant values:

- visGluedShapesAll1D = 0
- visGluedShapesIncoming1D = 1
- visGluedShapesOutgoing1D = 2
- visGluedShapesAll2D = 3
- visGluedShapesIncoming2D = 4
- visGluedShapesOutgoing2D = 5

Consequently, if you have an unconnected connector in your test diagram then it will raise an issue.

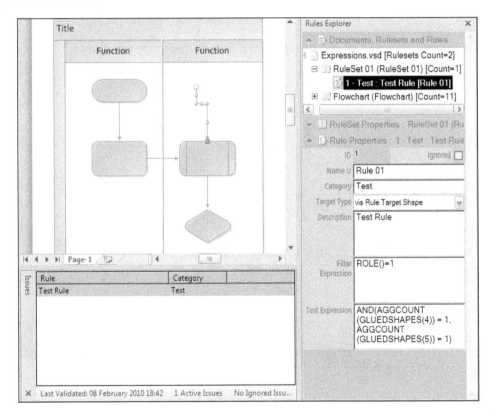

Checking that shapes have correct connections

A shape can be glued directly to other shapes, as is the case with connectors, or they can be connected via a connector to another shape.

You may want to ensure that certain shapes have incoming connections. For example, you could just filter for the **Decision** shapes by using the following formula:

```
OR(HASCATEGORY("Decision"),STRSAME(LEFT(MASTERNAME(750),LEN("Decision"
)),"Decision"))
```

Then you can test that there is at least one incoming connection using the following formula:

```
AGGCOUNT(GLUEDSHAPES(1)) > 0
```

This is entered in **Test Expression** as shown in the following screenshot:

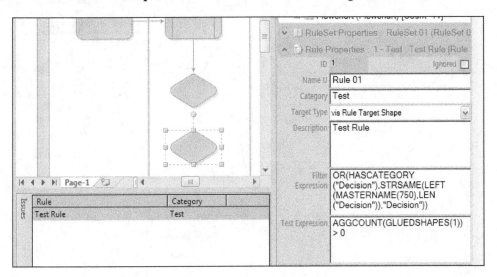

Similarly, you could ensure that each **Decision** shape has two outgoing connections using the **Test Expression**:

```
AGGCOUNT(GLUEDSHAPES(2)) = 2
```

Alternatively, you may want to try the following formula for the **Filter Expression** because it tests for all shapes on the **Flowchart** layer, except for **Start/End** shapes:

```
AND(ONLAYER("Flowchart"),NOT(STRSAME(LEFT(MASTERNAME(750),LEN("Start/
End")),"Start/End")))
```

The `ConnectedShapes()` function will return a collection of shapes at the other end of the glued connector.

```
AGGCOUNT(CONNECTEDSHAPES(0)) > 0
```

The `ConnectedShapes(n)` function has the following `Visio.`
`VisConnectedShapesFlags` constant values:

- `visConnectedShapesAllNodes = 0`
- `visConnectedShapesIncomingNodes = 1`
- `visConnectedShapesOutgoingNodes = 2`

Checking if shapes are outside containers

In a **Cross-functional Flowchart** diagram, you should ensure that all flowchart shapes are actually inside a swimlane. Visio 2010 has a new cell in the **Shape Layout** section called `Relationships` that stores the values of related containers and lists.

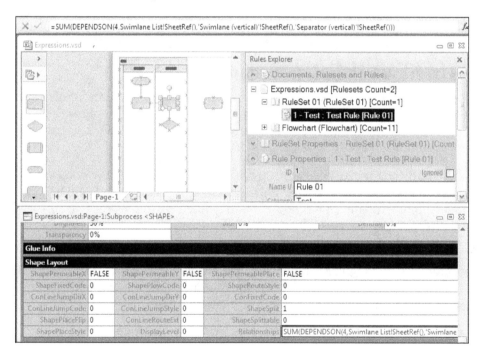

If you look at the `Relationships` cell for the **Process** shape to the right of the swimlanes, then you will find that there is no formula in there.

You first need to check that the page has at least one swimlane on it. This can be done with the following **Filter Expression** formula:

```
AGGCOUNT(FILTERSET(SHAPESONPAGE(),"HASCATEGORY(""Swimlane"")"))>0
```

However, you do need to change the **Target Type** to the page for this filter to work efficiently because you only want the rule to be validated once per page, not once per shape on the page.

Now, you need to test if there are any **Flowchart** shapes that are not within a swimlane. To do this, you need to use the PARENTCONTAINERS() function to get a collection of each shapes' containers, then filter this set by the category Swimlane. So, this is a complete formula for the **Test Expression**:

```
AGGCOUNT(FILTERSET(SHAPESONPAGE(),"AND(OR(HASCATEGORY(""Flowchart""),
   ONLAYER(""Flowchart"")),AGGCOUNT(FILTERSET(PARENTCONTAINERS(),
   ""HASCATEGORY(""""Swimlane"""")"")=0)"))=0
```

You can use a similar formula for checking if shapes are on a boundary or not, using:

```
ONBOUNDARYOF()
```

Custom validation rules in code

Previously in *Chapter 4*, you learnt that you can add custom validation rules in code. You would need to do this if the validation rule is too complex to phrase as Filter and Test Expressions. For example, you might want to ensure that there are no cycles (paths which return back to where they start from).

You could add code into a Visio add-in, but I will demonstrate how you can put some custom code into the drawing document as VBA because this will be in the document along with any rule set that you may have written using **Filter Expression** and **Test Expression**.

First, you need to listen for the RuleSetValidated event of the document, which can be added easily to the ThisDocument class in the VBA project. I have used the getRule() method from *Chapter 4* to ensure that there is a rule named CheckCycle present. If there is, then the CheckCycle() method is called.

```
Private Sub Document_RuleSetValidated(ByVal ruleSet As
   IVValidationRuleSet)
Dim rule As Visio.ValidationRule
    'Check for custom validation
    Set rule = getRule(ruleSet, "CheckCycle")
    If Not rule Is Nothing Then
        CheckCycle rule
```

```
        End If
    End Sub
```

The `CheckCycle()` method initially deletes any existing issues for the specified rule, then creates a new `CustomValidation` object before calling the `DoCycleValidation()` method.

```
    Private Sub CheckCycle(ByVal rule As Visio.ValidationRule)
        ClearRuleIssues rule
    Dim myCustomValidation As CustomValidation
        Set myCustomValidation = New CustomValidation
    Dim valid As Boolean
        valid = myCustomValidation.DoCycleValidation(rule)
    End Sub
```

The `ClearRuleIssues()` method steps backwards through the collection of `Validation.Issues` to delete any that are associated with the specified rule. Any other issues are left intact.

```
    Private Sub ClearRuleIssues(ByVal ruleToClear As Visio.ValidationRule)
    Dim val As Visio.validation
    Dim issue As Visio.ValidationIssue
    Dim rule As Visio.ValidationRule
    Dim i As Integer
        Set val = Visio.ActiveDocument.validation
        For i = val.Issues.count To 1 Step -1
            Set issue = val.Issues.Item(i)
            Set rule = issue.rule
            If rule Is ruleToClear Then
                issue.Delete
            End If
        Next
    End Sub
```

The `DoCycleValidation()` method loops through the whole of the page, and if the page is a foreground type, calls the `findCycle()` method.

```
    Public Function DoCycleValidation(ByVal cycleRule As Visio.
    ValidationRule) As Boolean

        'Declare variables
        Dim validationErrors As Boolean
        Dim issue As Visio.ValidationIssue
        Dim doc As Visio.Document
        Dim pag As Visio.page
```

```
'Use findCycle method to look for cycles"
'Add issue if cycle is found on a page
Set doc = cycleRule.Document
For Each pag In doc.Pages
    If pag.Type = visTypeForeground Then
        validationErrors = findCycle(pag, cycleRule)
    End If
Next

End Function
```

The findCycle() method is too long to list here (it's available in the code download for this book), but it will add an issue for the first shape in any cycle found, along with an issue for each connector in the cycle.

Now that the code exists it will be activated if a rule called **CheckCycle** is validated. The **Target Type** can be set to vis Rule Target Document, and the **Filter Expression** can be False because it will not need to do any validation.

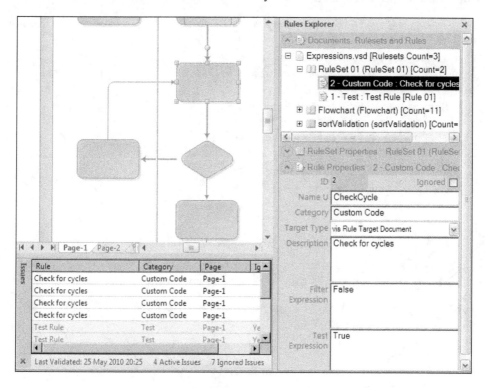

Of course, there could be many other validation rules in your custom code.

Summary

In this chapter, we have learned how to use the **Target Type** to set the context for a rule. We then learned how to write a few **Filter Expressions** to reduce the shapes that need to be processed, and finally how to write **Test Expressions** that can raise issues. There are probably more expressions that could be written, but we can work those out when we have specific requirements.

In the next chapter, we are going to learn how to publish our rules for others to use by providing them in Visio templates or documents. We will learn how to make these templates available to the normal user in the Visio user interface.

8
Publishing Validation Rules and Diagrams

In the last chapter, we learned how to write validation rules for structured diagrams. In particular, we looked at the quasi-ShapeSheet formulae that are used to define **Filter Expressions** and **Test Expressions**. You should now know how to write validation rules for most implementations.

In this chapter, we will go through methods for publishing Visio validation rules for others to use.

Overview of the Visio categories and templates

The normal Visio user selects a Visio template from a category, in the Backstage Getting Started view, of the Visio user interface, as opened by the **File | New** option,

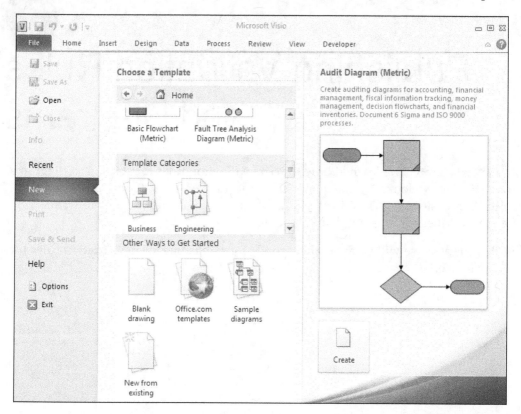

If you were to read the diagram template name, then you may think that there is a Visio template called `Audit Diagram (Metric).vst` in a folder called `Business`, somewhere on your hard-drive. However, that is not correct. In fact, there is a file called `Audit_M.vst` in `<Program Files>\Microsoft Office\Office14\Visio Content\1033`. The `<Program Files>` folder is usually `C:\Program Files`, and `1033` is the major language group ID. In my case, although UK English is `2047`, the major language is US English, which is `1033`. Therefore, my Microsoft Office content is installed under the `1033` sub-folder.

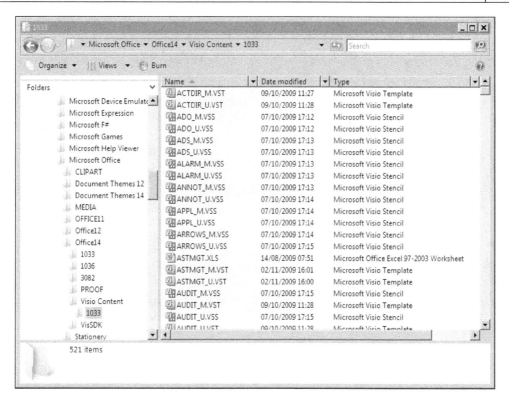

When Visio is installed, it has a files table in the installation file, which contains the mapping of the terse name to the more verbose one, along with the long description. This mapping is then installed into the registry and so the Visio interfaces then understand how to display the contents.

Some of this interpretation is hardcoded into Visio. For example, the built-in Visio templates and stencils all conform to the old **DOS 8.3** format, and the first part ends in _M or _U. This is how the Visio interface understands whether to display **(Metric)** or **(US Units)**. It may be that the content is slightly different for each version, perhaps defaulting to *mm* rather than *inches,* or sized slightly different to fit on grid, for example, but the display in the Backstage view is controlled by the last two characters of the terse file name.

You may notice that there is an option to create a Visio document from an existing one by selecting **New from existing** at the bottom of the Backstage view. This will offer you the chance to browse for all types of Visio files, as listed in the following table.

Extension	Format	Description
*.vsd	Binary	Visio drawing file
*.vdx	XML	Visio drawing file
*.vss	Binary	Visio stencil file
*.vsx	XML	Visio stencil file
*.vst	Binary	Visio template file
*.vtx	XML	Visio template file
*.vsw	Binary	Legacy Visio workspace file
*.vdw	Binary	Data-refreshable Visio drawing for use with Visio Services SharePoint 2010

However, if you want to present your users with a choice in one of the existing categories, or in a new one, then you need to create a template.

 Although most Visio file types can be saved in binary or XML format. The latter is typically 7 to 10 times larger in disk size.

Creating a custom template

We will create a new template, and then go through several ways that we can make it available to others for use as a template. Firstly, create a new drawing from the **Audit Diagram** template, then select **Process | Check Diagram | Import Rules From | Flowchart Rule Set**.

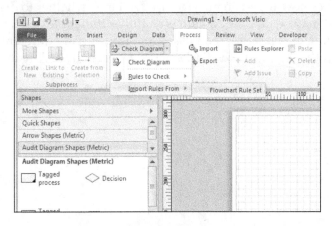

There is only one built-in rule set in Visio, so we will use an import of that for this example. In fact, the procedure shown in this chapter is exactly the same process that can be gone through in order to create Visio templates for companies who want customized versions of the ones supplied in Visio.

Adding embellishments

Most companies want to standardize the appearance of their Visio diagrams with, for example, company logos, borders, and titles. In this example, we are going to add a standard border and slightly modify it.

Select one of the **Borders & Titles** from the **Backgrounds** group on the **Design** tab.

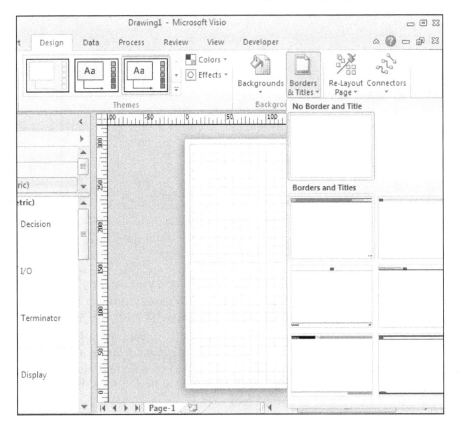

This action will automatically create a new background page, called **VBackground-1**. This will become the default background page for all new pages created in documents which are created from this template. In fact, you can add other backgrounds in a document and have pages of different sizes. Visio is very flexible, but you should consider whether you will be generally printing all pages in the document to the same printer using the same printed paper size.

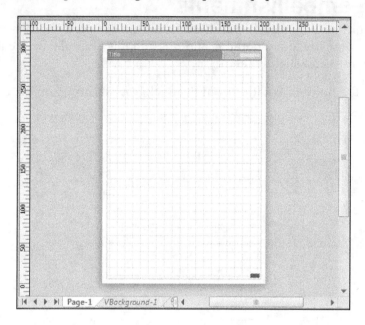

You can now select the **VBackground-1** tab and you will then be able to edit the shapes on the background page.

One of the best features in Visio is the ease with which you can create text that is automatically updated from a value in a cell. In this case, wouldn't it be nice if the page title automatically displayed the name of the page? Well, all you need to do is edit the text of the **Title** box on the background page. In this case, it is in the top left of the background page. Usually you can just double-click a shape to edit the text, but you can also just click to select it then press *F2* to go into text edit mode. You can then select **Field** from the **Insert** tab. This action will open up the **Field** dialog where you can select a **Category** and **Field name**, or enter a custom formula. In this case, you need to select **Page Info** from the **Category** and **Name** from the **Field name** sections respectively.

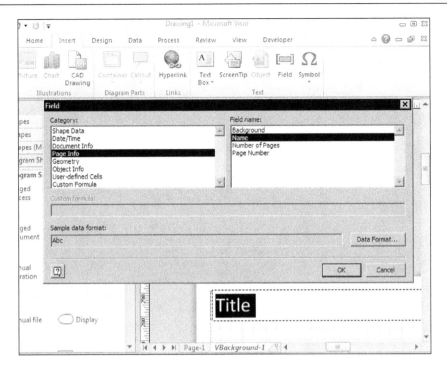

Actually, I will often add the **Document Info | Title** and **Document Info | Subject** with a hyphen between them before the **Page Info | Name** field. Of course, you may want to create a rule that reminds users that they should fill in a **Title** and **Subject** for every document that they create.

Although we just specified that the **Title** block displays the page name of the background page, Visio understands that you really want to display the page name of the foreground page. So when you click back onto **Page-1**, you will see that the text automatically displays **Page-1**:

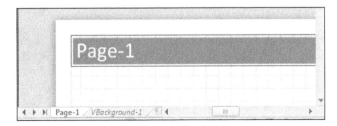

Clever isn't it? What is more, Visio 2010 will automatically change the size of the background page, if you change the size of the foreground page.

Adding the template description

You should now go into the Backstage view to edit the **Info** of the document. Once there, you can provide some information for future reference in the **Properties** panel.

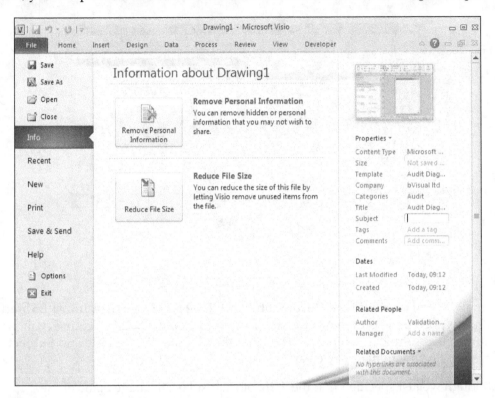

You should fill in the **Comments** section with a description that will help your users make the right choice of template because this will be displayed in the Visio user interface later.

 You can also get to edit the document properties from the right-mouse menu on the document node in the **Drawing Explorer** window, which can be opened from the checkbox on the **Developer** tab. In this case, it will open the old **Properties** dialog.

The simplest method to provide a template

Now save this document as a Visio template (*.vst) in a folder, let's say in a new folder called My Templates, with a sub-folder called Company Flowcharts, inside the special folder, Documents (or My Documents) folder.

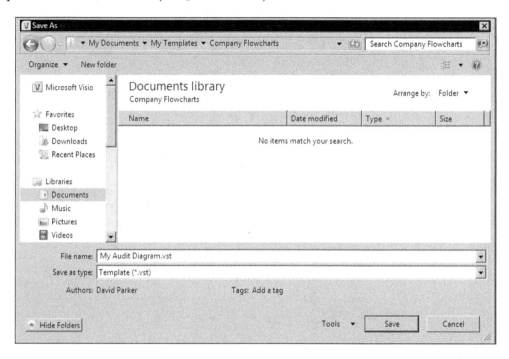

Ok, so we now have a custom template. However, the Visio interface does not know where to find the templates, even though it is inside the special folder Documents (or My Documents). There is a special folder called My Shapes in the Documents folder that is intended for Visio stencils, but it does not automatically display the contents for templates.

Editing the file paths for templates

Fortunately, we can tell Visio where to look for custom templates and other custom files from the **Visio Options** panel. Simply open the **File Locations** dialog from the **Advanced | General** section at the very bottom of the scrollable panel. You can then navigate to the **My Templates | Company Flowcharts** folder by clicking the ellipsis button ("**...**") to the right of the **Templates** text box.

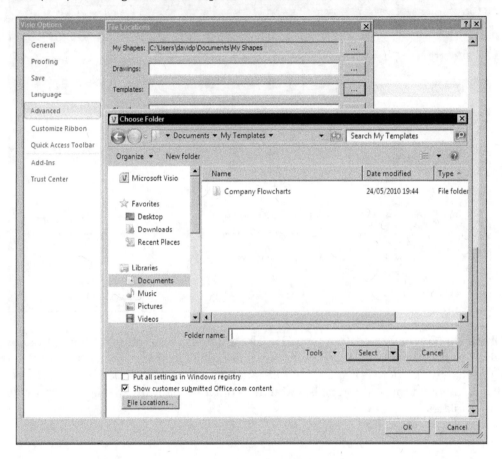

You should select the My Templates folder, not the Company Flowcharts sub-folder, because Company Flowcharts will be used as the category name in the Visio interface.

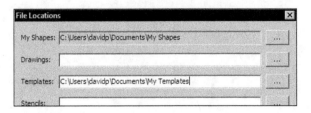

So, now when you want to select a template, you will find **My Audit Diagram** inside the Company Flowcharts folder.

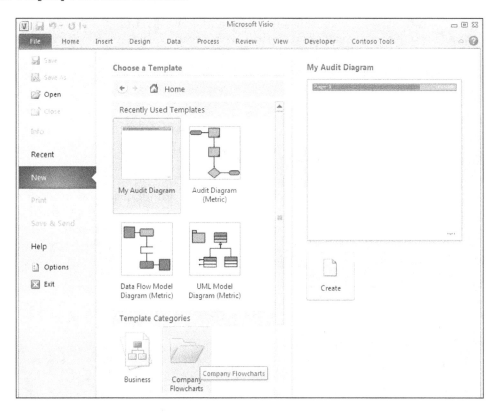

You should be aware that Visio will scan through every folder and sub-folder, for every path listed in the **File Locations** dialog. This can be a very slow process if there are a lot of folders and files within them. Therefore, this method of deploying custom templates is not recommended, but it is acceptable for certain situations (for example, when no installations are permitted) provided it is done with care. You can imagine the effect that entering C: in just one of these locations could have, since Visio will attempt to read every folder and sub-folder looking for suitable files. Visio will appear to stop responding, if you are lucky.

You may have noticed that you can specify a path called **Start-Up** in the **File Locations** dialog. If you set a path here, Visio will attempt to run every executable file it finds! Imagine doing that from C:! Believe me this has happened on more than one occasion. The only remedy is to shutdown as quickly as possible, restart the computer, then edit the registry below to remove this path before starting Visio again.

```
Computer\HKEY_CURRENT_USER\Software\Microsoft\
Office\14.0\Visio\Application\StartUpPath
```

Creating a template preview image

You will have noticed that our new template looks pretty boring in the Backstage view. The default preview image in Visio is generated automatically from the first foreground page in a document. Therefore, you can create a new preview image for the template by mocking-up a new drawing, created from the template, with a suitable arrangement of shapes on it. You will then be able to copy the image from the drawing to the template using a single line of VBA code.

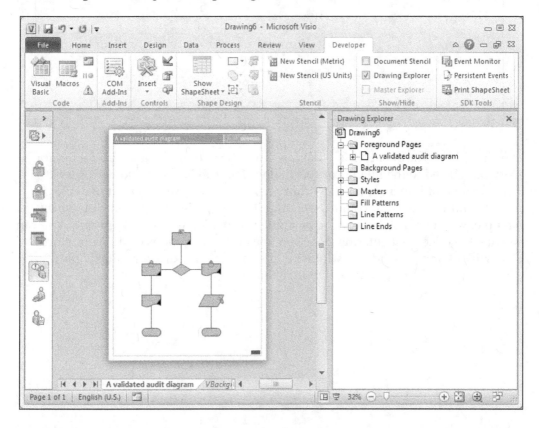

Now, open the **Page Setup** dialog from the right-mouse menu, on the foreground page node of the **Drawing Explorer** window, or from the **Size | More Page Sizes** option on the **Design** tab. Select **Custom size** on the **Page Size** tab, and edit the height to be the same as the width.

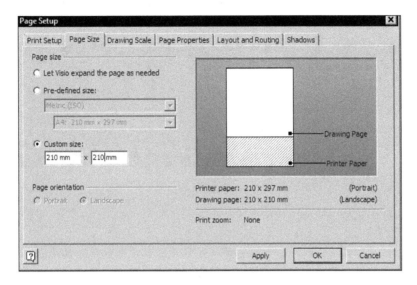

You are doing this because the preview image of the template in the Backstage view is square.

Open the Document Sheet by selecting **Show ShapeSheet** from the right-mouse menu of the document node, on the **Drawing Explorer** window.

Then edit the PreviewQuality to be 1 - visDocPreviewQualityDetailed. This will ensure that the size specified in ThumbnailDetailMaxSize registry key value is used.

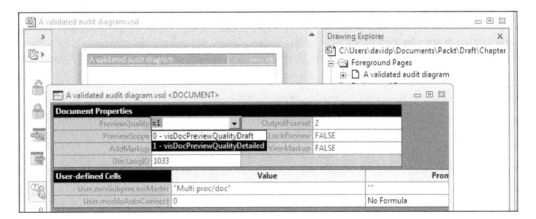

Close the ShapeSheet and then save the document as say, A validated audit diagram.vsd.

Next, you need to open the original My Audit Diagram.vst document by using the **File | Open** menu, and then select **Open Original** from the options on the **Open** button.

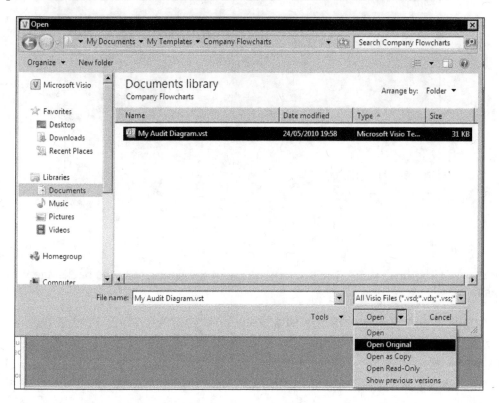

So, you now have two documents open. This is necessary because you are going to copy the preview image from one to the other! You can verify the names of the files that you have open from the menu on the **Switch Windows** button on the **View** tab.

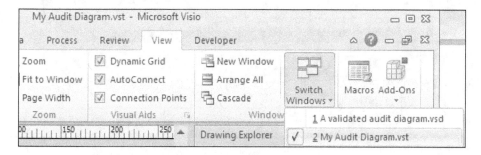

Go into the VBA environment—*Alt+F11* normally takes you straight there. You do not want to add any VBA code into the documents because you just need to type one line into the **Immediate Window** (*Ctrl+G*):

```
Visio.Documents("My Audit Diagram.vst").CopyPreviewPicture
Visio.Documents("A validated audit diagram.vsd")
```

You have now copied the preview image from A validated audit diagram.vsd to My Audit Diagram.vst, but the template will lose the preview unless you edit the LockPreview value to TRUE in the ShapeSheet of the My Audit Diagram.vst document.

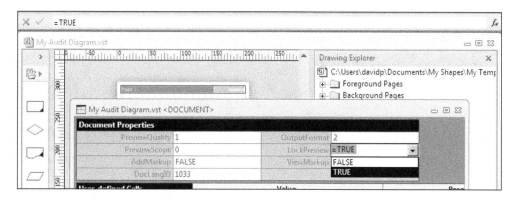

Now you can close the ShapeSheet and save the template, and this time you will see that there is a preview image.

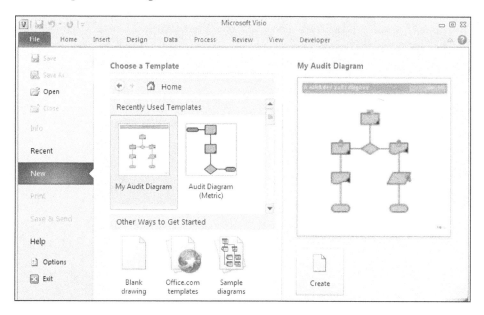

Remember that you will need to change the `LockPreview` back to `0` (`FALSE`) if you ever want to update the image.

Alternatively, you could save the following VBA code in the `ThisDocument` class of the `A validated audit diagram.vsd` file so that you can copy the preview image at a later date again. This method will assume that you also have the target template open.

```
Public Sub CopyPreview()
Dim docTarget As Visio.Document
Dim doc As Visio.Document
If Visio.Documents.Count < 2 Then
    Exit Sub
Else
    'Get the first writable drawing that is open
    For Each doc In Visio.Application.Documents
        If doc.Type = visTypeTemplate _
            And doc.ReadOnly = False _
            And Not doc Is ThisDocument Then
            Set docTarget = doc
            Exit For
        End If
    Next
    If docTarget Is Nothing Then
        Exit Sub
    End If
End If

If MsgBox("Do you want to copy the preview image from " & _
    ThisDocument.Name & " to " & docTarget.Name & "?", _
    vbYesNo) = vbYes Then
    docTarget.DocumentSheet.Cells("LockPreview").FormulaU = 0
    docTarget.CopyPreviewPicture ThisDocument
    docTarget.DocumentSheet.Cells("LockPreview").FormulaU = 1
End If

End Sub
```

Enhancing the quality of the preview image

You may be slightly disappointed with the quality of this image compared to the standard Visio ones. It is certainly less crisp, but there is a way that you can fix this. Visio is rendering to a fixed size by default.

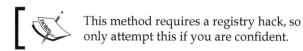

This method requires a registry hack, so only attempt this if you are confident.

First, you need to tell Visio to store all of its settings that it is holding in memory into the registry so that you can edit them. This is done by checking the **Put all settings in Windows registry** box in the **Visio Options** dialog, under the **Advanced | General** group.

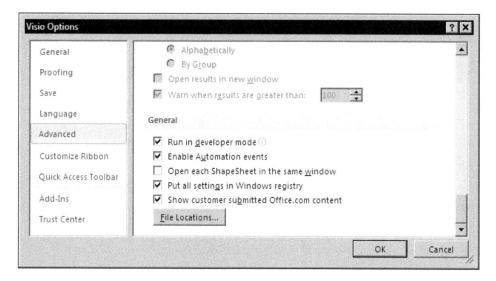

Then close Visio and start the **Registry Editor** (type `regedit` at the **Start** command). Navigate down to the following node:

```
Computer\HKEY_CURRENT_USER\Software\Microsoft\Office\14.0\
Visio\Application
```

Then edit one of the two Thumbnail values as follows:

```
ThumbnailDetailMaxSize = 5000000
```

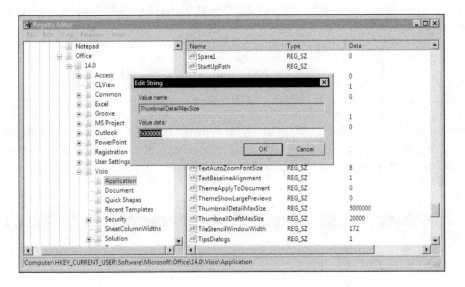

Now open the `A Validated Audit Diagram.vsd` that you previously created, and save the document again. You may then want to change the `LockPreview` value of this document to `TRUE` by using the ShapeSheet as described earlier, in case you want to use it again

Open the `My Audit Diagram.vst` document and set the `LockPreview` of this document to `FALSE`, before copying the preview image across, using the VBA line from above.

Set the `LockPreview` back to `TRUE` and save the document.

Now you will see that the preview picture of the document is much crisper and clearer.

Finally, you should edit the registry values back to their defaults, otherwise Visio will need to work harder and your file sizes will be increased.

```
ThumbnailDetailMaxSize = 60000
```

The best method for publishing templates

Now you know how to publish a template and category using a simple method, you will now learn how to do provide a setup package that can be distributed and installed. For this, you will need an application, such as Visual Studio, that can create an installation package (*.msi) file, and you will need to install the Microsoft Visio **SDK (Software Development Kit)**.

Creating a setup project

In Visual Studio, create a new project from **Other Project Types | Setup and Deployment | Visual Studio Installer | Setup Project** call it, say, MyAuditTemplateSetup.

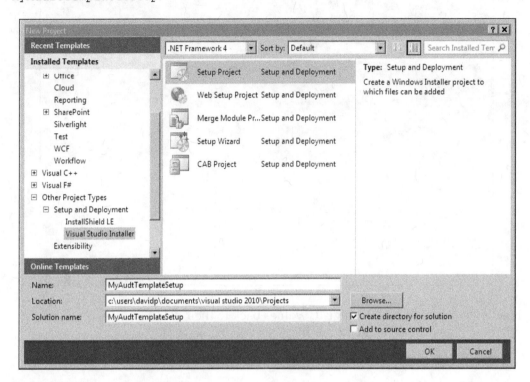

In Visio, save the My Audit Diagram.vst file as AuditR_M.vst, then in Visual Studio add the file to the Application folder in the **File System** of the MyAuditTemplateSetup project.

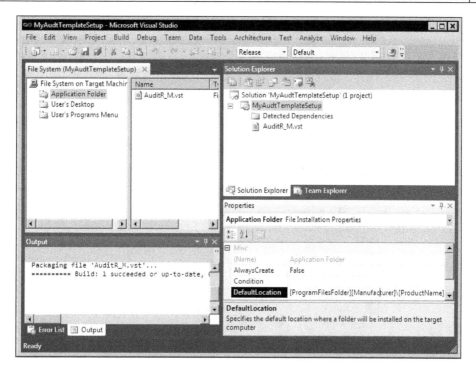

You may want to edit the `DefaultLocation` for the **Application Folder** because you are not installing any code, just a file. Your company may have a policy for keeping templates in particular locations on the hard drive, but I think the important factor is whether you are installing for all users, or just one user on the computer. If you are installing just for the user who is running the installation application, then you may wish to place the custom Visio files in the user hive, but if you are installing for all users, then you need a location that is available to all users, such as the `ProgramFilesFolder`.

 See the online article System Folder Properties (`http://msdn.microsoft.com/en-us/library/aa372057.aspx`) for more information about valid system folder codes.

You should edit the **Deployment Project Properties** with the product name, title, company name, and website, for example, and set the `InstallAllUsers` to `True` if you want the default installation to be for anyone who uses the target computer.

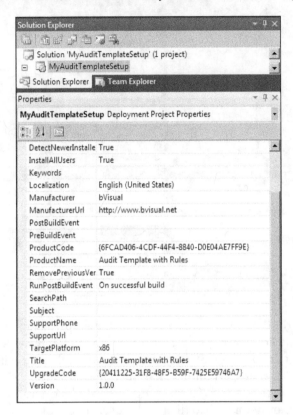

You can then build the release of this package and you should find that two files are created, namely `MyAudtTemplateSetup.msi` and `setup.exe`, in the `<Projects>\ MyAudtTemplateSetup\MyAudtTemplateSetup\Release` folder.

If you attempt to run the installation at this stage then the file will be installed, but it will not appear in the Visio user interface.

Amending the installation package

The Microsoft Visio Solution Publisher is installed as part of the Visio SDK, and I recommend that you add it as an external tool in Visual Studio because you will need to use this tool each and every time that you build or rebuild a setup project that includes Visio templates, stencils, and add-ons.

To do this, open the **External Tools** dialog from the **Tools** menu, then select **Add** and navigate to the `VisSolPublisher.exe` file that is in the `<ProgramFilesFolder>\`
`Microsoft Office\Office14\VisSDK` folder by default (it will be
`<ProgramFiles64Folder>` if you install the 64-bit version of the SDK).

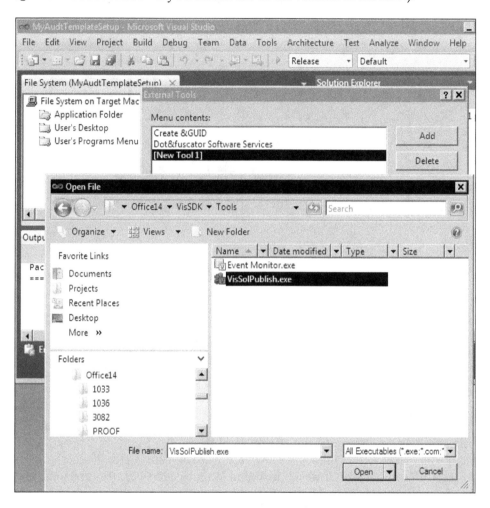

You can then start the Microsoft Visio Solution Publisher directly from the **Tools** menu. Initially, you will need to select **File | New** and navigate to the `MyAuditTemplateSetup.msi` file.

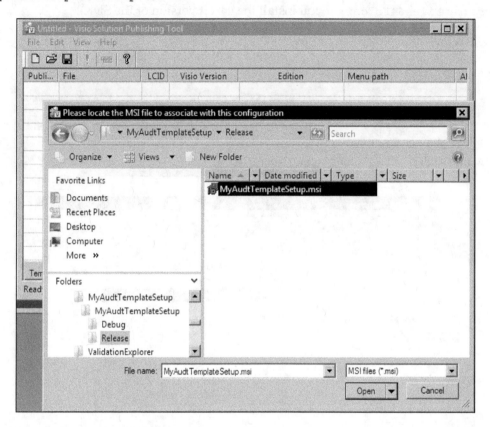

The Microsoft Visio Solution Publisher will read the `PublishComponent` table of the MSI file, and you can then edit the attributes of the file that it finds. Check the **All LCIDs** box near the top right of the **Template Information** dialog, unless you intend to create a different version for each installed language in your organization. Then you need to edit the **Menu path** to contain the category and verbose name that you want for your template in the Visio Backstage view. Notice that the category is **My Custom Templates**, and the template name is **Audit Diagram with Rules** in this example, with each separated by a backslash character (" \ ").

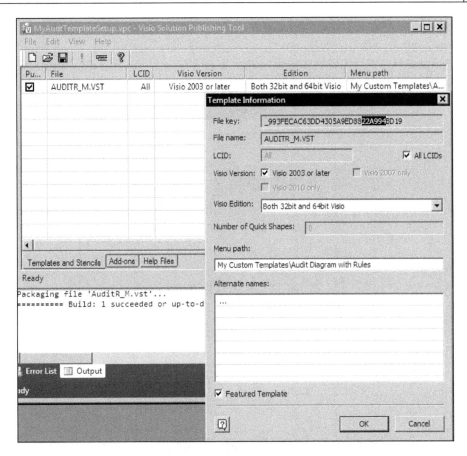

I decided to check the **Featured Template** too so that it is displayed more promptly in the Visio user interface. This setting only works in versions prior to Visio 2010 because the new Backstage view does not have featured templates.

You can now apply these changes to the MSI file with **File | Apply** (*F5*).

Running the installation

Locate the `setup.exe` file in the `Release` folder of the project, then select **Run as administrator** from the right-mouse menu on it. You may be asked to confirm the action, and when you do, the welcome dialog should appear as follows:

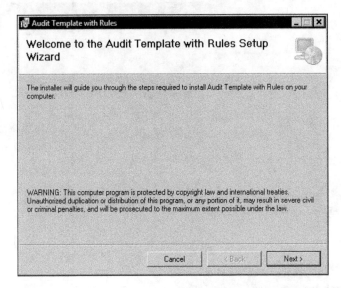

You will be prompted to confirm the installation folder, and whether to install for all users.

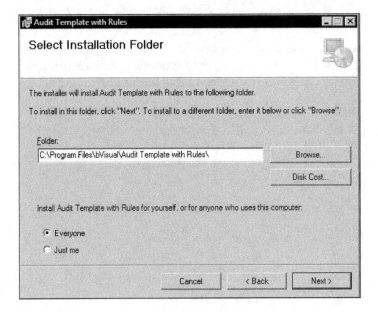

The installation should run through to completion now, and the `AuditR_M.vst` file will be placed into the folder:

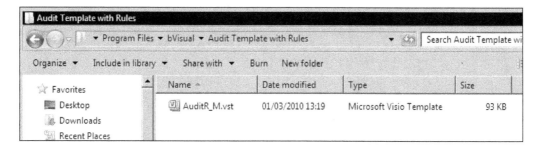

You can uninstall it from **Control Panel | Program and Features**.

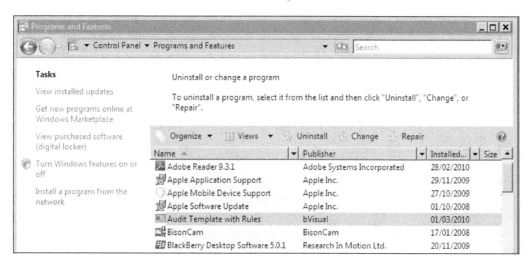

If you haven't gone straight for the uninstall option, then you can now start Visio and you will find that there is a new category, **My Custom Templates**, and that there is a new template **Audit Diagram with Rules** within it.

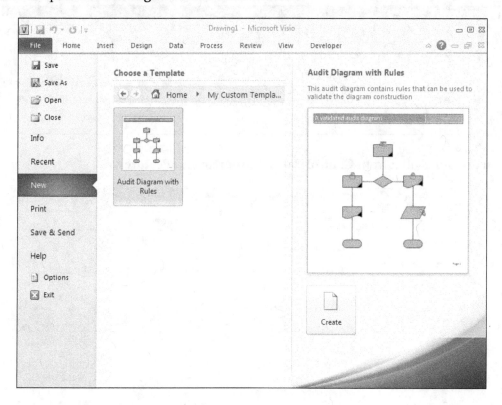

Quod Erat Demonstrandum as my teacher used to say.

The only niggle is that you currently cannot change the folder icon of the category. Perhaps this will be possible in the next version of the Visio SDK.

Of course, you do not have to have a separate installation package for each of your new templates because you can have multiple templates installed in one MSI file.

Also, the template could contain modified versions of standard Visio shapes, or even some extra ones on new stencils too. In this case there will be stencils to be deployed to the installation folder too, and each stencil will require name and description enhancements entered in the Microsoft Visio Solution Publisher tool.

And finally, if your rules are too complicated to be defined purely with Filter and Test Expressions then this method of installing custom templates could also contain custom validation code.

Summary

In this chapter, we learned two different ways of deploying custom Visio templates that contain validation rules. The first simple method does not require any extra tools besides Visio, but is more difficult to control. The second is more complex and requires additional skills and applications, but is more suitable for large-scale deployment and centralized control.

In the next and final chapter, we will walk through the creation and deployment of a new rule set for **Data Flow Model Diagrams**. We will convert some plain English rules into ones that Visio can understand, in order to ensure that well-constructed diagrams are created.

9
A Worked Example for Data Flow Model Diagrams

In the preceding chapters, we learned about the Visio object model, the new Validation API, how to write validation rules, and how to publish these rules for others to use.

In this chapter, we are going to present a complete cycle for writing validation rules for the **Data Flow Model Diagram** methodology. I chose this template because there used to be an add-on associated with it in Visio, but this add-on is no longer provided, and there are no rules for it either.

As we are going to be producing a new template, we can take the opportunity to enhance the Master shapes too. I know that some of these enhancements are usually done by a ShapeSheet developer rather than a rules developer, but I include fairly-detailed steps because they give valuable insight into Visio shape behavior.

So, in this chapter, we will go through the following steps:

- Examining the existing template
- Making any shape enhancements we may want
- Analyzing the rules requirements
- Writing the rules
- Publishing the new template.

What are Data Flow Diagrams?

A quick search on the Web reveals that **Data Flow Diagrams** (**DFDs**) are a graphical representation of the flow of data into, around, and out of a system.

Refer to the following links for more information on DFDs:

- `http://www.agilemodeling.com/artifacts/`
  `dataFlowDiagram.htm`
- `http://www.mckinnonsc.vic.edu.au/vceit/`
  `designtools/dfd/dfd.htm`

Throughout the seventies, various academics developed methodologies for modeling data flows. The one by **Gane** and **Sarson** is utilized in the **Data Flow Model Diagrams** template in Visio. This methodology has the following four elements:

- Squares representing external entities, which are sources or destinations of data. These are the places that provide the organization with data, or have data sent to them by the organization (for example, customers, partners, government bodies).
- Rounded rectangles representing processes, which take data as input, do something to it, and output it.
- Arrows representing the data flows, which can be either electronic data or physical items. The arrows should be labeled with the name of the data that moves through it.
- Open-ended rectangles representing data stores, including electronic stores such as databases or XML files, and physical stores such as or filing cabinets or stacks of paper. They can be manual, digital, or temporary.

With a dataflow diagram, developers can map how a system will operate, what the system will accomplish, and how the system will be implemented. It's important to have a clear idea of where and how data is processed in a system to avoid double-handling and bottlenecks. A DFD also helps management organize and prioritize data handling procedures and staffing requirements.

A DFD lets a system analyst study how existing systems work, locate possible areas prone to failure, track faulty procedures, and reorganize components to achieve better efficiency or effectiveness.

There are a number of rules that are commonly followed when creating DFDs:

- All processes must have at least one data flow in, and one data flow out
- All processes should modify the incoming data, producing new forms of outgoing data
- Each data store must be involved with at least one data flow
- Each external entity must be involved with at least one data flow
- A data flow must be attached to at least one process

- Data flows cannot go directly from one external entity to another external entity; such flows need to go through at least one process.

There are also a couple of conventions that could be considered. They are:

- Do not allow a single page of a data flow diagram to get too complex—it should have no more than ten components. If it has more than this, combine some components into a single, self-contained unit and create a new DFD for that unit.
- Each component should be labeled with a suitable description.
- Each data flow should be labeled describing the data flowing through it.
- Each component and subcomponent should be numbered in a top-down manner.

Finally, there are two other connectivity rules that could be added:

- A data flow must be connected to two data components
- A flow must not cycle back to itself

Examining the standard template

You can find the standard **Data Flow Model Diagram** template in the **Software and Databases** category.

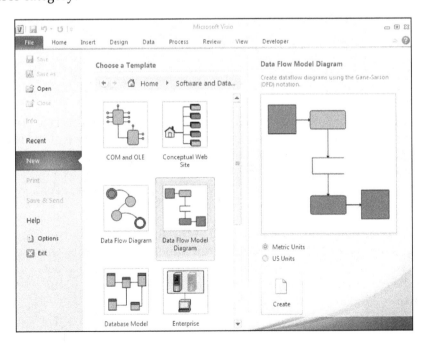

If you create a new document from this template, you will see that there are just four masters on the **Gane-Sarson** stencil, and there are no rules associated with it at all.

If you then drag-and-drop just one of each shape onto the page, you will see that the graphics are not complicated either.

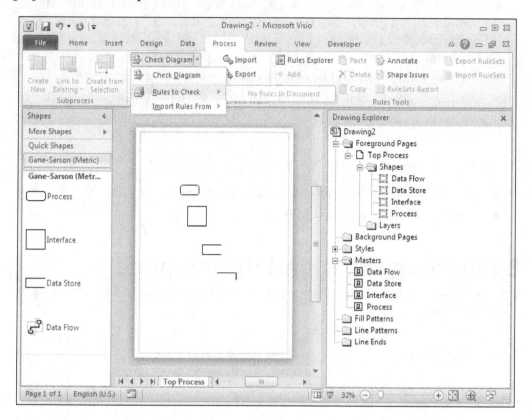

You now need to review the current shapes, and one way to do this is to create a quick report in Visio. I started by reviewing the ShapeSheet of each of the shapes and saw that each of them contain a few **User-defined Cells** that point to their role within UML diagrams. For example, the User.UMLShapeType cell contains a numerical value that specifies the type of UML shape, and the User.visDescription cell contains a text description of this type.

So, you can create a new report that lists all of the shapes on the current page using the **Shape Reports** button in the **Reports** group on the **Review** tab. Then you can select the **Advanced** button to open the dialog to set a filter. In this case, you can check for the existence of the UMLShapeType cell by selecting the **Value** = TRUE for the **Condition** = exists, before clicking **Add**.

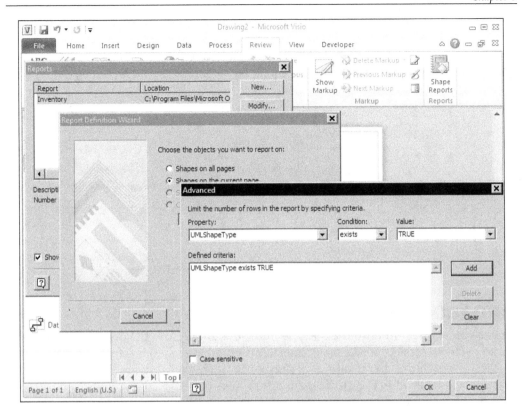

You can then proceed to select the properties that you want to display as columns in the report on the next panel. You should select **<MasterName>**, **UMLShapeType**, and **visDescription**. You will need to check the **Show all properties** option in order to see the last two, because User-defined cells are not displayed by default.

You can then proceed to save the report definition as, say **DFD Shapes**, and then run it as an Excel report format. You should get a report that looks as follows:

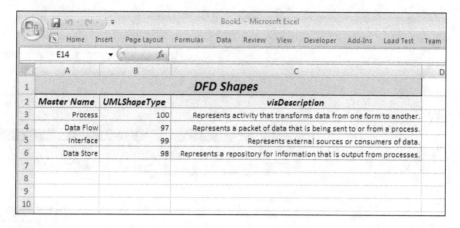

Enhancing the masters

Before you start to enhance the masters in the document (not the original **Gane-Sarson** stencil), open the **Master Properties** dialog for each of the four masters and check the **Match master by name on drop** option. This will ensure that the enhanced masters will be used in this document, rather than the original masters, even if the user drags-and-drops it from the original stencil.

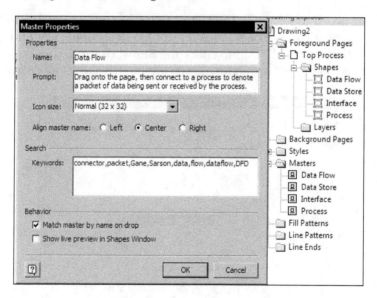

You can now edit each master in turn.

Editing the Data Flow master

The **Data Flow** master is used to connect **Process**, **Data Store**, and **Interface** shapes. The user should enter some text on each **Data Flow** to name the data that is flowing along it.

The **Data Flow** shape looks like a simple connector with an arrow head denoting the flow direction.

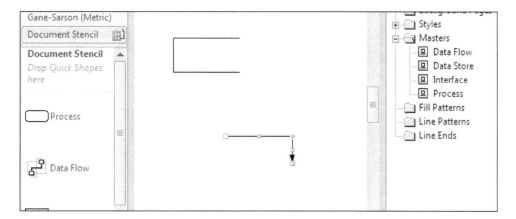

Now open the master shape by selecting **Edit Master Shape** on the right-mouse menu of the **Data Flow** node, in the **Masters** branch of the **Drawing Explorer** window.

Then ensure that the **Master Explorer** window is open and select the shape.

These shapes were created for an earlier version of Visio, before Microsoft added the ability for 2-D shapes to automatically split 1-D connectors when they are dropped on them. It would be useful to add this capability to the **Data Flow** shape by modifying its behavior. Click the **Behavior** button in the **Shape Design** group of the **Developer** tab. Check the **Connector can be split by shapes** option.

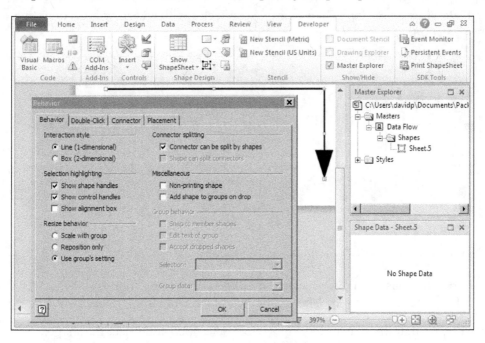

You can now click on **OK** and close the master edit window.

Preparing for AutoConnect

You will want to ensure that the user does indeed use the **Data Flow** shape to connect the DFD shapes together. Therefore, we need to understand how a user can make connections.

The easiest method is to use the new **AutoConnect** feature. This displays blue triangles around an existing shape as you hover over it. These triangles can be used to connect to an existing adjacent shape, or to even drop a new shape by using the **Quick Shapes** selector.

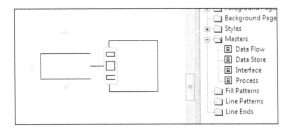

However, there is an unfortunate consequence of using this feature. It will automatically create and use a new master called **Dynamic connector**.

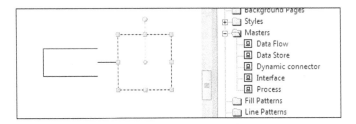

The **Dynamic connector** master is a rare hardcoded master in Visio, and it is also used by the **Connector Tool** in the **Tools** group on the **Home** tab (unless you have preselected an alternative connector master on the active stencil).

Therefore, we need to anticipate how Visio works, and avoid having the wrong connector between our shapes. To do this, we will change the **NameU** of the **Data Flow** connector.

So, first ensure that there is no **Dynamic connector** master present in the document, and then open the **Immediate Window** in the **VB Editor**.

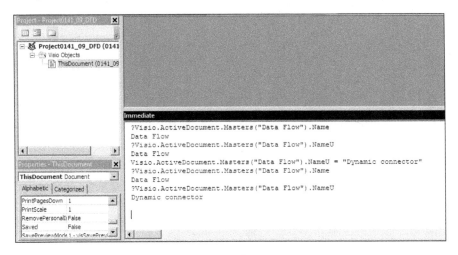

Initially, if you type `?Visio.ActiveDocument.Masters("Data Flow").Name` or `?Visio.ActiveDocument.Masters("Data Flow").NameU` in the **Immediate Window**, then you will get the words **Data Flow** on the response line.

If you then type `Visio.ActiveDocument.Masters("Data Flow").NameU = "Dynamic connector"` into the window, and repeat the first two lines, you will find that the `NameU` is now **Dynamic connector**.

Now, when you use the **Quick Shapes**, **AutoConnect**, or the **Connector Tool**, you should find that the **Data Flow** master is used in all cases!

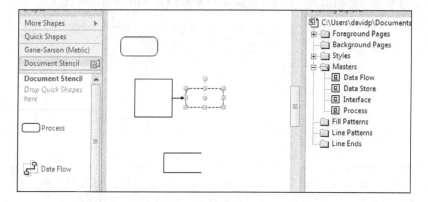

Editing the Data Store master

Select **Edit Master Shape** from the right-mouse menu on the **Data Store** master in the **Master Explorer** window, and you will see that the shape is a very simple three-sided rectangle.

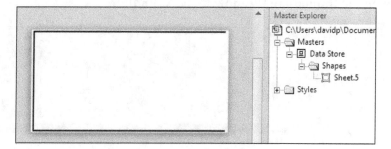

Adding the Data Store Shape Data

Whilst looking at examples of DFDs on the web, it is clear that there is an alternate appearance for the Data Store shape that has a square containing an identifier to the left of the shape. Therefore, we can take the opportunity to add this option to the shape.

Since we need to have two distinct text areas in the shape, it will need to be a group shape. Therefore, select the shape in the Master Edit window and then select **Convert to Group** from the **Group** dropdown in the **Arrange** group of the **Home** tab. It is important to convert to a group rather than just grouping the shape, because the converting will maintain the user-defined cells at the top level shape. You should notice a subtle change in the icon of the **Sheet.5** shape in the **Master Explorer** window after you have converted it to a group.

In order to provide the user with the option to display the ID boxes on the shape, I am suggesting that you should add a **Boolean Shape Data** row to the page.

So, on the **View** tab open the **Shape Data** window from the **Task Panes** dropdown in the **Show** group. Alternatively, you can check the **Shape Data Window** option on the **Show/Hide** group on the **Data** tab. Then select the page by clicking on the gray area around the shape.

You will see that there is no shape data in the **Shape Data** window, so open the **Define Shape Data** dialog from the right-mouse menu on the header caption of this window.

You need to enter the following text into the boxes on the **Define Shape Data** dialog:

- **Label:** Display DFD IDs
- **Name:** DisplayID
- **Type:** Boolean
- **Value:** True
- **Prompt:** Select True to display the IDs in the DFD shapes

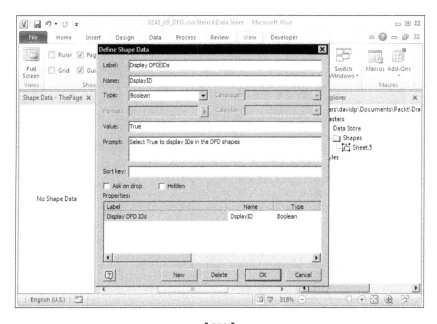

If you do not see the **Name** textbox in the **Define Shape Data** dialog, then you have not ticked **Run in developer mode** on the **File | Options | Advanced** panel.

Select **OK** to save this Shape Data in the page of the master. You now need to add a new **Shape Data** row called **ID** to the shape (called **Sheet.5)** by selecting it and then opening the **Define Shape Data** as before.

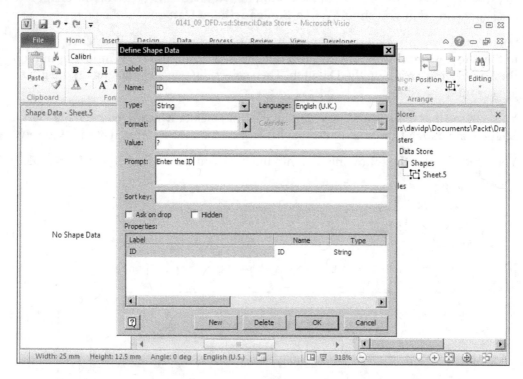

Enter a ? (question mark) for **Value**, just for testing purposes.

Creating Shape Data using the **Define Shape Data** dialog actually adds rows to the Shape Data section in the ShapeSheet. You can only enter text, not formulae, into these ShapeSheet cells using the **Define Shape Data** dialog, so you will need to open the ShapeSheet of the shape.

You should edit the formula in the **Invisible** cell of the Prop.ID Shape Data row and change it to:

```
=NOT(ThePage!Prop.DisplayID)
```

This will ensure that the `Prop.ID` Shape Data row is only visible if the value of the `Prop.DisplayID` shape data row is `True` for the page.

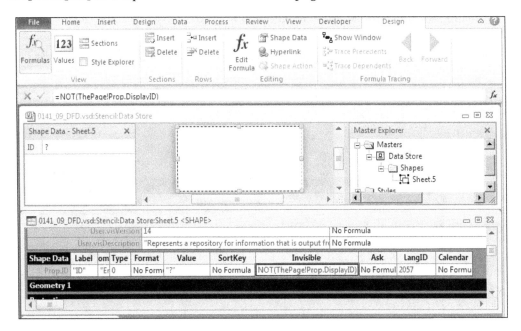

Enhancing the Data Store graphics

You now need to add a square into this master, so select **Group | Open Group** from the right-mouse menu on the master shape. Now roughly draw a square using the **Rectangle** button on the **Tools** group of the **Home** tab. You could change the **Line Weight** to **1/2 pt** at this stage, using the right-mouse menu item **Format | Line**.

Displaying the Data Store ID value

Use **Insert | Field** to add the **Custom Formula** value as =Sheet.5!Prop.ID. This will ensure that the text inside the rectangle always displays the value of the Prop. ID shape data row, in the top level of the group.

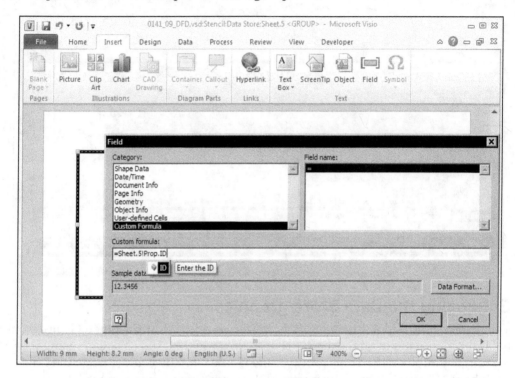

There are several formulae that you now need to edit in the ShapeSheet of the rectangle shape to ensure that it is always the right size, location, and to control the visibility of the lines and text.

In the **Shape Transform** section of the ShapeSheet, enter the formula =Sheet.5!Height*1 in the **Width** and **Height** cells and then enter the formula =Sheet.5!Height*0.5 in the **PinX** and **PinY** cells.

In the Geometry1.NoShow and HideText under **Miscellaneous** enter the formula =NOT(ThePage!Prop.DisplayID).

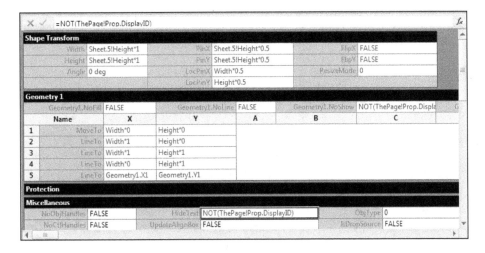

You can now close the ShapeSheet and group edit window in order to return to the main **Data Store** shape.

Improving the Data Store group shape

Use the **Size & Position** window that can be opened from the **View | Task Panes** menu or by clicking the **Height, Width**, or **Angle** display in the status bar, to enlarge the shape width to 35 mm. Enter some text into the shape, and then use the **Text Block Tool,** on the **Home | Tools** group to roughly resize the text block by selecting and moving one of the corners or mid-points of its edges. This last action will cause a new section, **Text Transform**, to be created in the ShapeSheet of this shape.

Navigate to this section and edit the TxtWidth cell formula to:

```
=GUARD(Width-IF(ThePage!Prop.DisplayID,Height*1,0))
```

Then edit the `TxtPinX` formula to:

```
=GUARD(TxtWidth*0.5+IF(ThePage!Prop.DisplayID,Height*1,0))
```

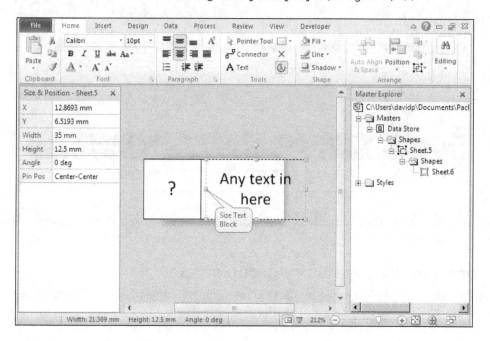

Close the ShapeSheet, and click the **Behavior** button on the **Shape Design** group on the **Developer** tab. In the **Group behavior** section, uncheck the **Snap to member shapes** option, then change **Selection** to **Group only**. Also check the **Shape can split connectors** option.

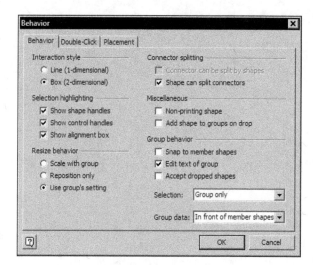

You can now delete the question mark in the `Prop.ID` Shape Data row using the **Shape Data window**, then close and save the **Data Flow** master.

Editing the Interface master

The **Interface** shape is used to represent external entities that are the source or destination of data. The only change required is to check the **Shape can split connectors** option on the **Behavior** dialog, as for the **Data Store** master so that the shape can automatically split the **Data Flow** connector when dropped on it.

Editing the Process master

The **Process** shape takes data as input, and then transforms it in some way, before sending it as output.

Adding the Process Shape Data

Edit the **Process** master shape, and add a `Prop.DisplayID` Shape Data row to the page, just like you did for the **Data Store** shape. Convert the shape to a group and add a `Prop.ID` shape data row. However, you should also add a new Shape Data row called **Category** with **Type** as `String`.

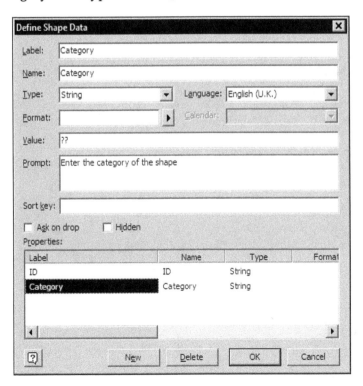

Like before, you should now open the ShapeSheet and edit the **Invisible** cell of these two Shape Data rows and enter the formula:

```
=NOT(ThePage!Prop.DisplayID)
```

Enhancing the Process graphics

Now you need to have the **ID** and the **Category** displayed optionally at the top of the shape. In the earlier Data Store shape, you added a new rectangle into the group shape, and you were able to see this rectangle and the text inside it. This worked because the group shape did not have any fill pattern. However, the **Process** shape is a solid shape, and therefore you need to remove the fill pattern. To do this, open the ShapeSheet of the **Process** shape, scroll to the **Geometry1** section, and change the `Geometry1.NoFill` formula to TRUE.

Having removed the fill from the group shape, you now need to add a new shape inside the group that can have a fill pattern. So, just like with the **Data Store** shape, open the group and draw a rough rectangle, then show the ShapeSheet of this rectangle.

You now need to edit the formula of the following:

- **Width**: `=Sheet.5!Width`
- **Height**: `=Sheet.5!Height*1`
- **PinX:** `=Sheet.5!Width*0.5`
- **PinY:** `=Sheet.5!Height*0.5`

Then edit `Geometry1.NoLine` to = TRUE, and `Rounding = Sheet.5!Rounding` in the **Line Format** section.

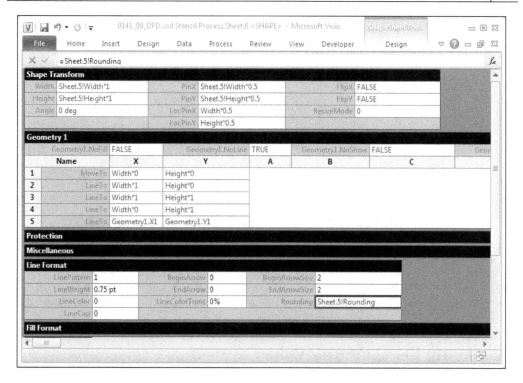

Displaying the ID value

Now you need to optionally display the Prop.ID value above a line at the top of the
shape, so draw a line inside the group, creating another shape like the rectangle, then
insert the =Sheet.5!Prop.ID formula using the **Insert | Field** action, just like for
the **Data Store** shape. Then open the ShapeSheet and scroll down to the **Text Block
Format** section to edit the TextBkgnd =0, VerticalAlign =2, and both TopMargin
and BottomMargin to =0 pt.

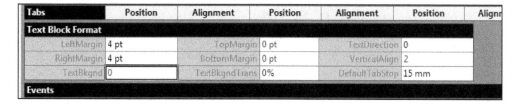

Then scroll back up to the **1-D Endpoints** section to edit the **BeginY** and **EndY** formula to =Sheet.5!Height*1-TEXTHEIGHT(TheText,750), and change the formulae of **BeginX** to =0 and **EndX** to =Sheet.5!Width*1.

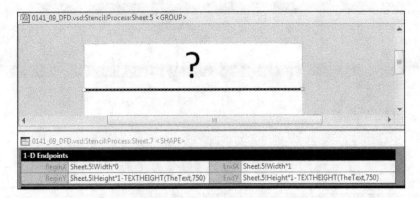

Lastly, you need to set the visibility of the line and text, as before, by putting the formula =NOT(ThePage!Prop.DisplayID) into the Geometry1.NoShow cell and the HideText cell in the **Miscellaneous** section.

Displaying the Category value

Close the ShapeSheet, and then duplicate the line using *Ctrl+D*. Open the ShapeSheet of this new line, and scroll down to the **Text Block Format** section to change the VerticalAlign value to 0.

Scroll up to the **Text Fields** section and change the Value cell to =Sheet.5!Prop. Category. Next scroll back up to the **1-D Endpoints** section to edit the **BeginY** and **EndY** formula to =TEXTHEIGHT(TheText,750), and **BeginX** to =0 and **EndX** to =Sheet.5!Width*1.

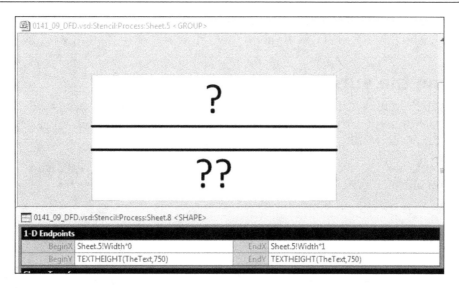

You can now close the ShapeSheet and the group window.

Improving the group shape

Use the **Size & Position** window to enlarge the shape to **35 mm** wide and **20 mm** high.

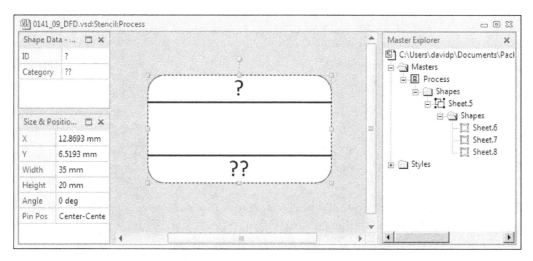

Again, click the **Behavior** button on the **Shape Design** group on the **Developer** tab. In the **Group behavior** section, uncheck the **Snap to member shapes** option, and then change the **Selection** to **Group only**. Also check the **Shape can split connectors** option.

You can now delete the question mark(s) in the `Prop.ID` and `Prop.Category` shape data row using the **Shape Data window**, then close and save the **Process** master.

Setting the sub-process master

Visio 2010 Premium edition has the ability to create a sub-process from a selection of shapes. Similarly to the **AutoConnect** feature discussed earlier, an unnecessary master can be accidently created by its use.

For example, if you select a few shapes on a document, then the **Create from Selection** button is enabled in the **Subprocess** group on the **Process** tab.

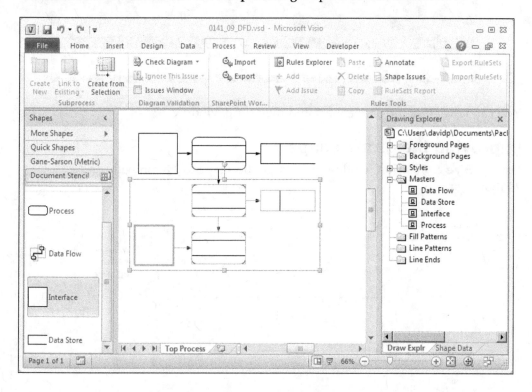

Clicking this button will move the selected shapes to a new page, and replace them with a sub-process shape in their place, with a hyperlink to the new page.

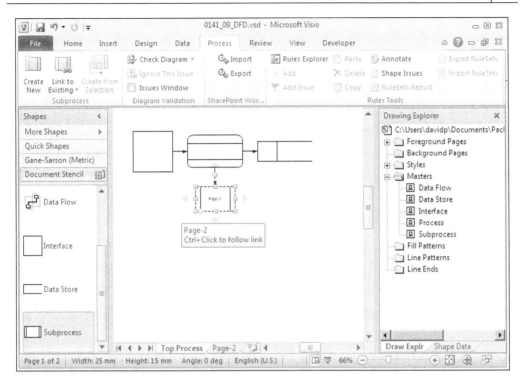

By default, a standard sub-process shape is used. We can change the default as follows.

First, open the ShapeSheet from the right-mouse menu of the document node in the **Drawing Explorer** window. Then create a new user-defined row and name it msvSubprocessMaster, then enter the formula =`"Process"`.

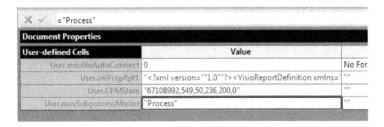

Now, when you use the **Subprocess** actions, you will find that your modified **Process** master is used.

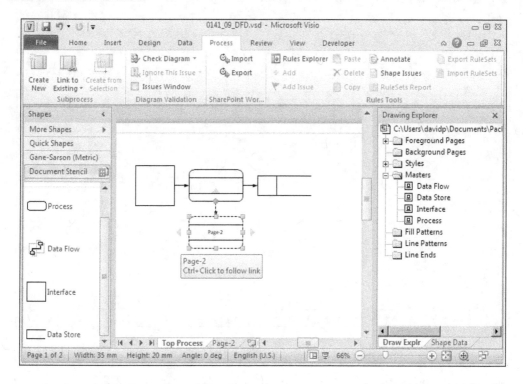

Now save your document!

Enhancing the page

As you have increased the size of a couple of the master shapes, you should now check the layout options for the page. You can take the opportunity to tweak the default spacing of shapes and connectors, as well as allowing shapes to split connectors.

So, select **Page Setup** from the right-mouse menu of the page node in the **Drawing Explorer** window. Check the **Enable connector splitting** on the **Layout and Routing** tab.

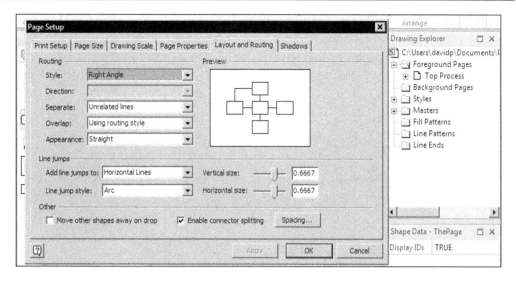

Select the **Spacing** button to open the **Layout and Routing Spacing** dialog. You should enter in suitable values for each of the settings. Of course, mine are shown in millimeters, but you could enter yours in inches (7.5 mm = 0.29 in, 15 mm = 0.59 in, 20 mm = 0.79 in, 25 mm = 0.98 in).

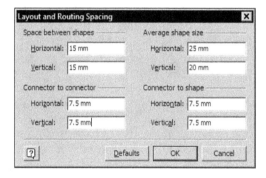

Select **OK** to close both dialogs.

You have ensured that the Data Flow connector can be split by a suitable 2-D shape, and that the three 2D shapes are splitters. You should also check that **Enable connector splitting** is ticked in the **Editing options** on the **File | Options | Advanced** panel.

Now when a user drops a DFD shape over an existing connector shape, it will automatically split, and reconnect to the added shape.

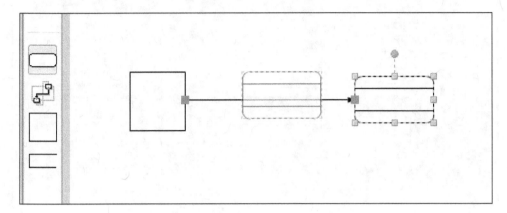

Writing the rule set

In *Chapter 4* you learned how to write VBA code to add a rule set and rules, and, although you could repeat this throughout the rest of this chapter, I prefer to use the user interface that we developed in chapters 6 and 7. Therefore, you will need to install the **Rules Tools** add-in or run the Validation Explorer solution from Visual Studio 2010, in order to write the rules easily. However, I have included VBA methods to add (or update) the rule set and rules, which can be written into the VBA project of any Visio document, but should be run when the document that you want to add the rules to is active.

Open the **Rules Explorer** window from the **Rules Tools** group on the **Process** tab.

With your document node selected in the **Rules Explorer** window, click the **Add** button, then enter the **Name**, **Name U**, and **Description** of this new rule set.

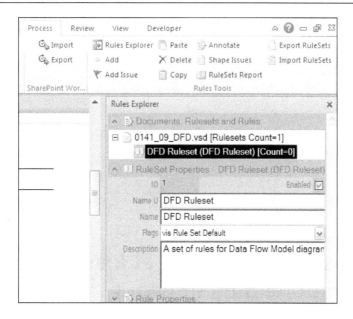

You can now add each of the new rules by translating the previous descriptions into validation formulae.

The equivalent VBA code is listed below, adapted from the code in *Chapter 4* (and requires the getRuleSet() method from there):

```
Public Sub AddOrUpdateRuleSet()
Dim ruleSet As Visio.ValidationRuleSet
Dim ruleSetNameU As String
Dim doc As Visio.Document
    Set doc = Visio.ActiveDocument
    ruleSetNameU = "DFD Ruleset"
    'Check if the rule set exists already
    Set ruleSet = getRuleSet(doc, ruleSetNameU)
    If ruleSet Is Nothing Then
        'Create the new rule set
        Set ruleSet = doc.Validation.RuleSets.Add(ruleSetNameU)
    End If
    ruleSet.Name = "DFD Ruleset"
    ruleSet.Description = _
        "A set of rules for Data Flow Model diagrams"
    ruleSet.Enabled = True
    ruleSet.RuleSetFlags = visRuleSetDefault

    'Uncomment a method below as required
    'AddOrUpdateRule1 ruleSet
```

```
        'AddOrUpdateRule2 ruleSet
        'AddOrUpdateRule3 ruleSet
        'AddOrUpdateRule4 ruleSet
        'AddOrUpdateRule5 ruleSet

        'AddOrUpdateRule7 ruleSet
        'AddOrUpdateRule8 ruleSet
        'AddOrUpdateRule9 ruleSet
        'AddOrUpdateRule10 ruleSet

        'AddOrUpdateRule11 ruleSet
        'AddOrUpdateRule12 ruleSet
End Sub
```

All processes must have at least one data flow in and one data flow out

A **Process** shape, `User.UMLShapeType=100`, must have the count of both the incoming and outgoing glued **Data Flow** connectors, `User.UMLShapeType=97`, greater than zero.

- **Name U:** `ProcessInOut`

- **Category:** `Connectivity`

- **Target Type:** `vis Rule Target Shape`

- **Description:** `All processes must have at least one data flow in and one data flow out`

- **Filter Expression:** `User.UMLShapeType=100`

- **Test Expression:** `AND(AGGCOUNT(FILTERSET(GLUEDSHAPES(1),"User.UMLShapeType=97"))>0,AGGCOUNT(FILTERSET(GLUEDSHAPES(2),"User.UMLShapeType=97"))>0)`

You can test this rule by having a **Process** shape without any Data Flow connections, or with only one Data Flow connection, or as shown in the following screenshot, with more than one Data Flow connection in the same direction.

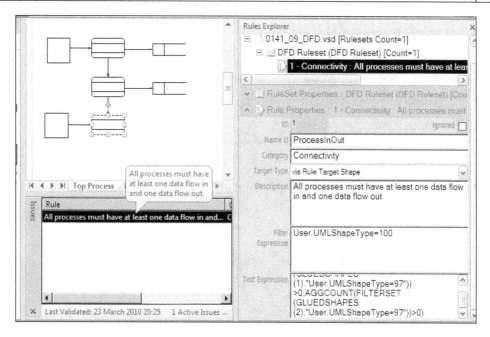

The equivalent VBA code is listed below, adapted from the code in *Chapter 4* (and requires the `getRule()` method from there):

```
Public Sub AddOrUpdateRule1( _
ByVal ruleSet As Visio.ValidationRuleSet)
Dim rule As Visio.ValidationRule
Dim ruleNameU As String
    ruleNameU = "ProcessInOut"
    Set rule = getRule(ruleSet, ruleNameU)
    If rule Is Nothing Then
        Set rule = ruleSet.Rules.Add(ruleNameU)
    End If
    rule.category = "Connectivity"
    rule.Description = _
        "All processes must have at least one data flow in and one
        data flow out"
    rule.TargetType = visRuleTargetShape
    rule.FilterExpression = _
        "User.UMLShapeType=100"
    rule.TestExpression = _
        "AND(AGGCOUNT(FILTERSET(GLUEDSHAPES(1),
          ""User.UMLShapeType=97""))>0,
          AGGCOUNT(FILTERSET(GLUEDSHAPES(2),
          ""User.UMLShapeType=97""))>0)"
End Sub
```

All processes should modify the incoming data, producing new forms of outgoing data

In other words, a **Process** shape must take input from a DFD component, and also send output to a DFD component.

A **Process** shape, `User.UMLShapeType=100`, must have the count of both the incoming and outgoing connected DFD components, `User.UMLShapeType=98`, or `User.UMLShapeType=99`, or `User.UMLShapeType=100`, greater than zero.

The values required for the Rule Properties panel are:

- **Name U:** `ProcessToDFD`
- **Category:** `Connectivity`
- **Target Type:** `vis Rule Target Shape`
- **Description:** `A Process shape must take input from a DFD component, and also send output to a DFD component`
- **Filter Expression:** `User.UMLShapeType=100`
- **Test Expression:** `AND(AGGCOUNT(FILTERSET(CONNECTEDSHAPES(1 ),"OR(User.UMLShapeType=98,User.UMLShapeType=99,User.UM LShapeType=100)"))>0,AGGCOUNT(FILTERSET(CONNECTEDSHAPES (2),"OR(User.UMLShapeType=98,User.UMLShapeType=99,User. UMLShapeType=100)"))>0)`

The parameter for the `ConnectedShapes()` method has the values of the constant `Visio.VisConnectedShapesFlags.visConnectedShapesIncomingNodes` (1) and `Visio.VisConnectedShapesFlags.visConnectedShapesOutgoingNodes` (2).

You can test this rule by having a **Process** shape connected with Data Flow connectors to non- DFD shapes.

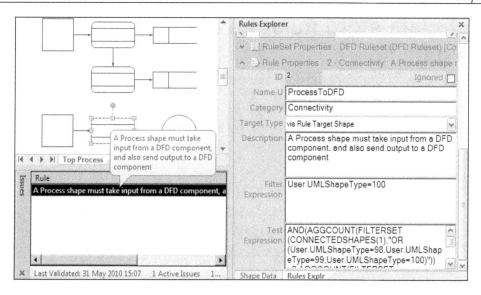

The equivalent VBA code is listed below, adapted from the code in *Chapter 4* (and requires the getRule() method from there):

```
Public Sub AddOrUpdateRule2( _
ByVal ruleSet As Visio.ValidationRuleSet)
Dim rule As Visio.ValidationRule
Dim ruleNameU As String
    ruleNameU = "ProcessToDFD"
    Set rule = getRule(ruleSet, ruleNameU)
    If rule Is Nothing Then
        Set rule = ruleSet.Rules.Add(ruleNameU)
    End If
    rule.category = "Connectivity"
    rule.Description = _
        "A Process shape must take input from a DFD component, and
            also send output to a DFD component"
    rule.TargetType = visRuleTargetShape
    rule.FilterExpression = _
        "User.UMLShapeType=100"
    rule.TestExpression = _
        "AND(AGGCOUNT(FILTERSET(CONNECTEDSHAPES(1),""OR(
            User.UMLShapeType=98,User.UMLShapeType=99,
            User.UMLShapeType=100)""))>0,AGGCOUNT(FILTERSET(
            CONNECTEDSHAPES(2),""OR(User.UMLShapeType=98,
            User.UMLShapeType=99,User.UMLShapeType=100)""))>0)"
End Sub
```

Each data store must be involved with at least one data flow

In other words, a Data Store must be connected to at least one data flow.

A **Data Store** shape, `User.UMLShapeType=98`, must have the count of glued **Data Flow** connectors, `User.UMLShapeType=97`, greater than zero.

- **Name U:** `DataStoreHasDataFlow`
- **Category:** `Connectivity`
- **Target Type:** `vis Rule Target Shape`
- **Description:** `A data store must be connected to at least one data flow`
- **Filter Expression:** `User.UMLShapeType=98`
- **Test Expression:** `AGGCOUNT(FILTERSET(GLUEDSHAPES(0),"User.UMLShapeType=97"))`

The parameter for the `GluedShapes` method is the value of the constant `Visio.VisGluedShapesFlags.visGluedShapesAll1D`.

You can test this rule by having a Data Store shape without any glued Data Flow connectors.

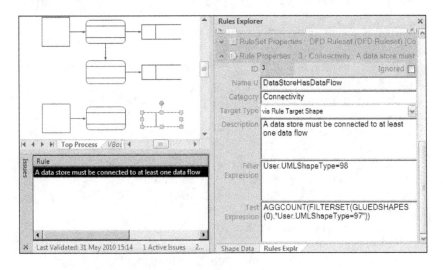

The equivalent VBA code is listed below, adapted from the code in *Chapter 4* (and requires the `getRule()` method from there):

```
Public Sub AddOrUpdateRule3( _
ByVal ruleSet As Visio.ValidationRuleSet)
Dim rule As Visio.ValidationRule
```

```
Dim ruleNameU As String
    ruleNameU = "DataStoreHasDataFlow"
    Set rule = getRule(ruleSet, ruleNameU)
    If rule Is Nothing Then
        Set rule = ruleSet.Rules.Add(ruleNameU)
    End If
    rule.category = "Connectivity"
    rule.Description = _
        "Each data store must be involved with at least one data
            flow"
    rule.TargetType = visRuleTargetShape
    rule.FilterExpression = _
        "User.UMLShapeType=98"
    rule.TestExpression = _
        "AGGCOUNT(FILTERSET(GLUEDSHAPES(0),
            ""User.UMLShapeType=97""))"
End Sub
```

Each external entity must be involved with at least one data flow

In other words, an interface must be connected to at least one data flow.

An **Interface** shape, User.UMLShapeType=99, must have the count of glued **Data Flow** connectors, User.UMLShapeType=97, greater than zero.

- **Name U:** InterfaceHasDataFlow
- **Category:** Connectivity
- **Target Type:** vis Rule Target Shape
- **Description:** An interface must be connected to at least one data flow
- **Filter Expression:** User.UMLShapeType=99
- **Test Expression:** AGGCOUNT(FILTERSET(GLUEDSHAPES(0),"User.UMLShapeType=97"))

The parameter for the GluedShapes() method is the value of the constant Visio.VisGluedShapesFlags.visGluedShapesAll1D(0).

You can test this rule by having a Data Store shape without any glued Data Flow connectors.

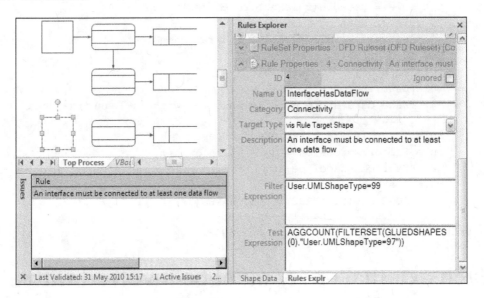

The equivalent VBA code is listed below, adapted from the code in *Chapter 4* (and requires the `getRule()` method from there):

```
Public Sub AddOrUpdateRule4( _
ByVal ruleSet As Visio.ValidationRuleSet)
Dim rule As Visio.ValidationRule
Dim ruleNameU As String
    ruleNameU = "InterfaceHasDataFlow"
    Set rule = getRule(ruleSet, ruleNameU)
    If rule Is Nothing Then
        Set rule = ruleSet.Rules.Add(ruleNameU)
    End If
    rule.category = "Connectivity"
    rule.Description = _
        " An interface must be connected to at least one data flow"
    rule.TargetType = visRuleTargetShape
    rule.FilterExpression = _
        "User.UMLShapeType=99"
    rule.TestExpression = _
        "AGGCOUNT(FILTERSET(GLUEDSHAPES(0),
          ""User.UMLShapeType=97""))"
End Sub
```

A data flow must be attached to at least one process

A **Data Flow** connector, User.UMLShapeType=97, must have the count of glued **Process** shapes, User.UMLShapeType=100, greater than zero.

- **Name U**: DataFlowToProcess
- **Category**: Connectivity
- **Target Type**: vis Rule Target Shape
- **Description**: A data flow must be attached to at least one process
- **Filter Expression**: User.UMLShapeType=97
- **Test Expression**: AGGCOUNT(FILTERSET(GLUEDSHAPES(3),"User.UMLShapeType=100"))

The parameter for the GluedShapes() method is the value of the constant Visio.VisGluedShapesFlags.visGluedShapesAll2D (3).

You can test this rule by having a **Data Flow** connector glued between two non-**Process** shapes.

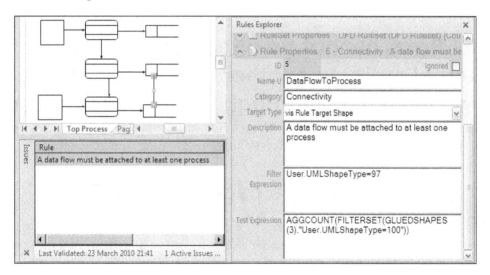

The equivalent VBA code is listed below, adapted from the code in *Chapter 4* (and requires the `getRule()` method from there):

```
Public Sub AddOrUpdateRule5( _
ByVal ruleSet As Visio.ValidationRuleSet)
Dim rule As Visio.ValidationRule
Dim ruleNameU As String
    ruleNameU = "DataFlowToProcess"
    Set rule = getRule(ruleSet, ruleNameU)
    If rule Is Nothing Then
        Set rule = ruleSet.Rules.Add(ruleNameU)
    End If
    rule.category = "Connectivity"
    rule.Description = _
        "A data flow must be attached to at least one process"
    rule.TargetType = visRuleTargetShape
    rule.FilterExpression = _
        "User.UMLShapeType=97"
    rule.TestExpression = _
        "AGGCOUNT(FILTERSET(GLUEDSHAPES(3),
          ""User.UMLShapeType=100""))"
End Sub
```

Data flows cannot go directly from one external entity to another external entity: such flows need to go through at least one process

This rule is already captured by the previous rule, since all **Data Flow** connectors must be connected to at least one **Process** shape.

Do not allow a single page of a DFD to get too complex

It should have no more than 10 components. If it has more than this, combine some components into a single self-contained unit and create a new DFD for that unit.

If there is a **Data Flow** connector, `User.UMLShapeType=97`, on the page then the total count of DFD component shapes, `User.UMLShapeType=98` or `User.UMLShapeType=99` or `User.UMLShapeType=100`, should be less than 11.

The values required for the Rule Properties panel are:

- **Name U:** `TooComplex`
- **Category:** `Count`
- **Target Type:** `vis Rule Target Page`
- **Description:** `This page is too complex. Combine some components into a single self-contained unit, and use a new page for this unit`
- **Filter Expression:** `AGGCOUNT(FILTERSET(SHAPESONPAGE(),"User.UMLShapeType=97"))>0`
- **Test Expression:** `AGGCOUNT(FILTERSET(SHAPESONPAGE()," OR(User.UMLShapeType=98,User.UMLShapeType=99,User.UMLShapeType=100)"))<11`

You can test this rule by having more than 10 DFD component shapes on a page, with at least one Data Flow connector shape on it

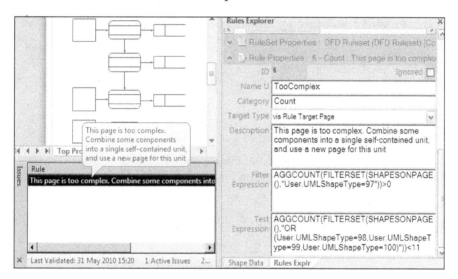

The equivalent VBA code is listed below, adapted from the code in Chapter 4 (and requires the `getRule()` methods from there):

```
Public Sub AddOrUpdateRule7( _
ByVal ruleSet As Visio.ValidationRuleSet)
Dim rule As Visio.ValidationRule
Dim ruleNameU As String
    ruleNameU = "TooComplex"
    Set rule = getRule(ruleSet, ruleNameU)
    If rule Is Nothing Then
        Set rule = ruleSet.Rules.Add(ruleNameU)
    End If
```

```
        rule.category = "Count"
        rule.Description = _
            "This page is too complex. Combine some components into a
            single self-contained unit, and use a new page for this unit"
        rule.TargetType = visRuleTargetPage
        rule.FilterExpression = _
            "AGGCOUNT(FILTERSET(SHAPESONPAGE(),
              ""User.UMLShapeType=97""))>0"
        rule.TestExpression = _
            "AGGCOUNT(FILTERSET(SHAPESONPAGE(),
              ""OR(User.UMLShapeType=98,User.UMLShapeType=99,
              User.UMLShapeType=100)""))<11"
End Sub
```

Each component should be labeled

Each DFD component shape, `User.UMLShapeType=98`, or `User.UMLShapeType=99`, or `User.UMLShapeType=100`, should have some text in it.

- **Name U:** `NoComponentLabel`

- **Category:** `Text`

- **Target Type:** `vis Rule Target Shape`

- **Description:** `Each component should be labelled`

- **Filter Expression:** `OR(User.UMLShapeType=98,User.UMLShapeType=99,User.UMLShapeType=100)`

- **Test Expression:** `NOT(STRSAME(SHAPETEXT(TheText),""))`

You can test this rule by omitting to add any text to a DFD component shape.

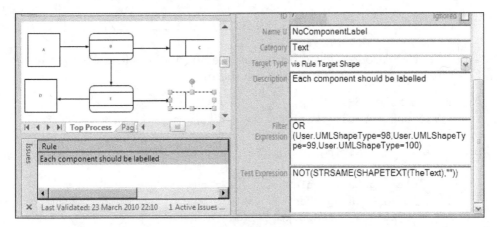

The equivalent VBA code is listed below, adapted from the code in *Chapter 4* (and requires the `getRule()` method from there):

```
Public Sub AddOrUpdateRule8( _
ByVal ruleSet As Visio.ValidationRuleSet)
Dim rule As Visio.ValidationRule
Dim ruleNameU As String
    ruleNameU = "NoComponentLabel"
    Set rule = getRule(ruleSet, ruleNameU)
    If rule Is Nothing Then
        Set rule = ruleSet.Rules.Add(ruleNameU)
    End If
    rule.category = "Text"
    rule.Description = _
        "Each component should be labelled"
    rule.TargetType = visRuleTargetShape
    rule.FilterExpression = _
        "OR(User.UMLShapeType=98,User.UMLShapeType=99,
          User.UMLShapeType=100)"
    rule.TestExpression = _
        "NOT(STRSAME(SHAPETEXT(TheText),""""))"
End Sub
```

Each data flow should be labeled describing the data that flows through it

Each **Data Flow** connector shape, `User.UMLShapeType=97`, should have some text in it.

The values required for the Rule Properties panel are:

- **Name U:** `NoDataFlowLabel`
- **Category:** `Text`
- **Target Type:** `vis Rule Target Shape`
- **Description:** `Each data flow should be labelled with the data that flows through it`
- **Filter Expression:** `User.UMLShapeType=97`
- **Test Expression:** `NOT(STRSAME(SHAPETEXT(TheText),""))`

You can test this rule by omitting to add any text to a DFD component shape.

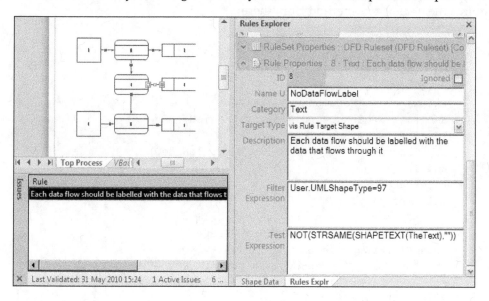

The equivalent VBA code is listed below, adapted from the code in *Chapter 4* (and requires the `getRule()` method from there):

```
Public Sub AddOrUpdateRule9( _
ByVal ruleSet As Visio.ValidationRuleSet)
Dim rule As Visio.ValidationRule
Dim ruleNameU As String
    ruleNameU = "NoDataFlowLabel"
    Set rule = getRule(ruleSet, ruleNameU)
    If rule Is Nothing Then
        Set rule = ruleSet.Rules.Add(ruleNameU)
    End If
    rule.category = "Text"
    rule.Description = _
        "Each data flow should be labelled with the data that flows
            through it"
    rule.TargetType = visRuleTargetShape
    rule.FilterExpression = _
        "User.UMLShapeType=97"
    rule.TestExpression = _
        "NOT(STRSAME(SHAPETEXT(TheText),""""))"
End Sub
```

Each component and subcomponent should be numbered

This rule continues with an example—a top level DFD has components 1, 2, 3, 4, and 5. The subcomponent DFD of component 3 would have components 3.1, 3.2, 3.3, and 3.4 and the sub-subcomponent DFD of component 3.2 would have components 3.2.1, 3.2.2, and 3.2.3. This enables a developer to plan in a top-down manner—starting with representing large concepts, and then repeatedly breaking these objects into their components.

Each **Process** or **Data Store** shape, `User.UMLShapeType=98` or `User.UMLShapeType=100`, should have a `Prop.ID` value if the page has a `Prop.DisplayID` value of `TRUE`.

- **Name U:** `NoID`
- **Category:** `Text`
- **Target Type:** `vis Rule Target Shape`
- **Description:** `Each component and subcomponent should be numbered.`
- **Filter Expression:** `AND(OR(User.UMLShapeType=98,User.UMLShapeType=100),Prop.ID.Invisible=False)`
- **Test Expression:** `NOT(STRSAME(Prop.ID,""))`

You can test this rule by omitting to add an **ID** value to any **Process** or **Data Store** shape, when the page has the **Display IDs** set to `TRUE`.

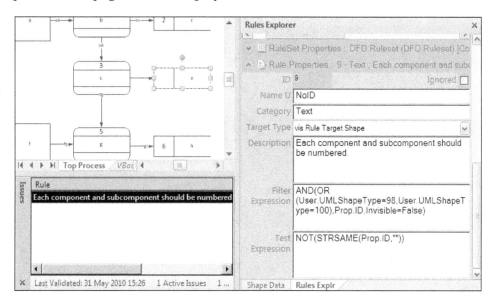

So, if you change the page **Display IDs Shape Data** to FALSE, and then run **Check Diagram** again, the page will pass validation because the Prop.ID Shape Data is invisible.

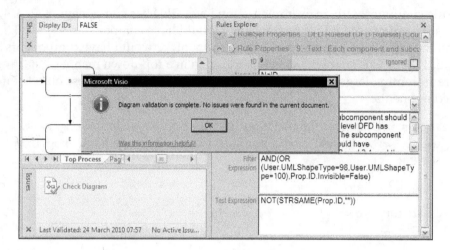

The equivalent VBA code is listed below, adapted from the code in *Chapter 4* (and requires the getRule() method from there):

```
Public Sub AddOrUpdateRule10( _
ByVal ruleSet As Visio.ValidationRuleSet)
Dim rule As Visio.ValidationRule
Dim ruleNameU As String
    ruleNameU = "NoID"
    Set rule = getRule(ruleSet, ruleNameU)
    If rule Is Nothing Then
        Set rule = ruleSet.Rules.Add(ruleNameU)
    End If
    rule.category = "Text"
    rule.Description = _
        "Each component and subcomponent should be numbered. E.g.
a top level DFD has components 1 2 3 4 5. The subcomponent DFD of
component 3 would have components 3.1, 3.2, 3.3, and 3.4; and the sub-
subcomponent DFD of component 3.2 would have components 3.2.1, 3.2.2,
and 3.2.3"
    rule.TargetType = visRuleTargetShape
    rule.FilterExpression = _
        "AND(OR(User.UMLShapeType=98,User.UMLShapeType=100),
          Prop.ID.Invisible=False)"
    rule.TestExpression = _
        "NOT(STRSAME(Prop.ID,""""))"
End Sub
```

A data flow must be connected between two components

The previous rule, **A data flow must be attached to at least one process**, does not check that both ends are connected to a data component, therefore an extra rule is required to check for this.

Each DFD component shape, `User.UMLShapeType=98`, or `User.UMLShapeType=99`, or `User.UMLShapeType=100`, should have some text in it.

- **Name U**: `DataFlowEnds`
- **Category**: `Connectivity`
- **Target Type**: `vis Rule Target Shape`
- **Description**: `A data flow must be attached to two data components`
- **Filter Expression**: `User.UMLShapeType=97`
- **Test Expression**: `AGGCOUNT(FILTERSET(GLUEDSHAPES(3),"` `OR(User.UMLShapeType=98,User.UMLShapeType=99,User.` `UMLShapeType=100)"))>1`

You can test this rule by omitting to add any text to a DFD component shape.

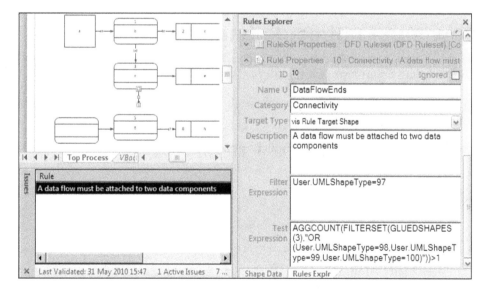

The equivalent VBA code is listed below, adapted from the code in *Chapter 4* (and requires the `getRule()` method from there):

```
Public Sub AddOrUpdateRule10( _
ByVal ruleSet As Visio.ValidationRuleSet)
Dim rule As Visio.ValidationRule
Dim ruleNameU As String
    ruleNameU = " DataFlowEnds"
    Set rule = getRule(ruleSet, ruleNameU)
    If rule Is Nothing Then
        Set rule = ruleSet.Rules.Add(ruleNameU)
    End If
    rule.category = "Connectivity"
    rule.Description = _
        "A data flow must be attached to two data components"
    rule.TargetType = visRuleTargetShape
    rule.FilterExpression = _
        " User.UMLShapeType=97"
    rule.TestExpression = _
        "AGGCOUNT(FILTERSET(GLUEDSHAPES(3),""OR(User.UMLShapeType=98,
            User.UMLShapeType=99,User.UMLShapeType=100)""))>1"
End Sub
```

A flow must not cycle back to itself

This rule is a variation of the one in *Chapter 7*, so the VBA code needs to be inserted into the template document that has all of the rules in it.

A DFD component shape must not cycle back to itself by following the flow direction through other DFD components.

The values required for the Rule Properties panel are:

- **Name U:** `CheckCycle`
- **Category:** `Connectivity`
- **Target Type:** `vis Rule Target Page`
- **Description:** `A flow must not cycle back to itself`
- **Filter Expression:** `False`
- **Test Expression:** `True`

You can test this rule by creating a connecting DFD component together in a cycle.

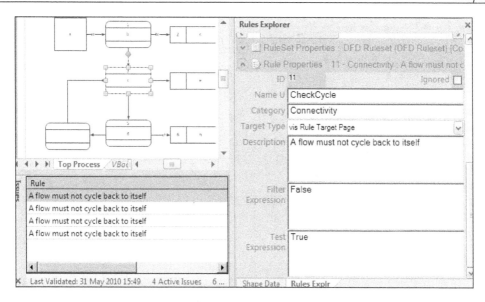

The `ThisDocument` class needs to include the `Document_RuleSetValidated()` event, `CheckCycle()`, `getRule()`, and `ClearRuleIssues()` methods as described in *Chapter 7*. Also, you must add a **Reference** to the **Microsoft Scripting Runtime**, as before.

The `CustomValidation` class needs to copied, but the `InitializeValues()` method needs to be modified because the data components are not on the Flowchart layer. Instead, the code checks for the value in the `User.UMLShapeType` cell if it exists.

```
Private Sub initializeValues(ByVal visPage As Visio.page)
    Dim shps As Visio.Shapes
    Set shps = visPage.Shapes
    Dim shapeID As Integer

    Set flowchartShapes = New Collection
    Set hshTable = New Dictionary
    cycleFound = False
    Dim shp As Visio.Shape
    Dim i As Integer
    For Each shp In shps
        If shp.CellExistsU("User.UMLShapeType",
            Visio.visExistsAnywhere) Then
            Select Case shp.Cells("User.UMLShapeType").ResultIU
                Case 97
                    shapeID = shp.ID
                Case 98, 99, 100
                    shapeID = shp.ID
```

```
                    flowchartShapes.Add shapeID
                    hshTable.Add shapeID, shapeStatus.[New]
            End Select
        End If

    Next
End Sub
```

The equivalent VBA code is listed below, adapted from the code in Chapter 4 (and requires the `getRule()` method from there):

```
Public Sub AddOrUpdateRule12( _
ByVal ruleSet As Visio.ValidationRuleSet)
Dim rule As Visio.ValidationRule
Dim ruleNameU As String
    ruleNameU = "CheckCycle"
    Set rule = getRule(ruleSet, ruleNameU)
    If rule Is Nothing Then
        Set rule = ruleSet.Rules.Add(ruleNameU)
    End If
    rule.category = " Connectivity"
    rule.Description = _
        " A flow must not cycle back to itself"
    rule.TargetType = visRuleTargetPage
    rule.FilterExpression = _
        "False
    rule.TestExpression = _
        "True
End Sub
```

Completing the template

Now that you have modified the masters, written the validation rules, and enhanced the first page, you need to put the finishing touches to the template before creating an installation file.

Follow the instructions in *Chapter 8* to add a title block, select a theme, and to insert the page name field into the title shape in the background page. Then save your document as a template `DFMD_M.vst`, if it is metric units, or `DFMD_U.vst`, if it is US units.

Test your template by creating a new document from it, and then resize the first page to be square.

> If you hold down the *Ctrl* key and move your mouse cursor to
> the top of the page, then you will see that the cursor changes to a
> vertical two-way arrow. You can then click and drag the top edge
> of the page downwards, whilst still holding down the *Ctrl* key,
> until the page looks square.

Now arrange some of the DFD shapes on the page as this page will be used as
the preview image on your new template. Follow the instructions in Chapter 8 for
enhancing the quality of the preview image, before saving it as a new document, say
as `0141_09_Image.vsd`. You can then copy the preview picture, as in Chapter 8,
with the `CopyPreview()` method or by the following command in the VBA
Immediate Window:

```
Visio.Documents("DFMD_M.vst").CopyPreviewPicture Visio.
Documents("0141_09_Image.vsd")
```

Of course, you need to ensure that the `LockPreview` cell in the document ShapeSheet
of your new template is changed to `TRUE` before saving your template again if you do
not use the `CopyPreview()` method. You should edit the document properties using
the **File | Info | Properties** panel. For example, I added **This is a Data Flow Model
Diagram template with validation rules** into the **Comments**.

Finally, ensure that you close the **Document Stencil** in your template before
saving it. You should still have the **Gane-Sarson** stencil docked when you save the
workspace, but you do not need to include this in your installer. Your target users
should already have this installed. The user will drag-and-drop shapes off this
stencil, but your modified ones in the document stencil will be dropped instead.

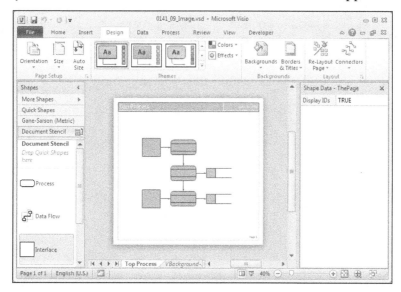

Creating the installer

In Visual Studio 2010, create a new **Setup and Deployment project** called
`DataFlowModelDiagramTemplate`. Add your new template to the **Application
Folder**. Then follow the instructions in *Chapter 8* for enhancing the properties of the
deployment package.

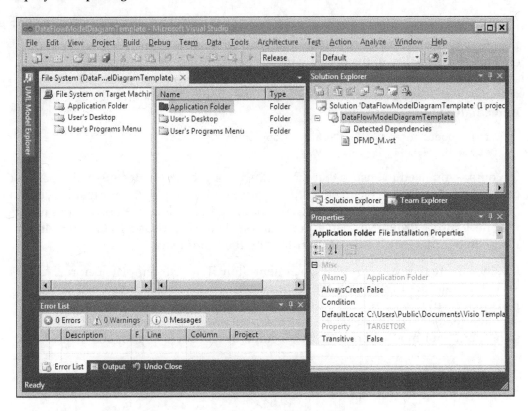

These are the steps to update the msi file after you have built it:

1. Start the Microsoft Visio Solution Publisher and select **File | New**.

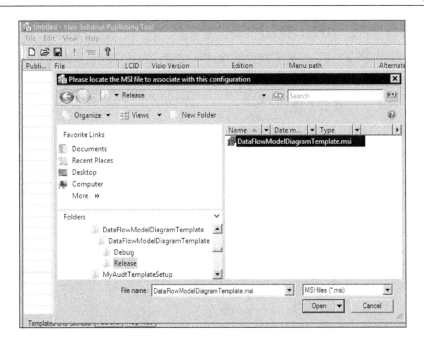

2. Double-click the template row to open the **Template Information** dialog, then tick the **All LCIDs** option and enter **Software and Database\Data Flow Model Diagram with Rules** as the **Menu Path**.

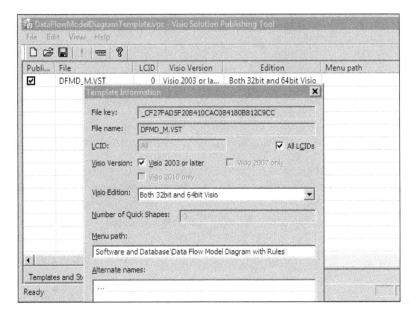

3. Close the dialog, then **Apply** the changes.

Testing the installation

All that remains is to test your installation package by navigating to the folder where the `setup.exe` and the `DataFlowModelDiagramTemplate.msi` file reside.

Run the `setup.exe` as an administrator, and install for all users.

When the installation has finished, you will find that there is a new template in the **Software and Database** category of the Visio Getting Started screen:

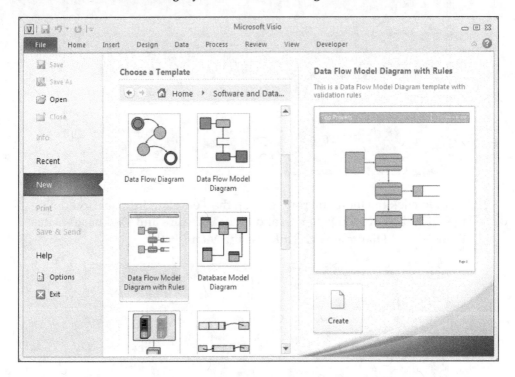

So, there you go. You have now created a professional template for your users!

Remember that our last rule, `CheckCycle`, requires VBA, so your users may be prompted to enable VBA when they open a document based on this template. If VBA is not allowed in your corporate environment, then you have only lost this rule, because all the rest is written as Filter and Test Expressions.

Should you ever want to uninstall this template, then you will find it listed under the **Programs and Features** panel of the **Control Panel**.

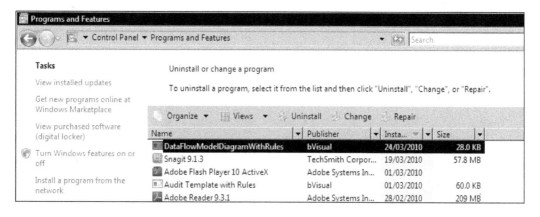

Summary

Well, that's all folks!

You have learnt a lot about how Visio works, both for the ShapeSheet and for automation. In particular, you have done the following:

- Written VBA code to examine the Visio objects and properties
- Written a VSTO add-in in C# to enable you to edit or export rule sets
- Analyzed how the built-in rule sets in Visio 2010 Premium edition are implemented
- Learned how to write validation rules that can enforce standards within your organization
- Learnt how to create a professional installation for a custom template, so that your rules can be easily used by others

Validation ensures that structured diagrams, such as business process flows, are well constructed. These validated diagrams could then be used to generate data for other systems now that you can be content that they have been correctly drawn, connected, labeled, or assigned data values.

I think that there are many other structured diagramming types that could benefit from having validation rules. These do not have to be business process diagrams but could be applied to facilities management, networks, or even organization charts. There are endless possibilities, so, this is just the beginning.

Index

Q

Quick Shapes 272

R

Result property 60
ReviewerID property 50
Ribbon class 158
Role() function 209
Rule.Delete() method 114
Rules 21
RuleSets 21
rule sets, exporting to XML
  steps 189-191
  XDocument object, obtaining 191-193
rule sets, importing from XML 195-198
RuleSets.xslt file 203
RuleSetValidated event 107
rule set, writing
  about 288
  component, labelling 300-302
  component, numbering 303, 304
  data flow, attaching to atleast one process
    297, 298
  data flow, connecting between two
    components 305, 306
  Data Flow connectors, connecting 298
  data flow in 290, 291
  data flow, involving in data store 294
  data flow out 290, 291
  DFD component, not cycling back to itself
    306, 307, 308
  DFD page complexity, avoiding 298-300
  external entity, involving with data flow
    295, 296
  incoming data, modifying 292, 293
  new outgoing data forms,
    producing 292, 293
  new rules, adding 289, 290
  subcomponent, numbering 303, 304
Rules Explorer window, creating
  about 149
  detail panel, linking 152
  Explorer actions 158
  tree-views 150
  tree-views, Informative tooltips 150, 152

rules set reports
  creating 198-200
  XSL stylesheet, obtaining 200-203
rules sets
  exporting, to XML 189-191
  importing, from XML 195-198
  reports, creating 198-203
rules validation
  Hyperlinks section 101
  Layer Membership 102
  Shape Data section 92
  User-defined Cells section 83

S

Scalable Vector Graphics. *See* SVG
SDK
  about 251
Section.Index property 57
Section Row Column 29
SelectedVEIssue property 168
SelectionChanged event 122, 133
Shape.CalloutsAssociated property,
    Connectivity API 67
shape.Characters.Text property 55
Shape.ConnectedShapes method,
    Connectivity API
  about 63-65
  CategoryFilte 64
  flags 64
Shape Data 15
  about 92, 93
  Boolean type 97
  Currency type 100, 101
  Date type 98, 99
  Duration type 100
  Fixed List type 95
  Number type 96, 97
  String type 94, 95
  types 92
  Variable List type 98
Shape.GluedShapes method, Connectivity
    API
  CategoryFilter 65
  Flags 65
  OtherConnectedShape 65
  using 66

W

Windows Presentation Foundation. *See* WPF
WPF 130

X

XAML 22, 30
XDocument object, obtaining
  VEIssue XElement, obtaining 194
  VERuleSet XElement, obtaining 193, 194
XML Notepad 19

Thank you for buying
Microsoft Visio 2010 Business Process Diagramming and Validation

About Packt Publishing

Packt, pronounced 'packed', published its first book "Mastering phpMyAdmin for Effective MySQL Management" in April 2004 and subsequently continued to specialize in publishing highly focused books on specific technologies and solutions.

Our books and publications share the experiences of your fellow IT professionals in adapting and customizing today's systems, applications, and frameworks. Our solution based books give you the knowledge and power to customize the software and technologies you're using to get the job done. Packt books are more specific and less general than the IT books you have seen in the past. Our unique business model allows us to bring you more focused information, giving you more of what you need to know, and less of what you don't.

Packt is a modern, yet unique publishing company, which focuses on producing quality, cutting-edge books for communities of developers, administrators, and newbies alike. For more information, please visit our website: www.packtpub.com.

About Packt Enterprise

In 2010, Packt launched two new brands, Packt Enterprise and Packt Open Source, in order to continue its focus on specialization. This book is part of the Packt Enterprise brand, home to books published on enterprise software – software created by major vendors, including (but not limited to) IBM, Microsoft and Oracle, often for use in other corporations. Its titles will offer information relevant to a range of users of this software, including administrators, developers, architects, and end users.

Writing for Packt

We welcome all inquiries from people who are interested in authoring. Book proposals should be sent to author@packtpub.com. If your book idea is still at an early stage and you would like to discuss it first before writing a formal book proposal, contact us; one of our commissioning editors will get in touch with you.

We're not just looking for published authors; if you have strong technical skills but no writing experience, our experienced editors can help you develop a writing career, or simply get some additional reward for your expertise.

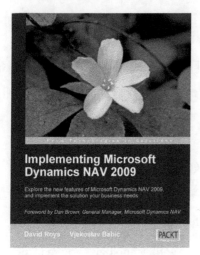

Implementing Microsoft Dynamics NAV 2009

ISBN: 978-1-847195-82-1   Paperback: 552 pages

Explore the new features of Microsoft Dynamics NAV 2009, and implement the solution your business needs

1. First book to show you how to implement Microsoft Dynamics NAV 2009 in your business

2. Meet the new features in Dynamics NAV 2009 that give your business the flexibility to adapt to new opportunities and growth

Learning SQL Server 2008 Reporting Services

ISBN: 978-1-847196-18-7   Paperback: pages

A step-by-step guide to getting the most of Microsoft SQL Server Reporting Services 2008

1. Everything you need to create and deliver data-rich reports with SQL Server 2008 Reporting Services as quickly as possible

2. Packed with hands-on-examples to learn and improve your skills

3. Connect and report from databases, spreadsheets, XML Data, and more

Please check **www.PacktPub.com** for information on our titles

Small Business Server 2008 – Installation, Migration, and Configuration

ISBN: 978-1-847196-30-9   Paperback: 408 pages

Set up and run your small business server making it deliver big business impact

1. Step-by-step guidance through the installation and configuration process with numerous pictures

2. Successfully install SBS 2008 into your business, either as a new installation or by migrating from SBS 2003

WCF Multi-tier Services Development with LINQ

ISBN: 978-1-847196-62-0   Paperback: 384 pages

Build SOA applications on the Microsoft platform in this hands-on guide

1. Master WCF and LINQ concepts by completing practical examples and apply them to your real-world assignments

2. First book to combine WCF and LINQ in a multi-tier real-world WCF service

Please check **www.PacktPub.com** for information on our titles